AF835455

ROUTLEDGE LIBRARY EDITIONS:
INTERNATIONAL SECURITY STUDIES

Volume 11

MARITIME STRATEGY FOR MEDIUM POWERS

MARITIME STRATEGY FOR MEDIUM POWERS

REAR ADMIRAL J.R. HILL

Routledge
Taylor & Francis Group
LONDON AND NEW YORK

First published in 1986 by Croom Helm Ltd

This edition first published in 2021
by Routledge
2 Park Square, Milton Park, Abingdon, Oxon OX14 4RN

and by Routledge
52 Vanderbilt Avenue, New York, NY 10017

Routledge is an imprint of the Taylor & Francis Group, an informa business

© 1986 Rear Admiral J.R. Hill

All rights reserved. No part of this book may be reprinted or reproduced or utilised in any form or by any electronic, mechanical, or other means, now known or hereafter invented, including photocopying and recording, or in any information storage or retrieval system, without permission in writing from the publishers.

Trademark notice: Product or corporate names may be trademarks or registered trademarks, and are used only for identification and explanation without intent to infringe.

British Library Cataloguing in Publication Data
A catalogue record for this book is available from the British Library

ISBN: 978-0-367-68499-0 (Set)
ISBN: 978-1-00-316169-1 (Set) (ebk)
ISBN: 978-0-367-71219-8 (Volume 11) (hbk)
ISBN: 978-0-367-71222-8 (Volume 11) (pbk)
ISBN: 978-1-00-314985-9 (Volume 11) (ebk)

Publisher's Note
The publisher has gone to great lengths to ensure the quality of this reprint but points out that some imperfections in the original copies may be apparent.

Disclaimer
The publisher has made every effort to trace copyright holders and would welcome correspondence from those they have been unable to trace.

MARITIME STRATEGY FOR MEDIUM POWERS

REAR ADMIRAL J.R. HILL

CROOM HELM
London & Sydney

© 1986 Rear Admiral J. R. Hill
Croom Helm Ltd, Provident House, Burrell Row,
Beckenham, Kent BR3 1AT
Croom Helm Australia Pty Ltd, Suite 4, 6th Floor,
64–76 Kippax Street, Surry Hills, NSW 2010, Australia

British Library Cataloguing in Publication Data

Hill, J. R. (John Richard)
Maritime strategy for medium powers.
1. Naval strategy
I. Title
359.4'3 V163

ISBN 0-7099-3719-9

Phototypeset by Patrick and Anne Murphy,
10 Bracken Way, Highcliffe-on-Sea, Dorset BH23 5LW
Printed and bound in Great Britain
by Billing & Sons Limited, Worcester.

CONTENTS

Part One: The Strategic Background

1. Introduction 3
2. Medium Power 7
3. Maritime Power 30
4. Threat and Alliances 51

Part Two: Tools of the Trade: Concepts and Materiel

5. General Concepts 79
6. Normal Conditions 88
7. Low Intensity Operations 111
8. Higher Level Operations 132
9. General War 145
10. Reach 149
11. Materiel 157

Part Three: Available Strategies

12. Planning, Organisation and Deployment 195
13. Towards a General Theory 218

Appendix 228
Bibliography 231
Index 236

PART ONE

THE STRATEGIC BACKGROUND

1 INTRODUCTION

The genesis of this book lies somewhere in 1968. It was a turbulent year, probably the most politically seminal of this half-century, and it saw among its many developments a critical change in Britain's defence policy.

Until then, in spite of the twists and turns imposed by internal and external events, Britain had a strategy that assumed her to be an independent actor on the world stage. The 1967 Supplementary Statement on Defence (its cover printed in ironic bright red) put more emphasis on peacekeeping, or 'brush fire wars' East of Suez, than it did on the NATO alliance. British measures were to protect, by a combination of defence and deterrence, British interests. The means provided were inadequate, but the intention remained.

In January 1968 that changed. As had been the case so often before, the motor of change was an economic crisis; but this time the reduced level and less comprehensive character of our forces were to be matched by a radical reduction in task. Thenceforth, British defence policy was linked to that of the Western alliance, and new force requirements could be justified only by reference to that policy.

As a ministerial statement of the period averred, British strategy (it was still called that) was now irreducible. The Alliance was the absolute core of British external security, the Soviet Union the only threat seriously considered in force planning. There was an assumption, more openly paraded by conservative than labour governments, that forces for operations beyond NATO's political and geographical boundaries could be found from among those provided for the core task. But of that task there was no doubt. A Secretary of State for Defence, fairly newly arrived in post in the mid-1970s and no doubt carefully briefed by his civil service advisers, was asked what British defence policy was. 'It is', he said, 'to make a contribution to NATO.' And stopped.

For a naval staff officer concerned with force planning in the Ministry of Defence, which — with a couple of remissions — I was from 1967 to 1980, this policy carried some difficulties. First, how big was a contribution? The Army and Royal Air Force had a simpler task than the Navy here. However artificial and pragmatic the premisses for the British force levels in mainland Europe might originally have been, the Treaty and its subsequent protocols could be quoted as authority. Back-up for those forces in the United Kingdom, too, was well-established and could be argued by direct reference to the NATO task. Moreover, the Army could, after 1969, point to a heavy internal security load in Northern Ireland. For the Navy, the bases of force requirements were less secure. At sea, there was no section of front allocated to the British to defend; NATO force goals were known to be a weak justification because they were arrived at by adjusting upwards the force levels that already existed; and NATO maritime forces were dominated by the US Navy in a way that had no parallel in central Europe. The mechanics of justification, then, were a serious intellectual difficulty.

But more important was a strategic crux. As the 1970s went on it was clear that Britain did not fit easily in the NATO box. The cod wars, Oman, Caribbean preoccupations, and flurries as far away as the South Atlantic and the New Hebrides showed the sensitivity of British interests to matters that were considered of no concern by the Alliance. Some of these could be presented as non-recurring residues of Empire, others clearly could not. It was evident that Britain's interests, as they came out in the wash, were of a different pattern from NATO's. Britain was not unique in that, of course; no NATO country could claim a complete identity of interest with the Alliance. But Britain's declared posture made it peculiarly difficult to do anything practical in planning for the anomalies; and Britain's geography and history ensured that many of the anomalies had a singularly maritime tinge.

Inevitably one began to live a kind of intellectual double life. Strategic realities demanded that our maritime forces should be responsive to a very wide range of demands, and the characteristics needed must all if possible be incorporated in our plans; but they had to be justified on the much narrower ground of a contribution to the Alliance. These justifications were not spurious (though sometimes the scenarios stretched reality to its limits) but they were incomplete. Attempts to reconcile the half-hidden, national requirements with the open, NATO ones were not welcomed by ministers, civil servants or the other services. The most serious, a carefully thought out and unclassified paper by the Naval Staff, vanished, after having been printed, in the mid-1970s.

Nicely-Nicely Jones, in Damon Runyon's immortal books, gets along by doing the best he can. The Naval Staff did the best it could. It was helped by the inertia both of naval forces — ships' lives being long and fleet patterns slow to change — and of what Chatfield called 'the power of the defensive in Whitehall'. Once a project was on the books, it took some shifting. So the fleet, and maritime air forces too, managed to maintain and even build many characteristics that served the national as well as the NATO end — afloat support, ship-based fixed-wing aircraft, a substantial specialised amphibious force. It did not — could not — succeed in providing ship-based airborne early warning, with results that were all too apparent in 1982.

But all this activity helped to set me thinking along broader and more theoretical lines. Britain was unique; all nations are unique. But surely she shared many characteristics and categories of interest with other medium-sized powers? There was no doubt that was what she was; superpower aspirations were not on the agenda — had not been since 1945. (I recall putting a motion at the Royal Naval College Debating Society in that year that 'Britain is no longer a First-Class Power'. It was heavily defeated, of course.) It was clear that the British experience was not unique, though it might not be typical; and, if France was anything to go by, Britain's solution was not the only one on offer. It seemed to me, as the 1970s went on, that there would be some value in gathering information on the ways in which other medium powers — both developed and developing — sought solutions to their strategic problems particularly in the maritime field, and attempting to formulate some principles, even perhaps a general theory.

The initial, tentative moves in this process could easily be predicted by anyone who has served in the Ministry of Defence: late-night gossip and philosophising over cheap sherry, with nearly all the ideas discarded next day but a nugget or two remaining. Nothing was ever written down; what was worthwhile stuck in the mind.

Later, I embarked on a series of articles for *The Naval Review*, a publication whose circulation is restricted to its members. They appeared in 1976–7, and were apparently well received, though no one accused me of finding, much less abusing, the philosopher's stone. A rather more mixed reception was given to a brainstorming paper called 'An Alternative Strategy for the United Kingdom', which I presented at a Cambridge Extramural Studies Seminar in

1979. The academics on the whole seemed to think it made some sense, some of the civil servants and serving officers smiled tolerantly, and one or two got quite cross. Finally, in my last post on the active list I had a little spare time and a very pleasant residence and mess, and this gave me the opportunity to conduct two seminars on 'Medium Maritime Power'. A flatteringly high proportion of those invited to attend did so, and some papers of high quality were presented.

Out of all that preliminary work the ideas in this book have grown. They, and particularly their imperfections, are mine; the modern vogue for composite books and contributory passages is not followed here. But they owe a debt, and it is here acknowledged, to many people who have given me the benefit of their knowledge and wisdom: among them Jonathan Alford, Clive Archer, Ken Booth, Sir James Cable, Ivan Cosby, Admiral Sir James Eberle, Rear Admiral Edward Gueritz, Captain Peter Kimm, Geoffrey Kinley, Captain Guy Liardet, James McConnell, Vice Admiral Sir Ian McGeoch, Professor Peter Nailor, Captain Richard Sharpe, Professor Bryan Ranft, Commander Michael Ranken, Geoffrey Till, Elizabeth Young. In France there has been much help from Hervé Coutau-Bégarie, Admiral Marcel Duval and Rear Admiral Olivier Sevaistre; in India, from Vice Admiral M. P. Awati; in Brazil from Captain Ruiz; in Japan, from Dr Seiichiro Onishi. As ever, my wife Patricia has tolerated, supported and encouraged throughout, as well as acting as secretary to the seminars. The book would not have happened if she had not been there.

2 MEDIUM POWER

It is a platitude that all nations are unique. Like most platitudes, though, the statement can do with examination. Certainly uniqueness is conferred by the cores of language; constitutional, cultural, social and economic structures; and geographical characteristics that go to make up the identity which lies at the heart of the idea of a nation-state. Sometimes the uniqueness is strong, apparent to the most casual traveller or observer; sometimes it is subtle, merging into the uniqueness of neighbouring countries; but it is always there.

But this is not to say that nation-states may not share common, or very similar, characteristics. The briefest scan of statistical data suggests that it is possible, for example, to group together those nations with a relatively high *per capita* income, and call them rich; and those with a relatively low one, to call them poor. At a rather less crude level of analysis, it may be possible to find groupings for nations' dependence on external trade or on certain types of economic activity. Whether it is possible to extend this kind of categorisation to the much more subtle matter of Power is a question this chapter has to answer.

Power is not the easiest of words to define; there are 14 heads of definition in the *Concise Oxford Dictionary*. This book is concerned with state power, and in general it treats states as entities with identifiable and coherent external policies. Contradictions and controversies within a state can of course have an effect on its power and its use of power; but generally the book's assumption will be that such forces are contained. It does not subscribe to class-based theories of ruling elites or internal struggle; the strategies of those who think along such lines are, inevitably, turned towards internal rather than external objectives.[1] The power of a state, then, is regarded here as directed, purposive, and in accordance with national policy. Its elements will be diverse, neither all military nor all economic nor all diplomatic in character, and all will not be active at the same time. But, in a properly-conceived strategy, they will work together in a way that provides us with a working definition of Power: they give a state *the ability to influence events.*

The Elements of Power

'Economic power' is almost as elusive a term as 'power' itself. It comprehends by far the largest manifestations of vigour in most nations. But, for the purposes of this book, such effort may not be particularly effective. Many busy, indeed thriving, economies are largely turned inward upon themselves. On the other hand, an economy such as Japan's has had a great deal of power in precisely the terms of this definition: it really does influence events in its effect on world markets, on levels of expectation, on the weight given to Japan in world counsels. But, and it is an important caveat, the events influenced are in the main economic ones.[2] Partly this is implicit in the workings of economic power itself; partly it is due to the fact that (more of course in capitalist economies than others) economic power lies under individual or corporate, and not state, control. Perhaps even more acutely, the influence of financial institutions tends to be less pervasive than might be imagined. Massive international debts, even if foreclosed, do not seem to inhibit states from military adventures. Economic power, therefore, is by no means a certain arbiter in security issues; it tends to feed upon, and influence, its own kind. But if this is its chief characteristic in external terms, it is of course internally an indispensable base for the other strong elements of a state.

More diffuse are the effects of a second and often underrated element: intellectual power. A strong educational base, a climate of intellectual activity and innovation, a rich and widespread language, articulated philosophies or ideologies, a cultivated approach to science and technology, are all tremendous assets to a state. The case of Israel, aided as it is by the immensely lively and fertile intellectual doings of international Jewry, is one of the most instructive in the modern world; but (since, earlier in this chapter, I abjured Marxist method) it is not inappropriate either to pay tribute to Marxism for its ability to influence the course of history. Nor, in the narrower intellectual field of diplomacy, is it possible to view the French foreign service as anything but the strongest yet most delicate of tools; its exploits under de Gaulle were so astonishing in their agility and stubbornness that they seem somewhat paler since, but they are still a remarkable manifestation of power. Increasingly, too, one sees that not only knowledge but the ability to organise knowledge in an efficient way is a major element of state power. Intellectual power is, in sum, pervasive, often slow-working, but always active if turned outward.

The third category of power is military. No states now admit to, and few pursue, a force-led foreign policy; conquest is not in fashion; wars there are, but they are often restrained and always full of protestations (from both sides) of legality and self-defence. Yet world armament is at its highest level ever, in any terms one cares to think of: firepower, allocation of resources (absolute, or *per capita*, or by comparison with national incomes) and public perception. The countervailing tensions, checks and balances that create this situaton will form a large part of the study that follows. It is enough to say here that military measures have the capacity to influence events in a radical and widespread way. When latent ('threat'), this influence is likely to be slow-acting and restrictive; when active ('conflict'), it is usually radical. Military power when used can be very widespread in its effects, affecting every part of the national life of its victim and, indeed, of the state projecting it.

Thus, in this analysis, there are three major classifications of state power: the power of goods and money, of knowledge and ideas, and of arms. The first is intrinsically desirable, and provides a base for other forms of power, but is often operationally unusable; the second powerful but slow-acting, not always controllable; the third dangerous and either menacing or violent. They may be thought an unholy trio, and they are certainly not the three Graces, but they are the means by which states seek to protect their vulnerabilities and promote their interests.

Vulnerabilities and Vital Interests

A nation-state will always seek to maintain its existence as an entity. That is another plonking platitude, and like the one with which this chapter began, it needs more than an assenting nod. States riven by communal tensions, whether ethnic, religious or political, may possess so little internal coherence that their impulse to maintain identity is very weak. By the same token, they are likely as states to be ineffective as actors on the international scene. This does not mean that their factions will have no influence, for they may generate support in other countries or communities; this is the power of ideas again. Nevertheless, for the purposes of this study such nations, and such influences, are not a central theme. The platitude will do, therefore, as a working hypothesis.

To maintain a state's existence as an entity there are two basic requirements, and these have never been better expressed than in the United Nations Charter:[3] Territorial Integrity and Political Independence.

Territorial Integrity

An Englishman may well be the worst sort of person in the world to discuss territorial integrity. The Island has for long been a practical entity. Its internal borders are marked by no more than courtesy signs; its economic and cultural diversities — however deeply felt — are relatively well-adjusted; it has not been successfully invaded certainly for three centuries, arguably for nine. Its territorial integrity has been built up and preserved with conspicuous effectiveness. It is not so with the other island, across the Irish Sea; there all the problems of faction, irredentism, insecure borders, uneasy sea frontiers, that are commonplace to other states are also a problem for the United Kingdom. But, mainly because they are remote from the mainland, they are seen by most Englishmen as less serious than perhaps they are.

For most nations, as I have suggested, territorial integrity is a much more sensitive issue. The majority of states in the world are of comparatively recent origin. They have the fundamental problem of putting themselves together, of nation-building; they are often stuck with frontiers that were fixed by others and cut across ethnic, as well as natural, boundaries. All this is likely to bring in its wake irredentism, border disputes, impatience and a desire for more or less radical solutions. On the whole, however, the inviolability of land frontiers is one of the strongest tenets of the United Nations, and outlets for border disputes may often be sought on sea frontiers.

States that are older — that may have existed, say, since before the early 1920s — tend to have territorial problems that are, in the medical sense, chronic rather than acute. Many of their disputed border areas will have changed hands several times. They will generally be sensitive, often more sensitive than pure logic would dictate, to the possibility of invasion across land frontiers. Their ethnic and other inter-community differences will tend to be deep-seated, sometimes dormant and sometimes festering. They will have established *vis-à-vis* their neighbours customary practices that may or may not be disputed; at sea these will tend to concern historic rights of user.

What is at once apparent is that territorial integrity, on land at any rate, is peculiarly sensitive to the military element of power. Except in the rare case of a state giving up, by genuinely voluntary action, part of its territory to the sovereignty of another, or the case (equally rare) of its doing so as a result of international arbitration, changes in territorial make-up are the product of the use or the threat of force.

The integrity of sea territory is a less simple matter. To begin with, there are various degrees of state sovereignty over it; over internal waters, it is virtually the same as land territory; over the territorial sea, qualified by certain rights of user by other nations; over the economic zone and continental shelf, limited to sovereign rights connected with resource enjoyment. Consequently the inviolability of territory tends to be a qualified notion at sea, and the absolute sanctions of force or threat of force tend not only to be blurred but supplemented by economic, diplomatic and legal pressures.

Political Independence

If the British experience is atypical with respect to territorial integrity, it may equally be thought so as regards political independence. While some sturdy souls are found to question current notions of 'interdependence' as a basis for international dealings, there is an assumption — more generally held the closer one gets to the western side of Whitehall — that independence is a 'highly stratified and variable phenomenon'[4] which can never be taken for granted and is likely to be heavily qualified by circumstances.

This sort of weary sophistication does not seem to me to be a characteristic of most countries in the world. Many are far too new to political independence to see it as anything but a glowing reality, a jewel as rich as territorial integrity, as nationhood itself. Others have spent far too long, devising shifts and manoeuvres to preserve political independence, to belittle it by allowing notions of dependence, however qualified, to become part of their policies. Those that clearly have no independence, that are tied to blocs or locked into hegemonies, shift uneasily and sometimes indulge in occasional, illusory flurries of solo diplomatic action.[5]

There is something to be said on the sophisticates' side, nevertheless. Political independence is itself a notion much less precise than territorial integrity. Is it merely the right of a state's people to choose their own form of government and rulers? Or the right of that government to formulate and act by its own policies? Or the right of a nation-state to resist undue pressures, from whatever kind of power, to make it change its policies?

Probably it is all these things. It is at once clear that, just as political independence is more imprecise and diffuse than territorial integrity, so the means by which it can be attacked are more diverse. It is evidently susceptible to all the elements of power that have been discussed in this chapter. It can be influenced by economic power; there is no doubt that, whatever Canadians like to think, Canada's freedom of political action is circumscribed by the economic power of the United States. It can be influenced by the power of ideas; the very phrase 'battle for hearts and minds' so often used by external powers about nations in turmoil is a clear indication of this kind of intervention. And it can be influenced by military power; the invasion of Czechoslovakia by the Soviet Union in 1968 was simply in order to snuff out the independence of the 'Prague spring'.

Naturally the question arises, much more than it does over territorial integrity, how far non-military uses of power, and influence amounting to less than total dominance, are activities prohibited by Article 2(4) of the United Nations Charter. That article speaks only of the 'threat or use of force'; and however stretched it may have been by appeals over the past 40 years to the Security Council or the General Assembly, that phrase surely does not cover the power of economic factors or ideas, provided that the threat of force is not used to back them. There are however other parts of the Charter, notably Articles 1(2), 2(1) and 33, as well as numerous General Assembly Resolutions, which condemn (either explicitly, or by implication) interference in the affairs and policies of another state; they add up to a general prohibition of the condition of dominance by one state over one or more others that is fashionably called hegemony. Moreover, it can be said that most hegemonies, if resisted, lead to a threat or use of force. Thus it can probably be said that even though hegemony is an overused and underdefined word, it surely was one of the contingencies Article 2(4) was designed to guard against.

The Extension of Vital Interests

Territorial integrity and political independence, then, may be taken as core interests of a state. But it may be questioned whether they exhaust the catalogue of vital interests. If they do, and if states embark upon conflict only when their vital interests are under severe threat (and this a pretty commonly held view), what can be made of such actions as Britain's in the Indonesian Confrontation with Malaysia; France's in Chad; or New Zealand's incursions into French nuclear testing zones in the Pacific? Even the Falklands campaign of 1982 would have required a pretty elastic description of territorial integrity where the United Kingdom was concerned. It must be that there is a third category of interests that states deem vital, more elusive than those in the Charter.

A pointer, maybe the most accurate pointer, lies in the notion of betterment. The overwhelming majority of governments, of whatever political persuasion, *desire that the governed shall flourish.* (Marxists profess not to believe this of capitalist governments, nor capitalists of Marxist governments; it is true nevertheless.) And in order to achieve that betterment, governments set objectives. They were described, idiosyncratically perhaps, by Lasswell in 1950:[6] Power, Wealth, Enlightenment, Well-being, Respect, Skill, Solidarity, Rectitude. The list is self-evidently imprecise and incomplete, and it has been well said that any set of terms that laid down objectives would do equally well;[7] the point is that it adds up to a list of Goods — some material, some operational, some cerebral — which states would regard as desirable and of which it would strongly wish to increase its stock (even of Rectitude and Solidarity, which can be painfully immobilising). If momentum towards these objectives is adversely changed, even reversed, a state may be in danger — of loss of international leverage, of loss of wealth, of loss of self-respect.[8] Such developments affect governments in two ways: a genuine sense of having failed the governed, often through weakness when strength might have availed; and a more self-serving appreciation of a risk to their own survival.

In consequence, states (and governments that are their operational arm) must regard as vital their aspirations towards betterment, and the key operations that realise those aspirations. Clearly questions of degree arise; a threat to a very small sliver of Wealth, a smidgeon of Well-being, a salami-slice of Rectitude, may not be regarded as vital. But the sum of such threats could be. Britain's experience in the Indonesian confrontation is instructive. She wished to preserve a carefully nurtured Malaysian state (Rectitude, Solidarity) which was an important source of raw materials (Wealth, Well-being) and lay on one side of an important strategic strait (Power), against a nation which was then perceived as likely to become a permanent member of an opposing bloc if it was allowed to succeed (Power again). Britain's credibility as an ally and as a decolonising state would have been gravely weakened had she abdicated responsibility (Respect). The sum of all these interests was rightly regarded as vital, in the face of much diplomatic hostility and domestic apathy.

Preserving Vital Interests

Since the whole of this book is about the preservation of vital interests — specifically those of medium powers — by sea, it would be absurd to attempt at this stage a summary of how states set out to do the job. It is enough to say that they should seek to assess their vulnerabilities — not only in the field of territorial integrity but in the much more difficult ones of political independence and of the package of objectives that have been characterised as the Extension of Vital Interests — and review the resources that are nationally available to ensure that the vulnerabilities are not exploited to their detriment. The inevitable mismatch will result in that amalgam of measures, devices and policies which, in the complexity of the modern world, form the strategies of the majority of states. But it is to the nature of those states, and in particular the characteristics of those which could be regarded as medium powers, that we must now turn.

The Classification of States

Since this discussion is about powers, and (as has been suggested above) power is a diverse, sometimes ill-defined, often unquantifiable thing, the search for classes or categories of powers is most unlikely to end in a statistical table. But it is not entirely illogical to begin with one; and since economic power is by far the most measurable of the kinds of power described, Table 2.1 gives population, *per capita* income and gross domestic product for 35 states in the world that appear to possess substantial economic power.

The figures and rankings will be familiar enough to students of international affairs. The USA and USSR stand out clearly as economic giants with Japan not far behind the Soviet Union in national income; India and China are prominent because of their vast populations; Western European countries figure prominently

Table 2.1: Economic Power, 1982

Country	Population (millions)	Gross Domestic Product ($ Bn.)	Per Capita Income ($)	Exports ($ Bn.)	As % GDP
Argentina	29.16	100.0[a]	3,500[a]	7.63	7.6
Australia	15.18	159.42	9,518	20.71	13.0
Austria	7.57	67.25	7,731	15.43	22.9
Belgium	9.86	86.23	7,870	51.25	59.4
Brazil	126.81	250.68	2,125	21.90	8.7
Canada	24.63	298.57	10,275	76.75	25.7
Chile	11.49	24.14	1,699	3.84	15.9
China	1,020.00	500.00[a]	490[a]	22.18	4.4
Denmark	5.12	56.38	9,606	16.00	28.4
Egypt	44.67	29.14	660	3.12	10.7
Finland	4.82	49.10	8,685	12.54	25.5
France	54.22	540.44	8,814	94.94	17.6
Germany, W.	61.64	660.39	9,341	169.45	25.7
Greece	9.79	37.69	3,614	4.41	11.7
India	711.66	172.92	219	9.36	5.4
Indonesia	153.03	88.46	578	21.15	23.9
Iran	40.24	104.06	2,223	19.50	18.7
Israel	4.02	22.98	5,098	5.06	22.0
Italy	56.74	347.36	5,512	72.77	21.0
Japan	118.45	1,060.50	7,677	146.96	13.9
Mexico	73.01	164.10	3,063	21.12	12.9
Netherlands	14.31	137.03	8,599	65.41	47.7
New Zealand	3.16	22.78	6,689	5.28	23.2
Nigeria	82.39	66.67	804	11.60	17.4
Norway	4.12	56.18	11,273	17.98	32.0
Pakistan	92.45	28.83	312	3.08	10.6
S. Africa	31.01	70.94	1,885	18.61	26.2
Soviet Union	269.99	1,500.00[a]	2,674	86.91	5.8
Spain	37.94	179.66	4,398	19.73	11.0
Sweden	8.33	99.11	10,223	27.42	27.7
Switzerland	6.48	96.54	14,093	25.59	26.5
Turkey	46.31	52.77	1,139	5.73	10.9
United Kingdom	56.28	459.70	7,548	91.83	20.0
USA	232.06	3,025.70	11,695	200.54	6.6
Venezuela	14.71	67.86	4,260	15.04	22.2

Note: a. Estimate.
Sources: Economist Intelligence Unit; *The Military Balance, 1984–85.*

for wealth both absolute and *per capita*; Brazil and Australia, in their different ways, look like young giants.

But in terms of power Table 2.1 looks raw and superficial. Near the bottom of the scale comes Israel; yet if power is defined as the ability to influence events, Israel has far more power in today's

Table 2.2: Military Power, 1984

Country	Men under arms (thousands)	Army (thousands)	Major Warships	Combat Aircraft	Defence Budget ($m.)
Argentina	153	100	20	170	1,900
Australia	72	33	19	133	4,945
Austria	50	45	–	32	767
Belgium	94	65	4	147	1,769
Brazil	274	183	24	215	2,000[a]
Canada	83	55	23	160	6,443
Chile	96	53	11	102	2,300[a]
China	4,000	3,160	138	5,300	8,200[a]
Denmark	31	18	10	96	1,127
Egypt	460	315	22	504	3,043
Finland	36	31	2	76	718
France	471	305	65	492	16,817
Germany, W.	495	336	44	486	17,396
Greece	178	135	31	303	2,287
India	1,120	960	36	920	5,684
Indonesia	281	210	12	83	2,527
Iran	555	250	9	95	17,370
Israel	141	104	7	555	5,000[a]
Italy	375	260	40	300	8,143
Japan	245	155	64	270	11,617
Mexico	370	344	15	85	582
Netherlands	103	65	28	174	4,227
New Zealand	13	6	4	33	470
Nigeria	133	120	6	42	1,240
Norway	37	20	21	114	1,657
Pakistan	479	450	19	314	1,873
S. Africa	83	67	4	304	2,700
Soviet Union	5,115	1,840	650	3,260	250,000[a]
Spain	330	240	35	215	3,350[a]
Sweden	66	47	14	410	2,589
Switzerland	20	580 (on mob.)	–	310	1,974
Turkey	602	500	31	458	1,635
United Kingdom	326	162	86	620	23,844
USA	2,136	781	340	3,700	273,400
Venezuela	44	27	11	85	1,200[a]

Notes: a. Estimate.

'Major Warships' include submarines and corvettes but not fast attack craft, minesweepers or amphibious vessels.

Source: *The Military Balance, 1984–85.*

world than the majority of the states in the table.

Military power too is to some extent susceptible to numerical analysis. Table 2.2 shows, for the same 35 countries, some of the more obvious military parameters. They are very crude and arbitrary, but give some indication of relative military power. Comparing the two tables, many sharp differences between economic and military power are apparent. Perhaps the most striking example is given by the cases of Egypt and New Zealand, who have similar gross domestic products but whose armed forces' weight differs by a factor that could be anything between 5 and 30, according to how it is viewed. Almost as dramatic is the difference, constantly quoted by defence commentators, between the top two economic powers — the United States and the Soviet Union — and the third, Japan. The first two are, simply from the figures, military giants, commanding forces of enormous weight. The third has extant military resources nowhere near this level, less by a factor of ten or more, comparable with those of a dozen much less rich nations.

Numerical analysis, then, can be helpful in establishing the limits of what may or may not be a medium power. Medium-ness, if one can put it that way, is more likely than not to be discovered in nations that appear in the tables; individual countries of less substance, that do not appear, may claim consideration, but prima facie they do not. It will be convenient, even if it is considered by many of them to be insulting, to call them small powers. They may, in the analysis which follows, be joined in the small power category by many of the nations that do appear in the table. At the other end of the scale stand out two, possibly three, states that cannot be considered as medium, and form a phenomenon of our age: the superpowers.

Superpowers

From de Tocqueville to Buchan, there has been no shortage of writers willing to discuss the nature of superpower, and this one has little new to add. Superpowers can be regarded as states 'with a stake in peace and freedom everywhere and the power to protect them';[9] as strategic monoliths capable of protecting all their vital interests from their own resources;[10] as diplomatic motors who believe that no problem in the world can be solved without their participation;[11] as economic giants whose collapse or weakening would bring about a catastrophe in the world's economy;[12] as rivals for the job of world policeman;[13] as leaders of rival ideologies.[14] In the terms of the view of power taken in this book, they can be summed up as wielders of all the three categories of power to an extent which, if fully deployed, is preponderant against any but another superpower.

As to who the superpowers are, the literature is as diverse as it is on the nature of superpower itself. Buchan, in his work in the early 1970s on a 'multipolar world', called Japan an economic superpower;[15] some writers equate power groupings such as the European Economic Community with economic and perhaps political (whatever that means) superpower; at the other end of the scale, serious doubts have been raised as to whether the Soviet Union is a superpower in anything but military terms. It seems to me that all these excursions are loose and ultimately defective. The first two falter because, as has been shown, economic power can be outflanked by military or, sometimes, intellectual power; a state or group of states that can so readily be outflanked cannot claim the attributes of superpower. Moreover, the coherence of non-federal groupings such as the EEC is too fragile to allow the unity of policy that a superpower needs.[16] Finally, the third excursion discounts the great intellectual power exercised by Marxism and the advantages it gives the Soviet Union, and it belittles the real economic strength of the USSR and the perceptions held of it in the Third World.

It can be held, then, that the USA and the USSR are without doubt superpowers in the meaning that has been given here to the term, and that neither Japan, nor any European state or grouping, nor any other nation in the world save arguably one, merits the title.

That one is China. With a land area similar to that of the United States, a population four times as great, a cultural tradition of unparalleled length, growing industries at all levels of technology, and military forces of great size and a wide range of capability (including a considerable inventory of nuclear weapons), China has a very good case for consideration as a superpower. Against this, however, are the facts that her *per capita* income is still very low, indicating that domestic problems will inhibit the external exercise of power; that she has not gathered round her a cluster of dependent, client or allied states to buttress or extend her power; and that her military power, except for the crudest nuclear forms, is incapable of world-wide projection.[17] The question remains open.

There will be some situations in which it is appropriate to regard China as a superpower; there will be others, perhaps more in the context of this book, in which she should be regarded as less than that. It will never be appropriate to consider her a medium power. As it has so often been through the centuries, China is *sui generis*.

Small Powers

If small powers occupy the bottom end of the hierarchy, clearly their distinguishing characteristic must be relative weakness. The effect of this weakness on their vital interests constitutes the limiting factor as to whether a nation is to be judged as a small or a medium power. It is appropriate when establishing this limit to confine oneself to the most basic of vital interests, that is to say, territorial integrity and political independence. The critical question is what a state can do, with its own resources, to safeguard these.

Small powers will be as unique as medium and superpowers. Their frontiers may be maritime or land or both; their land areas extensive or tiny; their populations numerous or sparse; their economies developed or emerging; their domestic situations stable or volatile. In any of these areas their vulnerabilities may be enough to make it impossible to secure them as entities without the guarantee of support from some outside agency. In the terms of the Charter this ought of course to be the United Nations, but as is well known that body's authority is moral and not, as it was meant to be, also potentially coercive. Small powers, then, may look for their guarantees to other states or groupings of states; or, if they are remote, strategically insignificant and not attractive economically, they may rely on those facts to avoid involvement and to preserve their treasured sovereignty. Luxembourg and Tuvalu could be taken to typify the extremes of small powers' solutions to the problem.

But it is the more substantial small powers that are of interest in this study because they lie near the limit between small and medium powers.

The case of Norway is instructive. Her large area, rugged terrain and independent, freedom-loving and hardy people are all characteristics that might put her into the medium-power category if she chose to realise her resources strategically. But, no doubt as a result not only of Norway's perception of a massive and ready threat just across the border but of her history and her view of the moral surrounds of the problem, she has chosen a more dependent role. By regarding herself as a small power, she has become one.

Medium Power

Medium powers then lie between the self-sufficient and the insufficient. Plainly, if they are going to be sufficient only in parts, they need to think even harder than their super- or small-power counterparts.

They need to think first about their vital interests. They are most unlikely to regard territorial integrity and political independence as a full catalogue; they will, that is to say, take much account of what this chapter has called the Extension of Vital Interest in the forms of material and economic gain and of international status and influence. They will do this for a variety of reasons, often co-existing, seldom mutually exclusive. One reason for states to hold such aspirations is because they are used to them: mature nations can be accustomed to wealth and power, even if they are perhaps as one commentator had it 'medium powers on the way down'.[18] Another reason is size of landmass, population or both; a medium power, more likely in this case a power 'on the way up', can look at itself and judge that it ought to command such wealth, wield such influence. Linked to this may be the notion of manifest destiny, that sustained the young United States (at one time, after all, a medium power) and now sustains beleaguered Israel. Finally, there is simply the amalgam of fact and history and prospects that suggests a many-sided, extensive set of interests, backed by powerful constituencies at home that will not easily forgo them, a set national and unique.

The other important part of a medium power's self-perception (and, it is to be hoped, self-knowledge) is that it can do something, of itself, to look after its interests, even the extended ones. It is not, and because it commands substantial resources need not be, content that their protection should be subject to the initiatives of an external guarantor. Realism will dictate that there are limits to the self-help that can be contemplated; but it is of the essence of medium power that it regards self-help, up to those limits, as possible.

The medium power then regards itself as of sufficient weight and substance to be in charge of its own destiny; and it realises that its uniqueness is complicated enough, and different enough, even from its closest friends', to ensure that, in some crises at any rate, coincidence of interest will not be enough to engage help on their side. Thus, the medium power will try *to create and keep under national control enough means of power to initiate and sustain coercive actions whose outcome will be the preservation of its vital interests.*

The words of this central statement need careful and critical examination and development, and this in effect will proceed through the rest of this book. At this stage, it will be useful to look at a few of them in more detail.

Vital Interests. As has been suggested, these will not be confined to territorial integrity and political independence; but the extended interests, those concerned with national betterment, will have to be carefully assessed if peripheral, non-vital matters are not to soak up scarce resources.

Means of Power. These will not all be military; the other elements of power must be available to their full potential, though as has been shown military power is usually a necessary backing for them.

National Control. Because its interests are not coincident even with those of its closest friends, the medium power must maintain control of the situation in its own hands. This requires an institutional structure *vis-à-vis* its colleagues which includes no power of veto on their part, and a power structure which gives the medium power the ability to command its own resources in crisis.

Initiate and Sustain. The initiative for safeguarding vital interests should lie with the medium power and not be abdicated to any other agency. But initiative will probably not be sufficient — particularly in cases where peculiarly national interests are involved — to ensure a satisfactory outcome. The ability to sustain pressure, at national level, will be needed. That such pressure may need to be applied to friends as well as opponents — even though it be pressure of two different kinds — goes without saying.

Coercive Action. The ultimate in power, as the ability to influence events, is evidently coercive action. Without the capacity to take such action, a state may find its earlier attempts to influence may be called as bluff. With it, a stable situation may be achieved without any action being necessary to coerce or even to influence.

This situation is the norm in a power-directed world; two of the more common ways of describing its main features are Balance of Power and Deterrence.

Some Examples of Medium Power Perceptions and Strategy

France. Shorn of its more pretentious references to *grandeur,* which are anyhow much less frequent as the great shadow of de Gaulle fades, French strategy is something of an exemplar of the principles above. It was determination to keep the levers, and many of the motors, of power in her own hands that made France leave the military structure of the NATO Alliance and to continue, at great expense, an independent nuclear weapons programme. She recognises that the Western Alliance is necessary to her, but most French strategic writers are rather coy about how they think it would operate on her behalf.[19] Instead they are ready to describe what France should be ready to do: *Dissuasion*, including the threat of quick recourse to nuclear weapons, to deter attack on metropolitan France; *Action*, at an appropriate level, for lesser and more remote contingencies of which Chad was a typical mid-1980s example.[20] French forces are structured accordingly, and in 1984 France announced the formation of a *Force d'action rapide* of 47,000 men which could more flexibly take on the *Action* task.[21] This of course outlines only the military side of French power. France has long used with some success her power in the economic field, offering a wide range of consumer goods including military hardware, and backed it with the third, intellectual arm of power — in her case the linguistic legacy of *France outre-mer*, a cultural and legal heritage, and highly skilled diplomacy.

India. As the largest of the ex-colonial and developing powers, India has always regarded herself as a leader among them, but also, for herself, as a power of natural weight in her own region. Many Indian writers refer to her as a medium, middle or regional power.[22] Her preferred stance is one of non-alignment; but she is willing to form associations with other states, including the most powerful, in order to maintain the strategic balance in her area of interest. 'A middle power-superpower interaction', writes Ashok Kapur, 'is first and foremost a study of engagement of the stronger by the weaker.'[23] This has, in the past decade and a half, been in India's case an engagement of the Soviet Union and the power involved has been mainly military in character. Two main reasons can be identified: American and British rejection of India's arms requirements in the early 1960s[24] and Indian perceptions, in the late 1970s and beyond, that the chief hegemonial threat in the Indian Ocean was the USA.[25] India recognises that her own forces are not sufficient to take on a superpower alone, but they must 'be so determined as to provide a credible threshold of deterrence to any belligerent country'.[26] Against regional states, however, Indian forces should be capable of reaching a successful outcome on their own.[27]

Japan. Since 1946 Japan's strategy has been dominated by her revulsion from militarism and consequent stress on self-defence as the only justification for forces or force. The legitimacy even of the Self Defence Force (SDF) has been frequently challenged within the country. However, the strategic basis of the SDF structure has in fact been quite clearly articulated in various national defence programmes and guidelines, notably in the late 1970s; in its latest form, it is to maintain surveillance and the capacity to defend against limited aggression but to call upon the United States (to whom facilities in Japan are made available) for help in case of larger-scale operations.[28] Nuclear deterrent cover is entirely in the hands of the United States. Japan, therefore, has deliberately downplayed the military element of power except in the strictest terms of so-called 'exclusive defence', and many commentators in that country profess to look down upon those who emphasise it.[29] She wields great economic power and, at present, appears to take the view that its vulnerable elements will take care of themselves. However, there are many influential voices in Japan who call for the country to be more self-sufficient both in home defence and in defence of extended vital interests.[30]

Brazil. Throughout the 1950s and 1960s Brazil maintained a client relationship with the United States. In the 1970s, however, perhaps more than any nation in this brief initial survey, she lived up to the predictions of the pundits who were forecasting a 'multi-polar world'.[31] Her industrial growth was considerable, in spite of rapid inflation; she adopted a steadily more independent line in organisations as different as the Organisation of American States and the Law of the Sea Conference; and at least one of her strategists gave as a primary aim the ability to avoid being drawn into a conflict involving the United States.[32] However, Brazil's force structures did not greatly change over this time and indeed she spends even less of her gross domestic product on armaments than does Japan.[33] There is not much published writing about strategy in Brazil, and her main military preoccupations at present are clearly frontier protection by land and sea (with the Franco-Brazilian spiny lobster war as the most far-reaching excursion so far) and internal security.[34] However, as will be suggested in later chapters, this could be on the change.

Australia is as subject as any two-party democracy to cyclical and relatively frequent shifts in strategy; from the end of the Second World War up to the late 1970s, this was based on her heavy dependence on US support in the case of anything but a small-scale local attack. However, size, distance and weak neighbours were on her side to the extent that she could adopt what was, in effect, a 'no-threat' strategy. This called for a core force of small size but considerable versatility around which, in the years of mounting tension and threat, an effective defence — although one which would still rely on the USA in major crisis — could be built.[35] About 1980 this view shifted markedly towards greater *immediate* self-reliance 'in defence of Australia's national sovereignty and interests, below a higher threshold for assistance from abroad than (she has) in the past been accustomed to contemplate',[36] though the idea of build-up under threat remained.[37]

At the time of writing it is too early to judge how the Hawke government's defence policy will in turn modify this view. Certainly Australia is unlikely to look to economics or ideas as very critical levers of power for her; on the other hand, sheer geography is in her case at once a useful tool and — given the possibility of casual and remote lodgments — an irritating vulnerability.

Israel. In the post-war world Israel has perhaps the most extraordinary strategic story of all to tell. It is very largely, as this chapter has previously indicated, a matter of the power of ideas: the Zionist vision, the extraordinary morale and energy of a nation of three million invested by opponents over 20 times that number, the clever, subtle, forceful and loyal backing of influential Jews throughout the West. These have earned Israel not only admirers, but effective and most powerful guarantors, most importantly the United States. The guarantee of Israel's existence is to all intents and purposes absolute, and this is a very secure base from which to conduct a dynamic strategy.[38] It has enabled Israel to spend money on high-quality armaments without too much fear of economic ruin, to carry out pre-emptive operations without much regard for 'international public opinion', and to expand her effective control over land areas (*pace* Kissinger) without respect for established frontiers. Israel has, in fact, a great measure of self-reliance in strategic actions; and no country of comparable size is so commonly reckoned to possess a nuclear weapon.[39] Moreover, there is probably no country in which such a high proportion of everyday doings have a strategic element.[40] But it is the ultimate American guarantee that gives the necessary confidence.[41]

Britain. From a reading of declared defence policy, it is not easy to place Britain in the medium power category at all. The insistence of successive Statements on the Defence Estimates, and other defence White Papers, on the primacy of the NATO alliance and the subordination of British defence structures to the NATO treaty and doctrine suggest that the United Kingdom regards itself as a small power.[42] This view is reinforced by the refusal of these same documents to make any appraisal of vital interests or of Britain's power potential. However, Britain's actions are at sharp variance with her declarations. In 1982 she fought a severe medium-power war some 8,000 miles away from the home base and (more significantly) 5,000 miles from the nearest point in the NATO area. She has embarked on admittedly limited conflict against her allies on several occasions.[43] She has frequently deployed land, sea and air forces, in situations short of conflict, apparently to uphold or further national interests, in areas remote from Europe.[44] And she has embarked on many economic activities with strong strategic connotations, also in such areas. There is evidence, therefore, of considerable confusion, or internal disagreement, about what British defence policy means, and about whether Britain has a strategy at all. It is hoped that this book may help in resolving the problem.

The Search for a Keyword

As academic devices, examples and summaries are fraught with pitfalls and dangers: question-begging, and new paths leading nowhere, and false elisions, like a coda to a sonata movement by an inexperienced composer. Even more perilous is the Keyword, the touchstone for all that has gone before. Yet in this case it is tempting to search for one, a word that will without adding new dimensions encapsulate most of what I have been trying to say about the nature, and basic strategic outlook, of medium powers.

It is clear that size, and population, and wealth can all be limiting parameters of medium power. But, as can be seen from the case of Israel, those limits are in effect set pretty low, and they are moreover very fluid; for it is most doubtful if Norway or The Netherlands, both of them more favoured than Israel in all these parameters and much more favoured in some, can be thought of as medium powers. No doubt they could be, if their perceived strategic needs and therefore their strategies and power structures were different; but they are not.

Therefore, given a certain minimum potential in basic resources of territory, people, skills and industrial development (and Israel probably represents something near that limit) medium-ness depends on a state's *perception of itself*. Independence, as has been suggested, is too all-embracing a term to mirror that perception; the smallest powers prize their independence, even though it lies in the gift or under the guarantee of more powerful organisations. What distinguishes the medium power's view is its desire to possess, of itself, the wherewithal to maintain its existence as an entity. It must be the prime mover of the actions required, even if other states or organisations are sooner or later engaged in its support. It must so far as possible maintain this control as long as its interests remain threatened.

The idea that needs to be encapsulated, then, is one of self-movement, of control. The Greeks did not, quite, have a word for it; their nearest, *automatos*, a thing acting of itself, has in any case become overlaid in its anglicising with all manner of mechanical associations. It is necessary to fall back on a related word, also from Greek and also somewhat distorted by its common English usage: Autonomy.

Autonomy will be used, probably far too often for comfort, in the pages that follow in order to describe in a shorthand way the aims and strategic aspirations of medium powers as they have been analysed above. It is worth reviewing some quotations that use the word to see how they fit the emerging concept of medium power.

Alastair Buchan, in his seminal work of the early 1970s

(particularly the Reith lectures of 1973),[45] spoke of 'the changing interests of the very largest powers in the position of the middle powers of the area, India, Indonesia, Australia, Iran, the Gulf States, whose influence and autonomy are rising'.[46] Here Buchan seems to be using the word very much in the sense described above.

Buchan's vision of a multipolar world was clearer, more accurate and less radical than that of some of his predecessors or followers in this field. Some, for example, have put forward the idea of groupings of small or medium powers as moving forces in the world. Liska wrote in 1967 that in 'regional subsystems . . . states must show the capacity to enjoy foreign policy autonomy as a group or groups',[47] and Ashok Kapur in 1982 of 'autonomous regional power centres' in the Indian Ocean area.[48] The evidence that such groupings or regional foci have sufficient strategic autonomy to matter is at present rather flimsy; rather, the very fact of grouping seems to keep the chances for coherence of strategy at a very low level. ASEAN's continued reluctance to face strategic matters is a case in point.[49]

Kapur, on the other hand, seems to have scored a bull's-eye when he wrote:

> If a middle-sized state is able to achieve some autonomy for itself from the great powers, is the achievement of autonomy rather than possession of middle size (or possession of medium power in the scale of international hierarchy) the true essence of a middle power?[50]

Just so, one is tempted to say. How the medium power is able to realise its requirements, particularly in the maritime side of strategy, is for the rest of this book to analyse. For the time being no further summary is needed except to say that, for the purposes of that analysis, the distinguishing characteristic in a medium power's strategic aspirations is autonomy.

Notes

1. See, for example, Dan Smith, *Defence of the Realm in the 1980s* (Croom Helm, London, 1980), p. 22.
2. Bruce Grant, *The Security of South-East Asia* (International Institute for Strategic Studies, Adelphi Paper No. 142, 1978), p. 16.
3. Charter of the United Nations, Art. 2(4).

4. P. Nailor, Gosport Seminar on Medium Maritime Power, November 1981, unpublished record.

5. These can quickly be damped. When Chancellor Honecker of the German Democratic Republic planned to visit Bonn in late 1984, he was brought into line by Russian opposition and the visit was called off.

6. Lasswell and Kaplan, *Power and Society* (Yale University Press, New Haven, 1950).

7. Myers S. McDougal and William T. Burke, *The Public Order of the Oceans* (Yale University Press, New Haven, 1962), p. 17, n. 45. Compare, for example, the statement of United Kingdom national objectives in *The UK's Overseas Representation*, Cmnd. 7308 (HMSO, London, 1978): 'To safeguard the security of our country, to protect its prosperity, to uphold and extend its basic values and freedoms, to honour commitments and obligations, to work for a peaceful and just world, and to contribute to the achievement of the above by providing assistance to developing countries.' When analysed, these do not turn out to be very different from Lasswell's objectives.

8. Michael Howard, in his brilliant essay on *The Causes of Wars* (Temple Smith, London, 1983), says (p. 16) that states go to war 'to maintain their power'. Given an elastic definition of state power such as has been adopted in this chapter, the statement holds.

9. Oscar Handlin, *The History of the United States*, Vol. 2 (Holt, Rinehart & Winston, New York, 1967), p. 655.

10. J. R. Hill, 'Maritime Forces for Medium Powers', *Naval Forces*, Vol. 5 (1984), p. 27.

11. Ashok Kapur, *The Indian Ocean: Regional and International Power Politics* (Praeger, New York, 1982), p. 104; Stephen E. Ambrose, *Rise to Globalism: American Foreign Policy since 1938*, 3rd revised edn (Penguin Books, London, 1983), p. 18.

12. Edward R. Fried in *The Next Phase in US Foreign Policy*, ed. Henry Owen (Brookings, Washington, 1973), pp. 157–202.

13. Ambrose, *Rise to Globalism*, p. 13.

14. C. Bolt, *A History of the USA* (Macmillan, London, 1974), pp. 590–5.

15. Alastair Buchan, *Change Without War* (Chatto and Windus, London, 1974), p. 21.

16. The compromises that emerge from smoke-filled rooms as a US or Soviet delegation's 'line' at any international conference may be tortuous; but they are at once more self-consistent and more comprehensive than anything a meeting of EEC delegations produces. This observation is based on the author's personal experience in Law of the Sea and Arms Control negotiations.

17. Harish Kapur, *The Awakening Giant* (Sijthoff and Noordhoff, Amsterdam, 1981), pp. 286–9.

18. P. Nailor, at a John Bell Systems seminar, 12 February 1985.

19. See, for example, *La Sécurité de L'Europe dans les années 80*, ed. Pierre Lellouche (Institut Français des Relations Internationales, 1980), particularly J. M. Daillet at p. 353 and M. Aurillac at p. 361.

20. Aurillac, ibid., p. 361; conversations with Admirals Duval and Sevaistre, September 1984.

21. *Le Monde*, 9 May 1984.

22. See, for example, P. K. S. Namboodiri, J. P. Anand and Sreedhar, in *Intervention in the Indian Ocean* (ABC Publishing House, New Delhi, 1982); Ashok Kapur, *The Indian Ocean*. The perception is also confirmed by Vice Admiral M. P. Awati in correspondence with the author.

23. Ashok Kapur, *The Indian Ocean*, p. 37.

24. Joel Larus, 'India: The Neglected Service Faces the Future', *United States*

Naval Institute Proceedings, March 1981, p. 78.

25. Namboodiri, Anand and Sreedhar, *Intervention in the Indian Ocean*, pp. 129–30.

26. Admiral S. N. Kohli, lecture to Indian Staff College, 1979.

27. Admiral S. N. Kohli, *Sea Power and the Indian Ocean* (Tata-McGraw Hill, New York, 1978), p. 91.

28. J. W. M. Chapman, R. Drifte and I. T. M. Gow, *Japan's Quest for Comprehensive Security* (Frances Pinter, London, 1983), pp. 53, 65–70.

29. Shimpei Fujimaki, 'Japan in the Eastern Sea', lecture at the Ninth Greenwich Forum, September 1983.

30. I. P. S. G. Cosby, 'Self-Defence as a Basis for Maritime Forces', Second Gosport Seminar on Medium Maritime Power, July 1982, unpublished record.

31. These predictions were so widespread, and sometimes so extreme, in the early 1970s that it is difficult to select examples: but see Buchan, *Change Without War*; Henry Owen, *The Next Phase in Foreign Policy*, pp. 1–8; A. Doak Barnett, *Uncertain Passage* (Brookings, Washington, 1973), pp. 243–315; George Liska, *Alliances and the Third World* (Johns Hopkins University Press, Baltimore, 1967), p. 8.

32. Domingos P. C. Ferreira, *The Navy of Brazil: an Emerging Power at Sea* (National Defense University, Washington, 1983), p. 40.

33. *The Military Balance, 1983–84* (International Institute for Strategic Studies, London), p. 127.

34. James Cable, *Gunboat Diplomacy*, 2nd edn (Macmillan, London, 1981), p. 119.

35. Australian Defence White Paper, 1979.

36. D. J. Killen in R. O'Neill and D. M. Horner (eds), *Australian Defence Policy for the 1980s* (University of Queensland Press, Queensland, 1982), p. 23.

37. Ibid., p. 31.

38. cf. Henry Kissinger, 1970: 'The United States is committed to defend Israel's existence, but not its conquests': quoted in Ambrose, *Rise to Globalism*, p. 341.

39. N. Safran, *Israel — The Embattled Ally* (Belknap Press, Harvard, 1978), p. 483.

40. Ibid., p. 230.

41. Liska, *Alliances*, p. 40.

42. Notably Cmnd. 8288, *Defence — The Way Forward* (HMSO, London, 1981).

43. Three 'cod wars' against Iceland: 1958; 1972; 1975.

44. For example, Oman 1970–75; Strait of Hormuz, 1980–5; Belize, 1977–82. These aspects are, admittedly, rather better explained in government documents, but they do not fully resolve the dichotomy.

45. Buchan, *Change Without War*, p. 21.

46. Ibid., p. 21.

47. Liska, *Alliances*, p. 44.

48. A. Kapur, *The Indian Ocean*, p. xiv.

49. A. Brionowski (ed.), *Understanding ASEAN* (Macmillan, London, 1982), pp. 17, 46, 179; Sqn Leader J. Clementson, 'No More Dominoes: ASEAN and Regional Security', RUSI, *Journal*, December 1984, p. 36.

50. A. Kapur, *The Indian Ocean*, p. 33.

3 MARITIME POWER

Most states use the sea. Of over 150 members of the United Nations, under 30 are landlocked (Switzerland is not a member of the United Nations: that makes one more). And there appears to be no instance of a state which possesses a sea coast ignoring the fact. However minimally, some of its people will apply the resources of the sea to their environment. Thus, if power is the ability to influence events, all states with a seacoast have some maritime power.[1]

The Components of Maritime Power

Trade and Access

Mahan called the sea a 'great common'; perhaps this was one of the phrases that made Rosinski consider him essentially an epigrammatic thinker.[2] Certainly it encapsulates several ideas that have to do with a major component of maritime power: Trade and access. The common leads to the places beyond it that are under others' jurisdiction; it is, perhaps, trackless; it is, legally, free for use; it is, sometimes, dangerous by reason of the elements or the fauna; it is, maybe, infested by highwaymen; parts of it may be under the control of armed bands. Its use may bring the user wealth, influence, fulfilment; if it did not, he would not venture there.

Mahan's analogy, as will be seen, is not as precise as it was when he wrote it, and even then it was not so exact as it would have been 100 years earlier. Nevertheless, the possession by a state of a flourishing seaborne trade, of access to routes and markets, is a very important element of economic power. Detailed figures of seaborne trade by value are surprisingly hard to come by, but analysis of published data indicates that for the majority of the world's 'top 30' economies, seaborne exports make up over 10 per cent of the national income (Table 3.1). This in itself is a very significant contribution to the economy, but as a motor for domestic economic power and a catalyst for development and modernisation it is even more important.

Table 3.1: Value of Exports by Sea as a Percentage of Gross National Product (1981)

Over 20 per cent:	Israel, The Netherlands, New Zealand, Norway, Nigeria, Sweden, United Kingdom, Venezuela
Between 10 and 20 per cent:	Argentina, Australia, Canada, Chile, Egypt, France, West Germany, Iran, Italy, Japan, South Africa
Under 10 per cent:	Brazil, India, Mexico, Spain, USA, USSR

A merchant marine, under the national flag and nationally owned and manned, was generally considered by the classical writers to be an essential constituent of this aspect of maritime power. It enabled the state to ensure the continuance of its trade; it earned profits, created wealth and provided employment; it maintained a pool of trained seamen. All these traits were regarded as particularly important in times of national crisis, when in addition it might be desirable for a state to requisition merchant ships for naval or auxiliary purposes.[3]

In practice if not in polemic, this view has been under challenge for about 50 years. Several governments in developed countries have deliberately acquiesced in the catastrophic decline of their merchant marine. The British Merchant Navy, with 1,600 ocean-going ships in 1975, was expected to number only 300 in the early 1990s.[4] It is not difficult to allow such a result to occur. The economics of merchant ship operation are complex, but it is clear that they are very sensitive both to market forces and to domestic legislation. Apparently small variations of freight rates, level of competition, crew costs, conditions of service and manning levels, and tax laws, can all critically affect economic viability. But why it was allowed to occur, in the British and several other cases, is another question.

The argument, largely unarticulated in Britain perhaps because no one in authority thought it prudent to do so, appears to run as follows: there is a world surplus of shipping; in this situation, market forces help to keep rates down; moreover, foreign-flag shipping will always be available; featherbedding of national shipping would increase the freight rates or tax burdens to the detriment of other industry; in any case there is a sizeable pool of flag-of-convenience shipping under British beneficial ownership; and the need for shipping and seamen in emergency is both exaggerated and unlikely.[5]

Such sentiments and outcomes appear to be confined to the developed West. In the rest of the world, a sizeable and flourishing merchant marine appears to be regarded as a good.[6] The emphasis given by developing countries to the UNCTAD liner code, whereby in principle 40 per cent of a trade is carried in bottoms of the supplying state, 40 per cent in those of the receiving state and 20 per cent in crosstraders, would otherwise be remarkable. It may be, of course, that this movement stems from developing states' resentment at their previous over-dependence on established shipping nations, rather than on any hard-headed economic or strategic assessment. But it seems unlikely that an irrational sentiment would be so articulated and so widespread. It thus appears that the traditional view of merchant shipping as part of the economic power base is still very generally held and that it has some validity.

The result is that most states seek to foster their merchant marine by a combination of subsidies, restrictive practices, discrimination against foreign shipping and favourable fiscal measures. Flag-of-convenience (or, as it is now coyly called, 'open registry') states adopt a different stance, setting generally rather low standards for crews and equipment and thereby giving the opportunity for cost-cutting which owners find attractive.[7] In general both sorts of state, the newly-developing and the open-registry, lead less complicated lives than developed nations and have little to lose in adopting such policies.

An ocean-going merchant marine is an excellent example of the dichotomy of maritime power and vulnerability. It does possess all the virtues claimed for it; it generally earns foreign exchange, it lessens dependence, it is a medium for access, it is valuable in emergency. Yet it can be unprofitable in domestic terms, can absorb valuable national resources for little immediate return, and can be a hostage to unfriendly powers. Even economically, therefore, the size, shape and employment of a merchant fleet is a matter for study by any state interested in the maritime component of its power.

Cabotage, the use of shipping as a means of moving goods within national boundaries, is far more a domestic element of a state's economy. Its effects on state power in peacetime are indirect; if it is efficient, it may release resources for external manifestations of power. In time of conflict it may be vulnerable in a way that some states would find embarrassingly sensitive.

Access to markets is an aspect of maritime power. Clearly this is a product of very many factors, which may be as diverse as ideological congruity; ease of language communication; price and quality of the goods on offer; ease of customs and health rules; effectiveness of trade missions. In the context of the current merchant shipping pattern, however, it seems likely that the availability in the participating states of suitable shipping is a powerful incentive to access. The increasing use of specialised shipping — container, roll-on/roll-off, barge and very large bulk carriers — may turn out to be too inflexible in operation to be attractive as an entrée to certain markets.

Shipbuilding

A national shipbuilding industry used to be regarded as an essential component of maritime power. The capacity to produce, more or less independently, the operational units of both economic and military power at sea was generally considered a vast financial asset in peace and a strategic necessity in war. But over the past two decades there has been a radical shift in the world shipbuilding pattern and far more fluidity in procurement. Nations, including medium powers, have accepted dependence they would never have countenanced before 1950, sometimes accompanied by catastrophic declines in their own shipbuilding industries. This must result in more vulnerability, but in modern economic and indeed operational conditions it may be less critical than in, say, the 1930s; and even then British ships depended on offshore procurement for side-armour.

Exploitation of Natural Resources

'Who can doubt,' thundered Vattel, 'that the pearl fisheries of Bahrain and Ceylon can lawfully fall under ownership?'[8] The exploitation of the resources in and under the sea has gone on for thousands of years and has generated a notion of coastal-state interest in such resources that is now firmly enshrined in international law. The detailed rules will be touched upon later in this chapter; here we are concerned with exploitation as an element of maritime power.

Exploitable resources are generally divided into living and non-living, sometimes into renewable and non-renewable; the former categorisation seems preferable. Both living and non-living resources can, in certain cases, enormously add to a state's economic power. Iceland throughout history, and Peru in the

1960s, could attribute over half their gross domestic products to exploitation of their coastal fisheries. In Japan over a quarter of the human protein intake is provided by fish. Many other countries, either historically or now, have used their fishing effort to contribute largely, if not in such extreme terms, both to their domestic economies and their exports.[9]

The exploitation of non-living resources is of later date, but nowadays is no less able to make a significant contribution to the economic power of many states. Oil extraction is the clearest example; rather over a quarter of all the world's oil at present comes from undersea installations.[10] Natural gas shows a similar incidence. Sand and gravel workings offshore are sometimes of considerable economic significance, while less humdrum exploitation concerns phosphorites, rare metals and precious stones. The future may hold prospect of further riches in deep-lying metalliferous muds and brines, and of course in the famous — almost fabled — manganese nodules, tennis-ball sized lumps of metal-bearing matter lying at great depths in the ocean basins.[11]

The power of resource exploitation, then, is ultimately economic. But the other kinds of power impinge upon it. First, exploitation often depends — particularly as it becomes more difficult — on an advanced technological base. Intellectual power is therefore important if a state is to develop its own resources; if it has not the necessary level of technological skills, it must either call upon organisations that have, or must forgo exploitation. Second, the ownership of certain resources may become a matter of dispute between states and here other forms of power — legal and diplomatic in the intellectual field and ultimately military if it comes to that — will be involved. Finally, the protection and preservation of resources and the agencies that exploit them will entail some constabulary function — a function of which the ultimate sanction must be military power.

Military Power at Sea

The existence of military power at sea is a fact of history and of the present day. The pertinent question is whether it is useful and, in the context of this book, in what way it is useful to medium powers.

Serious discussion of sea power began, no doubt, long before the American Admiral Mahan in 1890, but it was he who articulated it. He was followed by a roll-call of others: Corbett, Castex, Custance, Colomb, the list becomes alliterative. These writers shared two characteristics: they were interested in war, and they were interested in dominance. These preoccupations governed their theories: notably command of the sea, the importance of decisive ıttle, the efficacy of total blockade and the ineffectiveness of the harrying *guerre de* course against opposing trade. With refinements, this system of thought continued in the between-wars period.

It was a kind of argument *à outrance* and tended to lead to the view that if a maritime power could not do everything in war, it could do nothing. Such a philosophy allowed writers of a less maritime persusasion to argue that nothing was indeed what a second-rate maritime power could do.[12]

But, at the same time, another school of thought put forward the view that the kind of dominance at sea envisaged by the classical writers was unachievable anyway, mainly because of the power and diversity of modern systems. These writers analysed maritime military power much more in terms of discrete though interrelated functions.[13] They have generally concluded that the ability to perform these functions has utility when put into practice and tend to add (though all too often this most important point is taken as read) that it has even more utility when latent, since then it is acting in a deterrent way.

One such function is the protection of the economic elements of maritime power, which are, as has already been suggested, vulnerable to coercive pressure or simple predation. To describe at this point just how this may be achieved, particularly by a medium power, would be to trespass on succeeding chapters. However, it can be said here that safeguarding offshore resources and those who exploit them is in essence a direct and uncomplicated business however expensive and intricate it may be in practice; while the protection and, it may be, fostering of trade and access is a process that generally involves a subtle intermingling of military power with many other components.

But maritime military power can be provided for purposes other than safeguarding trade or resources. These purposes are in the broadest sense political, involving as they generally do the maintenance or enhancement of the state's position in the world (we return once more to Howard's analysis: states go to war — or embark on conflict at whatever level — 'to maintain their power'). Their execution can range from the assertion of sovereignty in one's own territorial sea to throwing amphibious forces half-way round the world; from placing a small vessel, suitably backed, in an exposed position, to deploying strategic nuclear weapons in ballistic missile submarines. It can include providing forces to support alliances. Such provision of power can take place in peace, or as near peace as the world is likely to get — in which case its very existence and abilities may deter any attempt by potential opponents to coerce; or in times of tension or crisis; or in war.[14] The modalities will often be complex and form the subject matter of later chapters. But as a general statement, it is safe to say that on all the evidence up to the present, maritime military power is an effective factor in the world's power make-up.

Law at Sea

All aspects of maritime power, whether economic or military, are influenced by international law. Indeed, were the code of international law comprehensive, fully agreed and universally respected, maritime power would be governed by law to the extent that the need for its military component would be much diminished. Regrettably, neither code nor respect is strong enough to bring this result about.

The history of the international law of the sea is the story of a search for accommodation between the interests of the coastal state on the one hand and the generality of sea users on the other. The search has taken the form of allotting and defining jurisdiction and rights, as matters of general principle, as between coastal states and sea users. But the obstacles have always been formidable. The untidiness of geography is one; the old dictum that there are no straight lines in nature is never so apparent as when studying a nautical chart. There may be some natural boundaries at sea but they are more likely to be recognised by fish than by man. The advance of technology is another; laws and rules that were appropriate in the days when steam drifters were the acme of fishing technology may be inadequate in the face of sonar-equipped purse seiners. The clash of doctrines is a third; it has involved not only the basic controversy between the followers of Grotius (freedom of the seas) and Selden (closed seas and exclusive use by the coastal state), but, in recent times, a maze of conflicting interests exacerbated by the emergence of many new states with no allegiance to any existing order.

The trend since 1945 has been overwhelmingly towards the coastal state's increased jurisdiction and resource enjoyment in the maritime zones off its shores. Particular aspects include the rapid evolution of a principle of sovereign rights over sea-bed and subsoil resources out to the edge of the continental margin; the recognition of the special interest, and subsequently of certain prescriptive rights, of a coastal state in the fisheries off its shores; the extension by the majority of coastal states of their territorial sea beyond the three-mile limit which previously was generally recognised; challenges to rights of passage, particularly by foreign warships, in coastal and archipelagic waters; and sensitivity by coastal states to vessel-source pollution leading, in some cases, to wide-ranging unilateral legislation.

Thus, it might be said, Mahan's 'great common' was indeed being enclosed, conceptually if not physically.[15] The distinction was, however, important; the difficulty of enforcing the more extreme claims to coastal-state jurisdiction meant that demonstrations of right by the generality of sea users were possible and, indeed, frequently made.[16] This may have had more value than many commentators at the time allowed, for when the Third United Nations Law of the Sea Conference hammered out, over eight arduous years, the convention opened for signature at Montego Bay in December 1982, the interests of the major maritime states were by no means left out of account.[17]

It is not easy to sum up a convention running to over 300 articles — some of them of great length and complexity — in a paragraph or two. Its essential elements include, for the coastal state, provision for a territorial sea up to twelve miles broad; for an exclusive economic zone up to 200 miles from the coast or coastal baselines; and for some rights of exploration and exploitation of continental margins beyond that limit. In the territorial sea the coastal state has sovereignty; in its economic zone, sovereign rights to enjoy resources and safeguard the marine environment. These coastal-state jurisdictions and rights are balanced by the rights of other sea users. They include, in the territorial sea, a right of innocent passage which the coastal state may not permanently hamper; in the exclusive economic zone, freedom of navigation and overflight in all areas except safety zones round oil rigs or similar structures; and beyond that, full high-seas freedoms of navigation, overflight and fishing. International straits through which no high-seas route exists are subject to a regime of transit passage which

Figure 3.1: Law of the Sea Convention, 1982. Coastal State Jurisdiction.

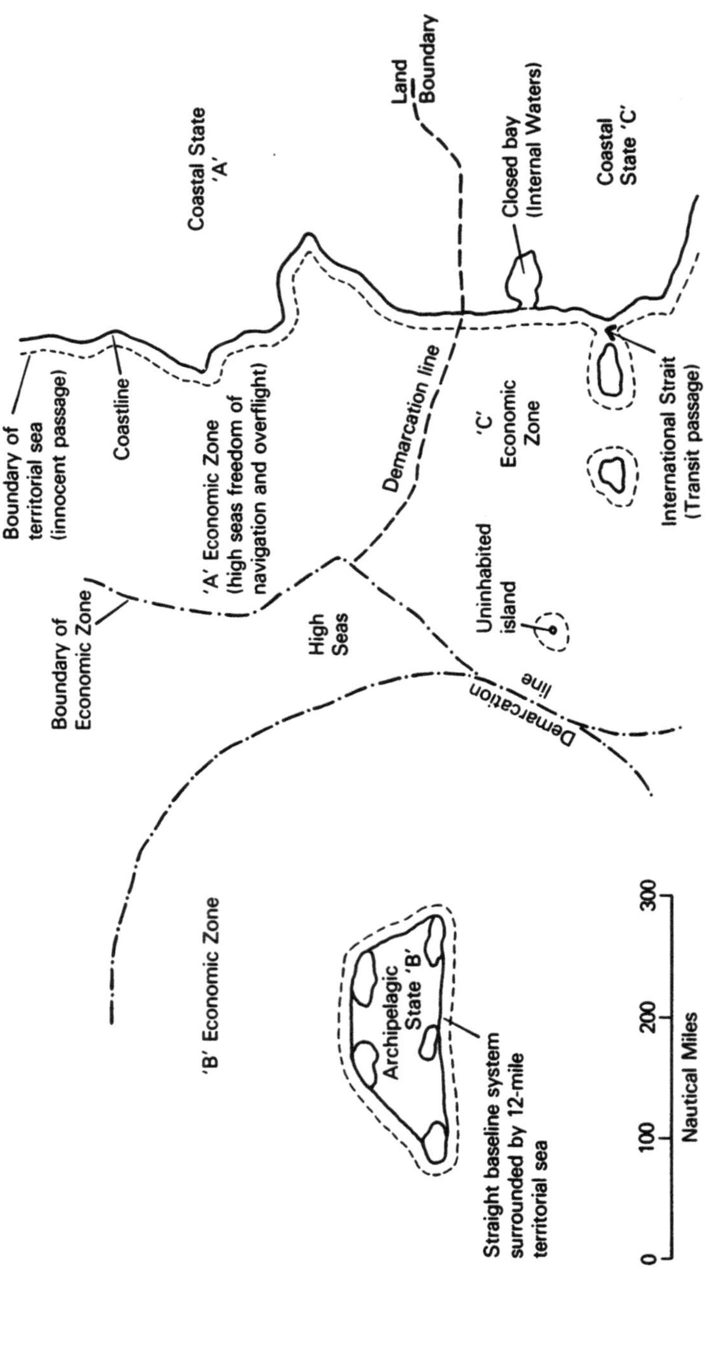

Note: Sources of dispute include demarcation lines, extent of passage rights, right to declare straight baseline systems.

is more liberal than innocent passage, since it is non-suspendable and allows both overflight and the submerged passage of submarines.

All these provisions — many of which embodied concepts new to international law — were acceptable, if not welcome, to the participants in the conference. What was not found acceptable by some was the regime proposed for the deep sea-bed beyond the limits of national jurisdiction, hailed by the United Nations General Assembly in the late 1960s as 'the common heritage of mankind'.[18] The setting up of a great International Sea-bed Authority and Enterprise to manage and exploit the resources of this area — between three-fifths and four-fifths of the sea floor — was, certainly in its detail and perhaps even in its principles, unacceptable to the United States administration of 1980–4.[19] Several close allies of the United States followed in refusing to sign the convention. Others, no less closely linked, did sign. It would be an interesting exercise in perceptions of medium power to analyse who did which, and why.[20] But that is doctoral-thesis stuff, and this chapter must move on.

The incompleteness of accession to the 1982 Convention is no doubt a possible source of dispute, even perhaps of conflict, in the future. But in truth there are plenty of seeds of conflict, within and beyond the Convention, that have nothing to do with the United States' refusal to sign. The length of the Convention certainly does not lead to clarity. As ever, variations in interpretation will depend on the interests of the interpreter, and the pattern of claim and counterclaim that has been a feature of sea business throughout history and intensified in the last few decades is most unlikely to be stilled by all the words; rather they will give increased opportunity for controversy. The root causes of dispute will no doubt be trade, resources, strategic positions, in fact those matters that have been characterised in this book as maritime power; but the focus of dispute will be the Law.[21]

The exercise of military power at sea is also much influenced by law, not only because it may arise out of law-based disputes but because it is itself governed by the international law of armed conflict and the use of force.

The basic supposition — codified to a degree since the Kellogg-Briand Pact of 1928 and enshrined in the UN Charter — is that to make war, or indeed to use force, is a bad action, justifiable only in exceptional circumstances in which the need for self-defence is central.[22] It follows that in planning and executing military operations at sea governments and commanders will feel the constraints that flow from this central restriction, and these will be reflected in what are commonly known as rules of engagement.[23] Such rules will vary with a great many factors, including critically the stakes, the existing intensity of conflict and the state of national and world opinion as well as the basic rules of law. It can certainly be said that the *mores* as to permissible levels of violence vary with time and place.[24] But, as a general rule, the political and legal premium in not firing the first shot is very high, and circumspection is a general feature of the early stages of conflict at sea.

Thus, although the law has not much power in the sense of international enforcement — the nations' record of submission to the judgements of the International Court of Justice and other tribunals is lamentable — it does have considerable influence on both the acquisition and the exercise of power at sea.

Sea Dependence

The maritime-ness of individual states, their dependence on the sea in various aspects of their national life, is a critical matter for enquiry in this book. It is a subject where a large degree of quantitative analysis ought to be possible, as well as qualitative assessment. The data are vast, diverse, sometimes apparently conflicting and often difficult to manage; and it is no wonder that the bulk of work in the field has concentrated on the sea-dependence of individual states rather than comparative studies.[25] Of the latter, clearly the work of Professor Couper's team at the University of Wales Institute of Science and Technology which culminated in *The Times Atlas of the Oceans*[26] is prominent, and is a most useful yardstick for comparison with the writer's own research on which the rest of this section is based.[27]

The figures used to produce Tables 3.2 and 3.3 were taken from UN statistical documents, except those for merchant marines where the *Fairplay Shipping Yearbook* was used. In all cases the year 1978 was taken as a base. While such an early date no doubt detracts from the value of the assessments now, it has the advantage at least of a certain comparability with the Couper team's 1980-based figures; and economic patterns, though they change more rapidly than they used to, have an inherent stability that in most cases survives the intervention of less than a decade.

The maritime parameters considered were, unsurprisingly, those covered in an earlier section of this chapter, namely seagoing trade, merchant marine, shipbuilding, fish catches (living resources), and offshore zones (both living and non-living resources). It was not considered appropriate to include the military components of maritime power, which are more a measure of a state's reaction to sea-dependence than of dependence itself.

The five maritime parameters, then, for each country were matched against two bases for comparison: the gross domestic product and the population. It is necessary to use both yardsticks, because otherwise oversimplification may creep in. Suppose, for example, that there are two countries, A and B, with similar GDPs. Seagoing trade in A accounts for 20 per cent of its GDP while in B it is only 10 per cent. It looks as though A is twice as dependent on seagoing trade as B. However, it turns out that A's population is ten times that of B; in A's near-subsistence economy, the level of seagoing trade per head is one-fifth that in B's more advanced one. Therefore, the impact of a constriction in A's seagoing trade will be heavier on the totality of the economy, but lighter on each individual citizen, than would be the same constriction in B. Consequently, two tables of comparison are presented here, the first based on GDP and the second on population. Cross-comparison reveals some interesting inferences.

The form of the tables will be familiar to any devotees of the British consumer magazine *Which?* For many years that admirable publication has put out comparative tables on everything from lawn mowers to insurance policies with the unforgettable legend — 'The more blobs the better'. The tables are, accordingly, in this form, though here it is 'the more blobs the greater the dependence'. For those interested in the methodology, some details and caveats are included in the Appendix.

Some points must be made here in the main text, nevertheless. First, it is notable that the UWIST ratings which are shown for comparison do not always tally with the blobs and indeed, in the case of the USA and the Scandinavian countries, are noticeably far out, as they are too with the ratings in Table 3.1 earlier in the chapter. It is clear from the legend why this should be: the UWIST rating is an 'Index of national interest in seaborne trade' and therefore takes account of the *absolute* amount of seaborne trade as a factor. This factor is not apparent in the present working, as

Table 3.2: Sea Dependence: Comparison with Gross Domestic Product

Country	Seaborne Trade	Merchant Marine	Ship-building	Fish Catch	Offshore Zone	UWIST Rating
Argentina	****	**	***	****	**	–
Australia	****	**	**	*	**	4.8
Belgium	***	**	**	*	*	4.0
Brazil	***	***	***	**	**	4.2
Canada	***	**	**	**	**	4.1
Chile	***	*	*	*****	**	–
Denmark	***	***	***	****	**	4.5
Egypt	****	*	*	*	****	–
Finland	***	***	***	*	*	–
France	**	**	**	**	*	6.2
Germany, W.	**	**	**	*	*	4.3
Greece	****	*****	*	**	**	5.9
India	**	**	**	**	**	3.4
Iran	*****	**	*	*	**	6.6
Israel	***	*	*	*	*	–
Italy	****	*	*	***	**	6.8
Japan	***	***	***	***	**	9.2
Mexico	**	**	*	**	**	–
Netherlands	*****	***	**	*	*	7.4
New Zealand	***	*	*	**	**	–
Nigeria	**	*	*	***	****	3.9
Norway	****	****	****	****	****	6.7
S. Africa	***	*	*	**	**	–
Soviet Union	n/a	n/a	n/a	n/a	n/a	5.2
Spain	**	***	***	**	**	5.4
Sweden	***	***	***	*	*	4.2
United Kingdom	**	***	**	*	***	7.3
USA	**	**	**	*	**	6.4
Venezuela	**	*	*	*	****	5.5

indeed it should not be when dependence as opposed to interest is under consideration, and it accounts for the discrepancy. The distorting effect is less when medium powers only come under consideration.

Second, and more seriously, there are many parameters that are not considered. Length of coastline, size of the offshore zones, strategic position, importance of entrepôt trade and cabotage, beneficial ownership of flag-of-convenience shipping, weight of offshore traffic, port facilities and usage, none of these appears in the tables. While some of them probably correspond closely with

Table 3.3: Sea Dependence: Comparison with Population

Country	Seaborne Trade	Merchant Marine	Ship-building	Fish Catch	Offshore Zone	UWIST Rating
Argentina	***	***	***	****	**	–
Australia	*****	***	***	**	****	4.8
Belgium	*****	****	****	**	*	4.0
Brazil	***	**	*	**	**	4.2
Canada	*****	***	***	*****	**	4.1
Chile	****	*	*	*****	**	–
Denmark	*****	*****	****	*****	***	4.5
Egypt	**	*	*	*	***	–
Finland	*****	****	****	****	*	–
France	****	****	****	***	**	6.2
Germany, W.	****	***	***	**	*	4.3
Greece	****	*****	*	***	*	5.9
India	*	**	**	**	**	3.4
Iran	***	**	*	*	**	6.6
Israel	****	*	*	**	*	–
Italy	****	****	***	**	**	6.8
Japan	*****	****	****	*****	**	9.2
Mexico	***	**	*	***	***	–
Netherlands	*****	****	****	****	**	7.4
New Zealand	****	*	*	****	**	–
Nigeria	**	*	*	**	**	3.9
Norway	*****	*****	*****	*****	****	6.7
S. Africa	****	*	*	****	***	–
Soviet Union	n/a	***	n/a	****	**	5.2
Spain	****	****	****	****	***	5.4
Sweden	*****	****	****	****	**	4.2
United Kingdom	****	****	****	***	****	7.3
USA	****	***	***	***	***	6.4
Venezuela	****	*	*	***	****	5.5

the ratings that exist, and others involve exceptionally difficult data management, there is clearly much work still to be done.

The conclusions are unspectacular, but useful. The most consistently sea-dependent nations are either islands or states with long coastlines and limited land frontiers. Of those in the tables, Japan, the Scandinavian countries and the United Kingdom stand out; the pattern is repeated in smaller states like Singapore, and probably would be for a state like Cuba if its figures were available. Other nations may be less consistently sea-dependent but still have a very marked dependence on one aspect or another of the sea affair. Liberia on merchant shipping, Saudi Arabia and Kuwait on shipborne trade, Iceland on fishing, Gabon on the offshore zone: for all these dependence is extremely marked, and though their population base and in some cases their national incomes do not put them into the medium-power category, their importance to the world economic and strategic situation makes their vulnerability of some significance. Finally, even on these crude ratings and assessments it is clear that some nations are relatively impervious to disturbances at sea. The difference between France, which has considerable sea-sensitivity, and West Germany is significant; while West Germany has a very large foreign trade and would undoubtedly feel a considerable blow to its economy if constraint were put upon that trade, it appears that it would not be perceived as so damaging as would a similar constraint upon France. But the difference between those two nations is nothing like as sharp as that between them and India, or even Brazil. It is important to emphasise, though, that patterns change and balances swing; the conscious effort in both Brazil and India to look outward and make use of the oceans will have its effects eventually in the form, for both these nations, of greater power, dependence and vulnerability at sea.

The Power/Vulnerability Equation

Of all the interactions and balances that make up the constantly-moving maritime framework, the equation between power and vulnerability is perhaps the most fascinating. It may be that the strategist, who spends a good deal of his time dealing with what are apparently zero-sum games (even though 'winning' and 'losing' are less fashionable words than they were) has much to learn from the businessman, who is more accustomed to thinking of margins and percentages. But for the strategist, the calculations are unlikely to be entirely financial, and will in any event be complex.

Some of the considerations surrounding the ownership of a merchant fleet have already been mentioned, but take that desirable item of maritime economic power, an offshore oil well. It is in essence a bonanza, a great big gift, fuel for free. But it is a little like the plot of *The Magic Flute*, or of a James Bond novel (the two have remarkable similarities): to win the gift, risks have to be taken. Exploration must be done; seismic tests conducted; holes drilled, of which statistically over 80 per cent will be dry; a production platform set up; wellheads constructed; pipelines or tanker moorings laid. Then the gift is won, the well is in production. But the risks have been considerable, and some will subsist. There has been technical risk, particularly in waters where depth or weather make for new problems.[28] There is, throughout, economic risk: the cost of development and production may exceed the total take, as world prices fluctuate. There is human risk: accident rates are not low. There is risk of damage to platforms, from weather, derelicts, carelessly handled vessels or aircraft; and to pipelines from trawls, anchors, even carelessly handled submarines. Finally, there is risk of damage by enemy action, whether by sabotage in peace or assault in war.

All these factors are taken into account by oil companies when considering offshore investment, and they generally get the percentages right. Whether governments — who must be in for part of the risk at any event — pay the same attention to the equations must be more doubtful, and the very different policies adopted by say the United Kingdom and Norway might be thought to indicate that someone is not being too clever; but again, their different sizes of population and aspirations may bring different factors into consideration.

The same balances of profit, risk, power and vulnerability operate in every economic activity at sea and, indeed, in every economic activity connected with the sea.[29] But even that does not exhaust the power/vulnerability interaction. It applies also to the existence and use of maritime forces. Leaving aside the question of cost of the forces themselves — for that is a question to be answered, if it can be answered at all, after the main arguments of this book have been considered — the practical vulnerabilities of partially-deployed military power at sea are sometimes considerable, and the penalties for exercising that power even in support of its own right to be there can be severe. The Corfu Channel incident of 1946 is perhaps the most notable example; in an attempt to demonstrate a right of innocent passage through an international strait, two British destroyers were mined with the loss of 44 lives. One writer called it, with unwarranted hyperbole, 'one of the most ignominious defeats inflicted on the Royal Navy'.[30] It certainly might have been thought a defeat, but in the subsequent case before the International Court of Justice, the right of innocent passage for warships through such straits was established as a principle of international law.[31] One could say that wars have been fought for less. The point is that unless naval power is always overwhelming, and not even the superpowers can manage that, it will on occasion be vulnerable. Navies are in the risk business.

It is fashionable, certainly in Britain, at the moment to say that little can be done in the way of constructing an overall maritime policy that correctly weighs all the potential gains against the vulnerabilities. The hour is long gone when, as Paul Kennedy said, there was a three-sided equation for the *Pax Britannica*:

> An adequate, not to say overwhelming, world naval force which utilised a whole host of bases and protected an ever-growing global trade; an expanding formal empire which offered harbour facilities for the Navy and focal centres of power, together with a far larger informal empire, both of which provided essential raw materials and markets for the British economy; and an industrial revolution which passed its products into the world, drew large overseas territories into its commercial and financial orbit, encouraged an enormous merchant marine, and provided the material strength to support its great fleets. It was an outstandingly strong framework for national and world power, and one which would remain effective, provided that no one side of it was so weakened that the whole edifice collapsed.[32]

As both Barnett and Kennedy himself have shown, the vast structure carried within it vast vulnerabilities, and Britain has since had to pick her way through a lot of its rubble, though without perhaps the need for quite the smug pessimism that these authors sometimes seem to display. But the crumbling of what was, after all, an empirically-erected structure of one nation's making does not seem to be any reason why a rational assessment of power, dependence, risk and vulnerability should not be made, now and subsequently, by medium powers and turned, not only into a coherent national policy, but a strategy as well.

Medium Maritime Powers

It is no coincidence that the powers identified in Chapter 2 as potentially medium, and featured in Tables 3.2 and 3.3, appear mostly to have a significant stake at sea. Medium-ness implies a certain level of development, and to achieve that level of development requires either the exploitation of a very large indigenous base, or the cross-fertilisation that is brought about by maritime use and intercourse. In fact, only the Soviet Union in the 1930s — and possibly the Chinese and Mughal Empires much earlier — achieved the first kind of development; the second is the norm. It is quite unsurprising, therefore, that medium-ness and maritime-ness are linked.

But the link is a loose one. As has been shown, there are marked variations in both sea-use and sea-dependence, and no doubt in sea-vulnerability too. These variations are very roughly demonstrable in quantitative terms, though there are many parameters yet to be investigated. At least it can be said that some medium powers are more maritime than others, and some sort of indication can be given of who the most maritime may be.

Equally important, however, is the medium power's perception of its own maritime-ness. Some nations, looking ahead perhaps, take a deliberately nautical slant to their national life; it is said that Brazilian schoolteachers are mandated to inculcate a regard for the sea in their pupils.[33] Others, reacting perhaps from what is perceived as too maritime a past and seeking shelter in the lagoon of continents, treat the sea with a sometimes malign neglect that can most kindly be characterised as sea-blindness.[34]

It might be thought that it is possible to quantify, however roughly, this self-perception in the same way as has been done for sea-dependence, or medium-ness, or the possession of military power. Something might be done by analysis of maritime forces and subsidies or other help given to maritime activity. It is highly doubtful if such an attempt would be successful. Information on naval budgets and subsidies is wayward and likely to be heavily classified, and governments often say what they do not think and vice versa.

Like many other things in the maritime scene, it tends to come out in the wash. However centralised government planning may be, the patterns of international trade and resource exploitation evolve through the action of many forces outside government control as well as some within it. Even a navy is an inheritance not only of hardware and men but history, traditions, methods and concepts, as well as an amalgam of plans and projects for time to come; it cannot, any more than can maritime economic power, be created overnight, nor in the normal state of affairs can its power be very quickly eroded. Governments can of course alter the direction and emphasis of policy, but their room for manoeuvre is limited by the inertia of events. Most of them will see clearly enough the part the sea plays in their affairs and endeavour to act accordingly; some will make a conscious effort to enlarge that part or diminish it, but many will let it run. It is with the efficiency of their efforts to make the sea work for them in the situation they find, rather than with the outside chance of their fostering a radical shift to a maritime-based national way of life, that this book is concerned.

Conclusion

Maritime power is the ability to use the sea. This can bring benefits to a state: in economic terms through trade and resource exploitation, and in military terms through the protection of the economic elements as well as the projection or threat of force against opponents. It also brings vulnerabilities: the economic elements can be threatened more easily than domestically-based assets, and the military elements may prove hostages in some situations. Even if a state judged that it could do without maritime power, it might find it extraordinarily difficult to do so; but the direction of policy can be changed to increase or decrease the emphasis on maritime power.

There are such things as medium maritime powers. If a medium power is a state that prizes autonomy and is able to manipulate power in order to preserve it, then the medium maritime power will aim to use the sea in order to enhance this ability. Just where the limits of the ability lie, and how much autonomy is in the event preservable, will depend on the medium power's use of resources towards this end: in other words, its strategy. How the sea comes into such a use of resources, in a way that will help secure medium maritime powers' strategies in the safeguarding of their vital interests, is the subject of the rest of the book.

Notes

1. In this chapter 'maritime power' will generally be used in preference to 'sea power' because the operational, even warlike, connotation often given to the latter term limits it in a way that is not acceptable when overall power-balances, vulnerabilities and strategies are under discussion. See Geoffrey Till, *Maritime Strategy and the Nuclear Age*, 2nd edn (Macmillan, London, 1984), p. 16.

2. Herbert Rosinski, 'Mahan and World War II' in *The Development of Naval Thought* (Naval War College Press, Newport, 1977), p. 21.

3. A. T. Mahan, *The Influence of Sea Power upon History* (Little, Brown, Boston, 1890), p. 23; Lord Haversham's dictum, quoted in Till, *Maritime Strategy and the Nuclear Age*, p. 76; memorandum to the Defence Committee of the House of Commons by the British Maritime League, 28 January 1985.

4. Admiral Sir Anthony Griffin, at a reception for the British Maritime Charitable Foundation, 15 November 1984.

5. British Maritime League: *Report* of a Conference on 21 June 1984, in rebuttal.

6. Lawrence O. F. Bereiweriso, 'New Maritime Policy and its Effect on Nigeria', *Seaways*, March 1985, pp. 12–13.

7. B. A. Boczek, *Flags of Convenience* (Harvard University Press, Harvard, 1962), p. 94.

8. Quoted in C. John Colombos, *International Law of the Sea*, 6th edn (Longmans, London, 1967), p. 404.

9. *The Times Atlas of the Oceans* (Times Books, London, 1983), p. 84.

10. Peter Odell, 'Offshore Resources: Oil and Gas' in *The Maritime Dimension*, ed. R. P. Barston and Patricia Birnie (George Allen and Unwin, London, 1980), pp. 76–107.

11. *The Times Atlas of the Oceans*, pp. 104–17.

12. Paul M. Kennedy, *The Rise and Fall of British Naval Mastery* (Allen Lane, London, 1976), p. 337; Julian Lider, *Military Thought of a Medium Power* (Institute of International Affairs, Stockholm, 1983), pp. 166–7. I have no doubt expressed their argument in more extreme terms than they would themselves.

13. K. Booth, *Navies and Foreign Policy* (Croom Helm, London, 1977); E. Luttwak, *The Political Uses of Sea Power* (Johns Hopkins University Press, Baltimore, 1974); Stansfield Turner, 'Missions of the US Navy' (*US Naval War College Review*, March 1974).

14. J. Cable, *Gunboat Diplomacy* (Macmillan, London, 1981), pp. 195–258, supplies a table detailing over 130 sets of events from 1945 to 1979.

15. Elizabeth Young, 'New Laws for Old Navies', *Survival*, November/December 1974, pp. 262–7; and J. R. Hill, 'Maritime Power and the Law of the Sea', *Survival*, March/April 1975, pp. 69–72.

16. Cable, *Gunboat Diplomacy*, pp. 195–258. Also Till, *Maritime Strategy and the Nuclear Age*, p. 208.

17. Cable, *Gunboat Diplomacy*, p. 224.

18. UN General Assembly Resolution 2574C (XXIV), 15 December 1969, later incorporated in the Law of the Sea Convention, Art. 136.

19. The objections are summarised by Bernard H. Oxman, quoting Ambassador Malone, in 'The Third UN Conference on the Law of the Sea: The Tenth Session (1981)', *American Journal of International Law*, Vol. 76 (1982), pp. 9–10. See for a contrary, also American, view, Elliot L. Richardson, 'The Case for the Convention — an American View', paper given at the Ninth Greenwich Forum, September 1983.

20. Tullio Treves, 'The UNLOS Convention of 1982: Prospects for Europe', paper given at the Ninth Greenwich Forum, September 1983.

21. In *A Sea of Troubles?* Buzan identifies nearly 50 areas of specific dispute around the world as well as a number of issues of general principle that, if applied to particular cases, could lead to conflict. There is no sign of general resolution since the signature of the 1982 Convention.

22. I. Brownlie, *International Law and the Use of Force by States* (Oxford University Press, Oxford, 1963), p. 75; D. W. Bowett, *Self-Defence in International Law* (Manchester University Press, Manchester, 1958), p. 135.

23. For a detailed discussion see below, Chapter 7.

24. Compare, for example, the fishery regulation modes in the Northeast Atlantic, where in the *Red Crusader* case (1961) a Danish fishery protection vessel was censured for the most limited and discriminating use of weapons to detain a

trawler which had kidnapped its boarding party, and those in the North Pacific where about five Japanese fishermen a year are killed in clashes with Soviet forces. The extreme sensitivity of Western public opinion at a higher level of conflict was pointed up in the ultimately tedious controversy over the sinking of the *General Belgrano*, even in the face of numerous acts of war by the Argentines over the previous 24 hours.

25. For example, the recent work of the British Maritime League.

26. *The Times Atlas of the Oceans*, pp. 144–5.

27. The work was first put forward at the Second Gosport Seminar on Medium Maritime Power, July 1982.

28. John S. Jennings, 'Problems Arising from North Sea Development', paper given at the Ninth Greenwich Forum, September 1983.

29. Roy Farndon, 'Does London Have a Future as a World Maritime Centre?', paper given at the Ninth Greenwich Forum, September 1983.

30. Eric Leggett, *The Corfu Incident* (Seeley Service, London, 1974), p. 24.

31. (1949) I.C.J. *Reports*, Corfu Channel Case (5 Vols).

32. P. M. Kennedy, *The Rise and Fall of British Naval Mastery* (Allen Lane, London, 1976), p. 157.

33. I am indebted to Professor Alec Smith for this information, which he gleaned from a visit to Patagonia in the company of South American academics in 1984.

34. Professor D. C. Watt, 'How British Governments have viewed the Sea', closing paper at the Ninth Greenwich Forum, September 1983.

4 THREAT AND ALLIANCES

Starting With The Threat is a Staff College short cut of dubious validity. Its effect on strategic thought is to invite numerous assumptions about the identity, nature and objectives of the opposition when analysis would be more beneficial. Applied to tactics, it is inclined to instil defensive and reactive ideas. All too often it is unrelated, in the study of either strategy or tactics, to the interests being protected or the national objectives being pursued.

Nevertheless, there must come a point in any strategic analysis where threat stands to be considered. This study, having discussed the nature, the interests, the objectives and in broadest terms the strategic principles of medium maritime powers, must now have reached that point. Since it concerns medium maritime powers in general, and not one such power in particular, it must confine itself to general statements about the nature of maritime threat except where specific examples give helpful illustration.

The essence of threat is an ability, and a willingness, to coerce; to make the victim do something he does not want to do, or submit to a course of action that is against his interests.

Threat can take any of the forms of power that were described in previous chapters. Even what I have inadequately called intellectual power can be deployed coercively; propaganda and subversion are obvious examples, but the normal traffic of diplomacy and negotiation too can often be coercive in nature. Anyone who has seen a superpower delegation at work in a conference consisting mostly of medium or small powers will recall well enough that the stamina of a large delegation generally outlasts that of a small one. Moreover, intellectual power can often be used in an indirect way to influence third parties; and it is a means of co-ordinating, maximising and if necessary publicising the other elements of coercion. But it is those other elements, the economic and the military, that will chiefly occupy this chapter.

There are two important general points to be made. First, once an adversary relationship is established, threat is most unlikely to be solely military in nature. The co-ordination of all elements of power against an opponent is at its most acute in war, particularly war between large and sophisticated states; it has been argued, persuasively, that too total a commitment of power has proved a bankrupting policy, but states in full-scale war have little opportunity to play the percentages, whatever hindsight may say.[1] Lower levels of conflict or confrontation are still likely to involve military, economic and intellectual elements, co-ordinated well or badly or not at all according to the skill of the threat nation. At the normal level of international rivalry that is called peace, military threats are latent even though they may be potent, while both economic and intellectual elements can still be active.

Secondly, threat need not be direct. The United States' preoccupation with the territories to their south — first Cuba, then the Central American republics — is a typical superpower reaction to a threat which was at one time perceived to be direct but is now regarded as indirect. Similarly, Britain's support of Oman during the 1960s was a response to a threat at two removes: had the Front for the Liberation of South Yemen (FLOSY) succeeded in overthrowing the regime of Sultan Qaboos, FLOSY forces would not have posed a direct threat to the UK, nor even immediately to Western shipping in the Gulf, but they would have been in a position to build up the power to do the latter, as well as having some potential to undermine friendly regimes further up the Gulf. Similarly, in the Soviet view no doubt an unstable Afghanistan that was even remotely vulnerable to take-over by a Western-leaning regime was an indirect threat that could not be tolerated. Reactions to threats of this kind are often subject to public censure, and require considerable strength of will to sustain. Even more do active measures to combat the most indirect of all threats: what is called in Soviet terminology an 'adverse change in the correlation of forces'. Such alterations in the international ambiance may not be brought on by adversary action at all but by spontaneous movements within states; the difference will in any case not be easy to identify. The use of power to counter them has come to be expected, if at all, from the superpowers alone; even in their hands it has to be subtle and carefully judged lest it do more harm than good.

Threats to Medium Powers

A favourite slogan on my study wall says 'Just because you're paranoid it doesn't mean they aren't out to get you'. Medium powers' paranoia about threat may be excusable. From their point of view, the range of their assailable interests is greater than that of either the superpowers or the small powers. They see the superpowers as possessing a greater carapace of military, economic and international political structure that will render them insensitive to pinpricks and deter mortal thrusts, the small powers as having only their territorial integrity, political independence and a relatively small package of extended interests to worry about; and they may not be of great interest to potential aggressors anyhow. But medium powers, as they see it, are subject to threats of great scope, both geographical and in nature.

First, because of their size and potential — whether developed or latent — medium powers are attractive to the superpowers, as members of 'their' economic systems, as providers of useful strategic assets, as backers of their policies; at the very least, as assets to be denied to opposing superpowers. Therefore, the superpower relationship is certain to impinge on medium powers. In the case of some, which incline in any case towards one superpower or another, this is a natural state of affairs. In other medium powers, which regard themselves as non-aligned, it is irksome. India and Brazil are notable cases in point. While one inclines somewhat to Moscow and the other to Washington, they do so because they see the main threat to their vital interests — in particular to their regional power-base — as coming from the other superpower, and not for ideological reasons or even any allegiance to an economic bloc. Gaullism in France, too, was a sign of unease with too close a client relationship with the American superpower, as well as being an exercise in opportunist political power-broking; *tous azimuts* meant what it said.[2]

Therefore, a superpower threat is a phenomenon that all medium powers must face. By its very nature it is bound to menace, in the ultimate, the whole fabric of the state. But at lower levels of conflict it can still be perceived as affecting political independence and extended vital interests, perhaps also territorial integrity itself.

Non-superpower threats to medium powers are conveniently divisible into two categories: those from neighbours and those from further afield.

Neighbours tend to be more of a problem for new medium powers than for older ones, and for continental rather than island states. In Western Europe the strategic issues between neighbours are largely resolved, or dissolved into intra-EEC economic tactics; and while there have been times when Australia and Indonesia looked at each other with some suspicion, the vast sea distances involved, even more than the limited resources of both states, have damped the possibility of confrontation.[3] Quite different was the danger to Malaysia in the 1960s; in that situation, some land frontiers in Sabah, and short sea passages in other sectors, allowed confrontation to be acute. In South America neighbour problems are a major preoccupation; it has been frequently suggested that in late 1981 and early 1982 the Argentine government, faced by discord at home and seeking a foreign adventure, virtually tossed a coin as to whether it took the Falklands by force or embarked on military action against Chile.[4] The Beagle Channel dispute with Chile certainly affected Argentine sensitivities in the late 1970s as much as did the Falklands.[5] But among the medium powers, Israel has the most acute neighbour problem, and reacts most sharply to it. The deployment of her resources, in every field, is governed by it.[6]

Non-neighbours tend to threaten medium powers more subtly, if not indirectly. The developed post-imperial medium powers may see such threats at their most acute. First, they have, whether they wish it or not, the territorial residue of empire scattered around the world: such areas tend to be embarrassing to keep and shaming to abandon, and principle and pragmatism are closely interwoven.[7] Second, they tend to have regional economic interests far afield; France would not have become involved in Chad had it not been for her interest in Francophone Africa as a whole, and Britain's special influence in the Gulf is a growth of both history and economic involvement.

As has been pointed out, the threats are as complex as the interests. They may grow from inside the countries concerned, giving the prospect of a change of regime inimical to the medium power's interests; they may be a spin-off from the conflicts of other states in the region (the Iran-Iraq war has had astonishingly little effect on the outside world, but only because it has occurred at a time of oil glut); they may come from regimes which are hostile for a variety of reasons to the medium power; they may spring from genuine differences of view over rights and responsibilities under public international law; or they may concern the expatriate economic interests of the medium power. While all such threats tend to be more telling when applied to fully-developed medium powers which have already built up a large network of interests far beyond their frontiers, the developing medium powers are by no means unaffected by them.[8]

Threat in the Maritime Arena

It is necessary now to examine more closely how threats to medium-power interests may operate at sea. The distinction must at once be made between two fundamentally different objects of threat: assets in the sea environment, such as fishing fleets, resource-exploiting installations, trade shipping, and amphibious and maritime forces; and interests in other environments, whether in metropolitan or overseas areas, which can be threatened from the sea.

Threats to sea-based assets may be at the administrative level ('. . . the sort of conflict which may start in the customs shed').[9] Examples in recent experience include the UNCTAD liner code, and the long-running differences of opinion between the UK and USA over liner shipping between the two countries.[10] How far such matters have contributed to the decline of the British merchant marine in the first half of the 1980s will be for historians to analyse, but there is no doubt that they have done it no good.

Administrative threats may also take the form of enactments in accordance with a certain interpretation of international law. These range from, at one end of the scale, claims to full sovereignty over a very wide patrimonial sea such as were made by Brazil, Ecuador and Peru in the 1950s and 1960s,[11] through fishery regulations which may or may not be disputed but nearly always have the effect of excluding some or all foreign fishermen,[12] to traffic and port entry regulations that bear exceptionally heavily on foreign traders.[13] While it is fair to say that up to now such enactments have had most effect on the distant-water fishing fleets of medium powers, it is possible that in future they could seriously impede merchant traffic, for example through the imposition of tolls as was at one time suggested for the Malacca Strait, or by the stipulation of unusually high standards of equipment as in the Canadian legislation of 1970.[14]

Given the sensitivity of many new nations to anything touching their sovereignty, it is surprising that more effort was not made in the Third UN Law of the Sea Conference to deny innocent passage through the territorial sea, without notification or authorisation, to the warships of foreign states. No such stipulation appears in the

Convention. However, the Gulf of Sidra incident on 19 August 1981, where American fighter aircraft from the carrier *Nimitz* shot down two Libyan SU-22s which had attacked them 60 miles from the coast, is instructive; Libya claimed these waters not as territorial but internal, on the grounds that the Gulf of Sidra penetrated Libyan territory.[15] Radical interpretations of international law such as this are by no means unique to Libya. Thus, administrative threats to the passage and manoeuvre of warships are likely to be relatively widespread in coastal waters in the future; and medium powers' forces will probably be more sensitive to them than superpowers', because they have less defensive potential.

Also in the arena of administrative threat are claims to areas of sea or sea-bed by neighbouring states. As Buzan has shown, such areas of rival claim are extremely numerous, and though some are now in process of settlement others will arise.[16]

The costs to a medium power of such administrative threats, if successfully prosecuted against it, can be severe. The extinction of the British distant-water fishing industry was no doubt due to a variety of factors of which only one was the successful attempt by Iceland, over three successive sets of legislation, to exclude it from a 200-mile zone round that country. But no one doubts that the exclusion was the critical blow to an industry already vulnerable.

Dealing with administrative threats is a pretty problem for medium powers and some thoughts on solutions will be offered in later chapters. It can be said here, though, that first, a military element, either in deterrence or in response, should not necessarily be ruled out simply because the threat purports to be in pursuit of law, since international law is subject to such varieties of interpretation; and second, disputes arising out of administrative measures may not be the sort of things that interest allies.

Administrative threats, then, are true threats, normally against extended vital interests and often cumulative in their effects. They probably do not accord with orthodox notions of threat but, on the evidence, no apology is needed for having introduced them here. It goes without saying that if resisted they may lead to some of the higher and more active threat levels now to be described.

Harassment is an elastic term and, like confrontation, is much less in vogue than it was a couple of decades ago. As a description of the niggling demonstrations of officiousness by coastal regulation forces of less-than-friendly states it is a trifle too strong; on the other hand, it is too weak to describe the tougher actions of blockade or interdiction. It appears, in fact, from the evidence of the 1970s and 1980s that seafarers, who are a pretty tough lot, have learnt to live with the irritating manoeuvres and menacing gestures that were considered to be effective in the 1960s. While, therefore, harassment — whether of fishing vessels, merchant ships or warships — still has a demonstrative role to play it can be thought of as an auxiliary rather than a basic threat.

Not so is the threat of being caught up in someone else's war. In spite of US and British naval presence in the approaches to the Gulf, the war between Iraq and Iran which began in 1980 had, by September 1984, claimed 60 neutral merchant vessels damaged or sunk. Both Iraqi and Iranian aircraft had carried out the attacks. Insurance rates for ships going to Bandar Khomeini at the head of the Gulf were quoted as 20 per cent of hull value, and 7.5 per cent for going to Kharg Island 80 miles southeast.[17] It is possible to draw all kinds of conclusion from these statements, and they are by no means all discouraging; for example, the world has not run short of oil, the insurance market has not collapsed and the war has not been extended to the Strait of Hormuz; the provenance of isolated mining incidents in the Red Sea is still obscure. But the lesson remains that other people's wars do, in a complex world, affect the interests of many medium powers.

The Gulf war anti-shipping operations might be described as an exceptionally crude form of blockade, but blockade is really a much more precise and restrictive kind of operation with, in classical warfare terms, well-defined rules.[18] If blockade concerned someone else's war, a third-party medium power would, in most modern conditions, not be vitally affected — unless, of course, either the war or the practice spread. On the other hand, a medium maritime power itself subjected to effective blockade might quickly find itself in great difficulty. This would, self-evidently, apply with more force to island states. Naturally, the blockade would need to be applied to neutral shipping as well as that of the victim state.

But, one is bound to ask, what sort of power is it that could mount a blockade on a medium power of a scale sufficient to be effective? The answer at present looks to be that a superpower only could do it; even the mining of coastal waters, the crudest form of blockade, would have to be of an extent beyond the capacity of a medium power save in the most exceptional circumstances.

Piracy is another threat to assets at sea which may well affect medium powers. The sporadic nature of piracy suggests that it is most unlikely to affect them vitally; however, it must be said that the scale of the problem has markedly increased during the last decade, to the extent that the Nigerian coast was, in 1983, regarded as highly dangerous and the Singapore Strait saw one merchant ship attacked every three days.[19] While on the high seas and, it appears, in the Economic Zone, a pirate is *hostis humani generis* and can be taken by any person or agency, in the Territorial Sea his apprehension is the responsibility of the coastal state, and medium powers may find the ineffectiveness of many coastal states in this regard a matter for irritation at the least.[20]

Sabotage and hijacking are not technically piracy (which is a precise term in law and a highly imprecise one as used by both press and politicians). Neither, probably, is likely to affect the vital interests of a medium power except in one aspect. That aspect is its offshore installations, if they exist in sufficient volume. The damage that can be done by a single oil spill from an offshore well is very considerable, and a concerted operation against either well-heads or pipelines that caused several such spills at once might be regarded as a severe assault on civil order. Similarly, simultaneous hijacking of several oil platforms could have disruptive effects on the policy of a medium power.

Last among the threats of action against various individual aspects of the maritime assets of a medium power, it is necessary to count action taken in support of administrative claims: that is to say, the detention and, it may be, punishment in the courts of alleged transgressions by fishing or merchant vessels; or attacks on warships. While in many cases action of this kind can be expected to be limited in its scope and effect, this limitation of force is tending to become less restrained.[21]

Finally, then, it remains to consider the generalised threat to assets at sea that would occur if a medium maritime power was involved in war. Here it is necessary to distinguish between situations where a superpower is included in the opposition and those where it is not.

If a superpower opponent is involved, the medium power's assets at sea could be subjected to the full gamut of capability. True, it is possible that in certain parts of the world, shorebased aircraft of the superpower — particularly those armed with anti-ship missiles — might not immediately menace medium-power assets. But a similar capability would almost certainly be available from other parts of the superpower armoury. Maritime assets would therefore be subject to attack by submarine, surface craft and aircraft, by torpedo, missile, mine, gun and bomb, both conventional and nuclear, and in large numbers. The whole would be backed by reconnaissance, command and control facilities of a comprehensiveness unmatched by any except the other superpower.

Non-superpower opponents in war would offer a variety of threats but all would be an order of magnitude less than those of a superpower. That said, their peculiar abilities would of course be critically important. Some non-superpowers' maritime forces are suitable for general action far from their shores; many are not. Over 40 have submarines in their armouries, but numbers tend to be in single figures and the level of training may not be high.[22] Over 50 operate aircraft dedicated to or primarily for maritime roles, but in most forces these are shore-based and there are no in-flight refuelling facilities.[23] In about half the cases the aircraft are primarily for a surveillance role, and any armament would have to be strapped on. About 70 states operate vessels carrying surface-to-surface missiles, typically of horizon range.[24] The great majority of such vessels are fast attack craft which could not conduct operations at great distances (say more than 200–300 miles) from their bases. Command, control and communications are in some cases suitable for operations of great geographical scope, but in the majority are unlikely to be operationally effective more than a few hundred miles from base. Hardly any non-superpowers have effective bases outside their own territories. Britain's possession of Ascension Island, a key element in the South Atlantic campaign of 1982, was an accident of history rather than a strategically conceived facility; Gibraltar is still of marked strategic importance even though the dockyard is closed and it is now more firmly within the NATO ambit with Spain's accession; at one or two points in the Indian Ocean, France has toeholds that could be useful to her; and the Netherlands has a similar outpost in the Antilles. Apart from that, islands forming part of national territory and deployed alliance or United Nations forces (none of them maritime) are the only overseas footholds on land of the non-superpowers.

It is worth noting that the very brief catalogue above did not refer only to medium powers, much less medium maritime powers. This is because the opponent or opponents of a medium power are not necessarily going to be medium powers themselves. States as small as Iceland and Surinam appear in the table of incidents at the end of Cable's *Gunboat Diplomacy*: what is more, they appear as assailants not victims.[25] Davids and Goliaths come in all shapes and sizes nowadays. The ability and readiness of small states, particularly on or near their home ground, to challenge much larger and more powerful ones is not a new phenomenon, of course. But it has been helped along by many of the developments described above, notably the emphasis on sovereignty as a fundamental right of states; insistence on self-defence as a criterion to justify warlike action; the existence of a built-in majority of small states in the General Assembly of the United Nations; the speed and comprehensiveness of modern media communications; and, in the field of maritime armouries, the relatively small size and cost of powerful weapon systems.

Medium maritime powers, then, may see in a turbulent future many and diverse threats to their assets at sea. That does not exhaust the catalogue, however, for the sea can also be used by some opponents to threaten medium-power interests on land.

What has been called 'island-grabbing' is perhaps the least serious of such threats.[26] It is still, in all conscience, serious enough to take by force or threat of arms a territory which is claimed by another power, as happened in the cases in the 1970s alone of the Tunbs in the Gulf, the Paracels and the Spratly Islands in the South China Sea, and Portuguese Timor. All were invasions, not on a particularly large scale but large enough to be successful. Their effect was of course much more far-reaching than the occupation of small pieces of land which in all cases but one were sparsely inhabited or not inhabited at all; they would not have been prizes if that was all they were — their real value was that they generated or might be held to generate offshore zones of great extent and possible riches.[27]

Moreover, questions of principle arose; did seizure confer title? if the occupation amounted to aggression, was aggression to be allowed to end in profit for the aggressor? what part was the international community, embodied in the United Nations, to play in ensuring just outcomes? Did the claim to be taking decolonising action, as in the case of the Indonesian occupation of East Timor, nullify all other objections?

All these factors were again apparent, with in many cases added sharpness, when Argentine forces occupied the Falkland Islands on 2 April 1982. The outcome of that operation is well enough known to need no further analysis, but the reasons for the British reaction, and reoccupation of the Islands in a highly risky campaign, are of some importance to the theme of this book.

Discounting the domestic reasons — bluntly, that no government could have remained long in office after the humiliation of acquiescing in Argentine occupation of the Falklands, and therefore British forces had to be risked if the administration was to have a chance of survival — the more legitimate reasons were those of extended vital interest. The re-establishment of an atmosphere of deterrence, the upholding of the principle of self-determination for the islanders, the defence of a legal title perceived as sound, the determination that aggression should not pay, and the reinforcement of the rule of international law as the UK saw it, were all reasons for the British action that went straight back to the deeper motivations outlined in Chapter 2: in Lasswell's terms Power, Respect, Solidarity and Rectitude. It is not impossible that, in the long term, Wealth and Well-being could be involved too, if the riches of the Falklands continental shelf are properly developed, perhaps jointly with Argentina.

Islands, then, are one part of a medium power's assets that are vulnerable from the sea. But so, in many cases, is its mainland. It has been pointed out, by the most eminent of Russian writers on sea power no less, that of the very numerous amphibious operations carried out in the Second World War, almost all were successful;[28] the pattern has been repeated since.[29] Naturally the full scale seaborne invasion of a medium-sized state is an act of war fraught, even after initial softening-up, with considerable risk for the attacker; nevertheless it is not a contingency that an island medium power, or one with a vulnerable sea coast, can ignore. It is worth remembering that for long periods of British history the Navy's primary role and justification was the prevention of invasion; and failure to guard adequately against invasion has been the cause of defeat in wars from the Iron Age onwards.

More widespread, though, would be the threat of landings from the sea of relatively small units of the opposition. This is a threat which, in confrontation or war, could be posed to the majority of medium powers, and — unlike full-scale seaborne invasion — by a wide variety of opponents. Typical objectives of such raids are the command and control centres and key logistic points of the metropolitan power; but in a situation short of war, more public objectives including the civilian population may be attractive particularly to terrorists working from another state's territory. The success of raids has historically varied very widely from the near-farcical, as in most of the Indonesian efforts against Malaya during confrontation,[31] to the brilliant, as in the Israeli commando attack on Palestinian guerrilla bases in Lebanon in June 1984.[32]

Small-scale operations of this kind, which depend so much on individuals and on special circumstances in which chance plays an important part, will always be subject to these wide variations. But powers with considerable resources, both human and material, can well spare enough to train special forces with a wide variety of skills; the Soviet Spetsnaz and British SAS/SBS are cases in point. Resources available to terrorist organisations are fortunately more often limited, and because the sea is a quite demanding medium terrorists have generally fought shy of using it except for transporting armaments from their sources of supply to their forward bases. There are, nevertheless, plenty of situations where a medium power may see terrorist options as including infiltration of people and supplies from the sea.

Finally among the threats to a metropolitan state from the sea is the most extreme of all: the destruction of all or parts of its fabric by bombardment, both conventional and nuclear.

Conventional bombardment from the sea can be carried out by gunfire, aerodynamic missiles or ship-based aircraft. Against a medium power it is likely to be selective rather than indiscriminate in nature simply because medium powers have widespread resources, and conventional explosive power, even that possessed by a superpower, is limited by the levels of ammunition stocks that can be carried at sea. So the most likely targets are military, or at least strategic, ones. A heavy attack could cause severe disruption to a medium power's economy and strategic potential; putting out of action several selected ports, a couple of shipyards, three or four key electronics factories and half a dozen airfields would cripple any medium power one cared to mention. That weight of conventional attack from the sea, in a single operation, is at present available only to the superpowers.

Nuclear bombardment from the sea is at present the prerogative of five states, which also happen (it is not entirely a coincidence) to be the permanent members of the Security Council of the United Nations. Two are superpowers (USA, USSR); two are medium powers (UK, France); and one is China. All can, in theory, deploy strategic nuclear threat world-wide, though for some the practical constraints at great distances from the homeland are severe. There seems little doubt that all medium powers are deeply aware of, and concerned about, the threat to the fabric of their societies that the strategic nuclear threat represents. Many are unconvinced by the deterrent theory that, at least in the West, reconciles the possession of such weapons with the desire to maintain peace; but even when they subscribe to the theory they will be sensitive to any sign of its breaking down and will seek as many safeguards as they can find against that contingency. They are, for the most part, somewhat suspicious particularly of the superpowers, who with their great extent of land and population might conceivably expect to survive as political entities at the end of a nuclear conflict; most medium powers, with far less extensive resources, cannot believe they would so survive. The perception is sharpened by a feeling of helplessness in the face of a threat that is borne in the least detectable and therefore least vulnerable vehicle at present in existence, the nuclear-powered submarine, and delivered by ballistic missiles against which defences, if achievable at all, can be managed only by the superpowers.

Threat: A Summary

Medium powers may face a very wide variety of threats at sea and by sea. The less severe threats — administrative pinpricks and harassment — if isolated, cannot be said to affect vital interest; but if widespread or systematic may sap confidence and weaken economic positions. *A fortiori* this applies to the effects of major wars involving medium-power assets at sea, even if the medium power is not a belligerent. The resource-exploiting assets of medium powers may also be under threat, even in conditions of uneasy peace, through the operation of claim and counterclaim in international law and in the attempted enforcement of such claims. If a medium power becomes involved in hostilities, all these threats are of course greatly sharpened and generalised; there is a wide distinction between the severity of threats from a superpower opponent and those from another medium, or a small, power. Threats to the medium power's land possessions, resources and population are also posed from the sea — from, again, minor pinpricks (though these will be against spots more sensitive than assets at sea) to nuclear threat against the fabric of society itself.

Before discussing what a medium power may do about the sea-based threats that encompass it, it is necessary to make one point.

Threat is often characterised as 'latent' or 'potential', or as 'consisting of capability plus intention'. In my experience there is a tendency to derive from such formulations the implication that nothing need therefore be done to provide against threats of this sort. But it takes a deal of time and resources to build up the military elements of power, and therefore the implication will not do. It may be an exaggeration to say that intentions can change overnight; it is no exaggeration that threats can change from latent to actual in a very short space of time. It is, therefore, incumbent on governments not only to provide against the more obvious contingencies, but to produce a machinery of power that can respond in time to threats that their intelligence and external affairs departments either characterised as latent or did not perceive at all, when these become acute.

Medium-power Dilemmas

Producing such a machinery is easier said than done. The basic problem faced by a medium power is coping with the vulnerability of its interests, and the diveristy of the threats to them, from its available resources; subsidiary problems arise out of attempts to solve this basic one.

Because military power is expensive and cannot directly be used to advance national well-being but only to protect it, there are great attractions in deploying the other elements of power in order to minimise or neutralise threats. At its extreme, such a policy is encapsulated in the dictum that 'trade protects itself'. Japanese arguments about defence often seem to tend in this direction.[33] Extended, they seem to say that a nation can become so useful that the rest of the world regards its weakening to be against the public interest. Alternatively, its influence in world economic fora — on which so many states, particularly developing countries, depend — is held to be so great that otherwise hostile nations must keep on the right side of it.

Other nations, notably France and increasingly West Germany, Italy and Brazil, seek to use economic power in this way regionally or as opportunity offers. The sort of economic dependency imposed by being a client for, say, civil nuclear know-how or armament supplies deemed to be crucial, is held to be a powerful deterrent to unfriendly action against the supplier. In the same way, co-operation in education can be a useful threat-minimising influence as well as desirable in itself. So can diplomatic co-operation; the links established in the complex network of international conferences and the machinery of the United Nations agencies are often helpful if they are allowed to be so; this is one of the reasons why the display of pique by the United States, British and West German mining interests, resulting in non-signature of the 1982 Law of the Sea Convention, is so potentially damaging, particularly for the non-superpowers involved.

Thus there are ways in which a medium power can seek by its own non-military efforts to minimise threat, and some of these — because they are to do with trade and commerce — may be particularly applicable to the minor threats to sea assets. Some medium powers may judge that their efforts, coupled with the sporadic nature of the threats, reduce to vanishing point the threat to vital interests in this field. It appears that those who think about these matters in, for instance, Japan and West Germany (there are probably not very many of them) have reached that conclusion.

Analysis of recent experience scarcely bears it out, however. As an example: the British Nautical Institute's monthly magazine *Seaways* is a professional, many would say technical, publication. Yet in the years 1983–4 nine separate issues contained items detailing multiple examples of discrimination, restriction, piracy and state acts of violence against trade shipping not only of British flag but many others as well.[34] Seafarers and shipowners clearly do not, on the evidence before them, believe that trade protects itself. Understandably, they call for more protection rather than less. While accepting that many situations are not susceptible to military measures, and that in others containing and localising conflict is the best that can be done, they require in order to maintain their confidence a minimum assurance that help from national sources will be available when circumstances become extreme.[35]

Against other threats, the situation is more clear-cut. The more overtly military they are in character, the more unlikely it becomes that any but military means will be effective against them; and the more intense they become, the greater the military effort needed to counter them. Special circumstances, notably distance from the metropolitan bases of the medium power and the possession of particular capabilities by the threat nation or nations, sharpen the military problem. It is like a set of hilltops increasingly high, steep and difficult to climb. And then, round the shoulder of what perhaps appeared the last summit, there looms a far higher, quite unscalable peak: the menace of superpower.

The dimensions of superpower threat at sea have already been touched upon in this chapter, but at this point it is worth drawing attention to them once more. The United States can field 14 carrier battle groups, 34 ballistic missile submarines, 93 nuclear-powered attack submarines, over 60 ocean-going amphibious ships with a marine corps of 195,000 to suit.[36] The Soviet Union similarly has four carriers, 64 nuclear-powered ballistic missile submarines, 300 attack submarines of which 120 are nuclear-powered and 64 armed with antiship missiles, 37 cruisers many of which are missile-armed, 80 amphibious ships and 4,500 naval infantry.[37]

This brief quantification must be qualified by reference to two limitations when threats to medium powers are under consideration. First, whatever the state of *détente* at the time, each superpower will be preoccupied with the other to some extent. Second, dispersal (particularly of the Soviet Navy, which geography and strategic realities demand should be divided into four fleets) does to some extent dilute the threat that can be brought to bear against a medium power.

It is cold comfort. Both the mobility and the staying power of such huge forces are enough to ensure that, if opposed only by a medium power, they will eventually prevail.

Faced by such a threat, a medium power has few choices. It can of course plan to submit if the threat is foreclosed; but, by definition, submission will make it do something to its detriment, and one payment may lead to more. Sooner or later vital interests will be involved even if they are not at first. Or it can choose to ally itself with like-minded small or medium powers. Collective security of this sort, as exercised by relatively weak states, has a bad record, and a quick scrutiny of numbers and quality of maritime forces suggests that it would fare no better in future.[38] Nor does the United Nations give much prospect of relief, especially as each superpower is a permanent member of the Security Council and therefore has a right of veto.

Alliances

The only remaining choice is obvious: so obvious, indeed, that it is seldom now argued in the official statements of medium powers.[39]

It is that, in conditions of superpower threat, another superpower must be engaged on behalf of the medium power.

For most medium powers, some formal arrangements exist that are designed to bring this engagement about. The formality, the level of commitment and the conditions vary a good deal.

Britain and France are both signatories of the North Atlantic Treaty of 1949, which mutually engages them and the USA (as well as the 13 other signatories) to consider an armed attack against one as an attack against all, to be met by such action as each of them deems necessary. Specifically this includes the use of armed force.

The Treaty applies within the North Atlantic area, which is defined in Article 6 as the territory of the parties, the islands under their jurisdiction in the North Atlantic north of the Tropic of Cancer and their vessels or aircraft in this area. In pursuance of the treaty an integrated military structure was set up and has grown steadily in the intervening 36 years, extending now to a planning and policy machinery including political and military committees at the highest level supported by a very large international staff; and an operational command structure including two supreme commanders, six commanders-in-chief and several dozen major subordinate commanders, supported by appropriate staffs.

The effect when applied to a medium power with extended vital interests is rather curious. Within the specified area there is as rigid a superpower commitment as can be provided by treaty arrangements; outside it there is nothing. The oddity is itensified when seen against the way the Tropic of Cancer limit evolved in the initial negotiations — as a means of including France's 'Algerian departments', at her insistence, in the Treaty area.[40]

Neither Britain nor France has, overtly, chafed too much under this strange abrasion. When France left the integrated military organisation in 1966 it was for other reasons, although in fact this loosening of the formal ties within the NATO area made more logical her necessarily independent stance outside it. Britain, up to 1968, pursued a defence policy outside the NATO area independent of the United States. She still had, just, enough resources to do so and the Soviet Navy was only beginning to emerge into the world oceans. After that date, those in charge of policy generally appear to have judged that by complementing (or supplementing; the words were often debated) US efforts beyond the NATO area, Britain was ensuring sufficient US engagement without any further formal commitment.

Japan has a mutual co-operation and security treaty with the United States, signed in 1960. While the basic terms of this are of a familiar kind ('Each party recognises that an armed attack against either party in the territories under the administration of Japan would be dangerous to its own peace and safety, and declares that it would act to meet the common danger in accordance with its constitutional practices and processes.'[41]), some aspects surrounding the arrangements are novel. First, it appears that, to satisfy the Japanese conscience, the basic policy enunciated in 1956 was that the bilateral agreement was to last only until a suitable United Nations machinery for guaranteeing Japanese security was available.[42] Second, although no formal command machinery was set up, several committees, all at ministerial or high official level, meet frequently to discuss security and the implementation of the US Status of Forces agreement.[43] Finally, the progressive distancing of US defence commitment that began with the Nixon doctrine in 1970 led to a more self-reliant stance by Japan in the so-called 'defence of sea lanes' by which, in 1981, the concept of self-defence was applied to Japanese shipping to a distance of 1,000 miles from the homeland.[44] There is still a wide gap between concept and implementation.[45]

India is the only medium power here under review that relies mainly on an agreement with the Soviet Union. The history of the events that led up to the Treaty of Friendship, Co-operation and Mutual Assistance of 1971 is complex and space does not allow analysis here. One salient if obvious point must however be made. Even if the initial impetus came from elsewhere — notably the Chinese invasions in the early 1960s, the Sino-Pakistan alliance, and US and UK reluctance to side with India — the agreement is now rationalised against the perception of a threat from US forces based at sea and supported (to add insult to potential injury) from Diego Garcia, within what India regards as its natural ambit of power.[46]

Nevertheless there are indications that India is by no means fully committed to a Soviet alliance in the way that Britain and Japan are to an American one. Some authoritative Indian writers, while seeing the US as the principal present threat, note a parallelism between US and Soviet policies in the Indian Ocean,[47] and Indian naval officers emphasise the essential non-alignment of their country.[48] Moreover the wording of the operative part of the Treaty ('in the event of either party being subjected to attack or threat thereof, the high contracting parties shall immediately enter into mutual consultations with a view to eliminating the threat and taking appropriate effective measures to ensure the peace and security of their countries')[49] is relatively non-committal.

Brazil relies for her superpower support on the engagement of the United States by a series of treaties that are relatively loosely worded and unsupported by permanent military infrastructure. These are the Act of Chapultepec (1945), its extension and consolidation by the Rio Treaty (1947), and further extension in the Charter of the Organisation of American States (1948). All these instruments involve the generality of the countries of South America, the later ones many Caribbean and Central American states as well.

Brazil, as the largest and most powerful of the non-superpowers involved, has occupied a slightly special position among them. On the one hand her forces, particularly her Navy, exercise more frequently with those of the United States than do the other states, and she is clearly thought capable of providing more control, both administrative and naval, in the South Atlantic in emergency than any other local power; on the other, she has shown considerable independence of spirit over a variety of matters where the OAS and US policies do not coincide. She has also shown a good deal of sensitivity about the possibility of being involved by the USA in global conflict. However, this is but one example of the price of superpower alliance: a subject to which this study, in later chapters, must return.

Australia, with New Zealand, bases her superpower security on the ANZUS treaty of 1952. Under this treaty the parties agree, in terms very similar to the US-Japanese treaty, to act together in the event of attack on their own territories, islands under their jurisdiction, or on their armed forces, public vessels or aircraft in the Pacific. Although from about 1980 onwards Australian defence policy was increasingly permeated by emphasis on 'self-reliance' and a withdrawal from her previous dependence on 'great and powerful friends', it was clear that this did not extend to dealing on her own with superpower threats.[50] Once again, however, one of the medium-powers' dilemmas was clearly visible: how to keep the superpower sufficiently engaged without becoming too heavily engaged in one's turn.

Israel presents one of the most extreme, and certainly one of the most interesting, examples of superpower counterbalances at present in existence. It began not with a treaty but with a tripartite guarantee by the USA, UK and France of 1950 when, at the end of the war which followed Israel's independence, armistice lines were drawn. The three powers guaranteed the armistice lines against forcible change. Subsequent history has, of course, added stratum upon stratum not only through war and conquest but through further negotiations, guarantees and agreements. *De facto* the situation is now that the United States gives an absolute guarantee of the existence of the state of Israel but does not necessarily back Israel's actions. However similar this may be in form to other superpower-mediumpower relationships, it has not worked out in the same way as any other. Israel has repeatedly used it as a guarantee not so much of her existence but of her freedom of action.

But Israel's relationship with her superpower ally has also a different emphasis of another sort. None of the medium powers mentioned above has a common frontier with the Soviet Union, and for all of them except Israel a very large part of the Soviet military threat must come from the sea. Israel does not seem to perceive matters so. Her maritime force structure shows either massive reliance on the deterrent effect of the US Sixth Fleet in the Mediterranean, or a conviction that Soviet intervention if it came would be through Syria or Lebanon, with airborne assistance.

Superpower alliances, then, in spite of their entangling effect, are generally embarked upon by medium powers who feel themselves menaced — as all of them do — by superpowers. The alliances apply quite as much in the maritime field as in others, and not only against strategic nuclear threat from the sea — indeed that may, given the existence of Negative Security Assurances, be rather far down the agenda of some medium powers — but against threats of less absolute character.[51]

The formality or otherwise of the alliance, as has been shown, can vary widely. The nation that relies most on its alliance in practical terms, Israel, has probably the least watertight guarantee — in terms of treaty instruments — of any. Developing countries appear to be more comfortable with relatively loose arrangements that allow them to maintain an independent image — not least to show to themselves — and there is some evidence that developed countries, too, chafe at alliances that threaten to impose a dependent relationship.[52] Actions, of course, can overturn words, theories and preconceptions; the British government did all that to at least the western side of Whitehall in 1982. But that paradox was possible only because the policies based on a dependent relationship, carried to an extreme and reflected in the 1981 plans greatly to reduce the independent power of the Royal Navy, had not had time to work through.

Even when considering its most severe and mortal threat, then, it seems the wise medium power will seek a solution that preserves to the maximum its freedom of action, while providing the necessary basic security. The form of the treaty or agreement may well matter less than the machinery of power that surrounds it — and that includes the power-structures of the medium power, its superpower ally and the threat superpower.

If threats to medium powers came solely from superpowers and could always be countered by the safeguards that have been described, the world would be a simpler place. As this chapter has already shown, that is not the case at all. Moreover, as has often been demonstrated, but seldom more cogently than in Stanley Hoffman's brilliant analysis to the International Institute for Strategic Studies' 1980 Conference, the pattern of power and threat is not only complex but becoming steadily more so.[53]

It is not easy to say whether sea-based threats and conflicts are more, or less, likely than others to concern, on both sides, non-superpowers. However, it is beyond doubt that such threats are perceived, such conflicts occur; a summary of conflict situations at sea from 1971–9 shows 20 involving one or more superpowers and 32 involving superpowers on neither side.[54]

If, against sea-based threats from other medium or small powers, a medium power seeks to depend on a superpower ally it may run into difficulty. First, the weight of help the superpower can provide may be quite inappropriate; the United States in particular has a record of heavy-footedness in small sea-based conflicts that might result in unnecessary damage to relations between the parties in contention.[55] Second, the involvement of a superpower in local quarrels could bring on the unwelcome attention of the other superpower. Third, the superpower may be entirely unwilling to guarantee local interests in this way; it is well known that the CENTO alliance was directed entirely against a threat from the Soviet Union, and this was not well received by Pakistan, a key member, who considered the Pact should also have safeguarded her against an Indian threat — and though this is an example that had particularly far-reaching consequences, it is by no means an isolated one.[56]

Thus, although a medium power may rely on a superpower ally to cope with non-superpower sea-based threats of a rather diffuse and far-flung kind — not least by promoting an atmosphere of maritime stability — it is unlikely to do so for threats that are more specific or closer to home. Can it then look to other means of ensuring security against such threats? The possibilities lie in two areas: international organisations or non-superpower allies.

International organisations, both regional and world-wide, provide a variety of fora for the peaceful settlement of disputes, and it is not their fault that too little use is made of them by those who have access to them. But it takes two sides to enter an arbitration, and all too often one or both is reluctant to put its case to that sort of test. A medium power therefore cannot *rely* on such machinery to relieve it of threat. Nor can it rely on collective intervention by international organisations in the event of sea-based aggression or attack. There have been a few such interventions in cases of land conflict over the past 40 years, but none at sea.[57]

Non-superpower alliances are rare in the world at present. Such as exist are mainly between the old colonial powers and their erstwhile dependent territories, and tend to play down guarantees of help in case of aggression. In South and Central America, to be sure, there are signs of groupings much smaller amd more directed than the very large and cumbersome OAS,[58] but they are a far cry from the very complex and sometimes influential multipower alliance systems of the pre-1914 and pre-1939 eras.[59]

It is not too easy to see why this should be so. Perhaps the desire for co-operation through large-scale international organisations, in pursuance of the principles of peaceful coexistence so often quoted by many governments, is more sincerely and genuinely held than the cynical observer might think. Or perhaps most states are too preoccupied with their domestic problems to enter upon delicate negotiations towards alliances that may never be called upon. Perhaps threats are perceived by the inner circles of government as less acute than national propaganda for public consumption suggests. Or perhaps the level of commitment implied by an alliance is unattractive, particularly to developing countries in a fluid international situation. Finally, there may not be a sufficient level of trust in any potential ally.

Whatever the reasons, it looks as if the medium power threatened at or from sea by a non-superpower is likely to be doing without any formal alliance directed at that threat. That does not mean that, if confrontation or conflict develops, allies — whether *ad hoc* or formal — may not become involved. It will be a matter, as indeed it really is in the case of superpower alliances, of the machinery of power and the way that machinery is operated.

Notes

1. Correlli Barnett, *The Collapse of British Power* (Methuen, London, 1972), pp. 586–7.
2. David S. Yost, *France's Deterrent Posture and Security in Europe* (International Institute for Strategic Studies, Adelphi Paper No. 194, 1984/5), p. 6.
3. Michael McGwire in *Insecurity! The Spread of Weapons in the the Indian and Pacific Oceans* (ed. R. C. O'Neill) (Australian National University Press, Canberra, 1978), p. 100.
4. *Strategic Survey, 1982–83* (International Institute for Strategic Studies, London), p. 117.
5. J. Cable, *Gunboat Diplomacy* (Macmillan, London, 1982), p. 256.
6. N. Safran, *Israel — The Embattled Ally* (Belknap Press, Harvard, 1978), p. 230.
7. The dichotomy in the British positions over Hong Kong and the Falklands is a case in point in the mid-1980s: see the *Sunday Times*, 23 December 1984.
8. In some areas, indeed, threats to the commercial interests of established medium powers may create opportunities for developing medium powers: see Peter M. Dawkins in *Controlling Future Arms Trade*, eds A. H. Cahn, P. M. Dawkins, J. J. Kruzel, J. Huntziger (McGraw-Hill, New York, 1980), p. 116.
9. J. R. Hill, 'The Role of Navies', *Brassey's Annual 1970* (William Clowes, London, 1970), pp. 127–37.
10. *Greenwich Forum VI* (ed. M. B. F. Ranken) (Westbury House, London, 1981), pp. 127–37.
11. *Admiralty Notice to Mariners*, No. 12/1982.
12. B. Buzan, *A Sea of Troubles? Sources of Dispute in the New Ocean Régime* (International Institute for Strategic Studies, London, 1978), p. 9.
13. In a letter to the British Prime Minister in June 1984, the President of the Nautical Institute said 'We know that some 25 nations actively discriminate against British shipping using their ports.' *Seaways*, August 1984, p. 27.
14. Canada, Arctic Waters Pollution Prevention Act, 1970.
15. Commander Denis R. Neutze, 'The Gulf of Sidra Incident', US Naval Institute, *Proceedings* (1982), pp. 26–31.
16. For example, the Case Concerning the Continental Shelf (Tunisia-Libyan Arab Jamahiriya), Judgement of 24 February 1982, ICJ Rep. 18.
17. Capt. B. E. D. Edwards, 'High Noon in the Gulf', *Seaways*, November 1984, p. 3.
18. C. J. Colombos, *International Law of the Sea* (Longmans, London, 1967), pp. 716–26.
19. Capt. C. W. Koburger, Jr, USCG (Retd.), 'Swords and Surfboats: Cost Effective Maritime Law Enforcement', Nautical Institute Seminar, 10 November 1983, *Report*, p. 6.
20. United Nations Convention on the Law of the Sea, 1982, Art. 58(2).
21. A striking example is the very narrow and force-limiting judgement in the *Red Crusader* case a quarter of a century ago, compared with the comparative unconcern

with which public opinion appeared to view the sinking of a Spanish fishing boat by an Irish patrol craft in 1984.

22. J. R. Hill, *Anti-Submarine Warfare* (Ian Allan, Shepperton, 1981), p. 35, for a 'non-aligned' list.

23. Jean Labayle-Couhat, ed., *Combat Fleets of the World 1984–85* (Arms and Armour Press, London, 1984), *passim*.

24. *The Military Balance, 1983–84*.

25. Cable, *Gunboat Diplomacy*, pp. 250, 254, 256.

26. Ibid., p. 21.

27. The 1982 Law of the Sea Convention states (Art. 121(3)) that 'Rocks which cannot sustain human habitation or economic life of their own shall have no exclusive economic zone or continental shelf.' Whether the Tunbs, Paracels or Spratlys fell under this definition would no doubt be a matter for interpretation: the questions at issue would not only be habitability and economic life but whether title had in fact been acquired by seizure.

28. Admiral of the Fleet of the Soviet Union S. G. Gorshkov, *The Sea Power of the State* (Pergamon Press, Oxford, 1978), p. 269.

29. Cable, *Gunboat Diplomacy*, pp. 228–56, counts only one unsuccessful assault among many successful ones.

30. Cable, *Britain's Naval Future* (Naval Institute Press, Annapolis, 1983), p. 39.

31. UNDOCs S/6034, S/6036, S/6054, S/6084, S/6111, S/6140, S/6167, S/6222, S/6388.

32. *Keesing's Contemporary Archives* (Longman's, London), p. 33062.

33. Shimpei Fujimaki, 'Japan in the Eastern Sea', paper given at the Ninth Greenwich Forum, September 1983.

34. *Seaways*, January 1983, p. 20; February 1983, p. 16; May 1983, p. 23; June 1983, pp. 5–10; September 1983, p. 23; December 1983, p. 21; July 1984, p. 4; September 1984, p. 27; November 1984, pp. 3–4.

35. As, for instance, in the Armilla Patrol in the Hormuz approaches conducted by US, British and French warships from 1980–5.

36. *Combat Fleets of the World 1984–85*, pp. 821–3; *The Military Balance, 1983–84*, p. 8.

37. *Combat Fleets of the World, 1984–85*, pp. 671–3; *The Military Balance, 1983–4*, p. 17.

38. L. B. Namier, *Diplomatic Prelude 1938–1939* (Macmillan, London, 1948), pp. xvi and 91–5.

39. The engagement of the USA in the defence of Western Europe, as a crucial element in the NATO structure, is for example nowhere mentioned in Cmnd. 9227–1, *Statement on the Defence Estimates 1984*, and in the writer's recollection has not been so mentioned for many years. Perhaps it is considered bad form.

40. Sir Nicholas Henderson, *The Birth of NATO* (Weidenfeld and Nicholson, London, 1983), p. 81.

41. Treaty of 19 January 1960, Art. 5.

42. J. W. M. Chapman, R. Drifte and I. T. M. Gow, *Japan's Quest for Comprehensive Security* (Frances Pinter, London, 1983), p. 58.

43. Japan, Defence White Paper, 1981.

44. I. S. P. G. Cosby, 'Self-Defence as a Basis for Maritime Forces', Gosport Seminar 1982.

45. Lieut. Joseph Bouchard and Lieut. Douglas J. Hess, 'The Japanese Navy and Sea Lanes Defence' in US Naval Institute, *Proceedings*, March 1984, pp. 90–7.

46. P. K. S. Namboodiri, J. P. Anand and Sreedhar, *Intervention in the Indian Ocean* (ABC Publishing House, Bombay, 1982), pp. 129–30.

47. A. Kapur, *The Indian Ocean: Regional and International Power Politics*

(Praeger, New York, 1965), p. xxiv.

48. Admiral S. N. Kohli, lecture II at the Indian Naval Staff College, 1979; letter to the author from Vice Admiral M. P. Awati, 16 August 1984. See also J. Larus, *US Naval Institute Proceedings*, March 1981, p. 79.

49. Treaty of 9 August 1971, Art. 9.

50. Noel Butlin in *Australian Defence Policy for the 1980s* (ed. O'Neill) (Australian National University Press, Canberra, 1978), p. 97.

51. 'Negative Security Assurances' is the term of art applied to the declarations made by all nuclear weapon states that they will not initiate nuclear action against non-nuclear weapon states, given certain conditions. The conditions vary from one nuclear weapon state to another; they may include the requirement to be a signatory of the Non-Proliferation Treaty, or not to allow nuclear weapons on one's soil, or not to be formally allied to a nuclear weapon state, or several of these.

52. James Cable, 'Interdependence — A Drug of Addiction?', *International Affairs*, Summer 1983, p. 372.

53. Stanley Hoffman, 'Security in an Age of Turbulence: Means of Response' in International Institute for Strategic Studies, Adelphi Paper No. 167, pp. 2 and 5–6.

54. Cable, *Gunboat Diplomacy*, pp. 249–58.

55. Ibid., p. 253; the *Mayaguez* incident in which, although they successfully recaptured a US merchant ship on 12 May 1975, the US Navy and US Marine Corps incurred and inflicted casualties that appeared disproportionate to the scale of the operation.

56. Quoting Alan Dowty, Shai Feldman wrote in 'Super Power Guarantees in the 1980s' (Adelphi Paper No. 167, p. 39) that only 17 out of the 104 great-power guarantees since 1815 had been directed at a *local* threat.

57. In particular United Nations peacekeeping forces, though there have also been isolated attempts by the Organisation of African Unity and the Organisation of American States to provide physical interventions.

58. *The Military Balance, 1984–85*, p. 114.

59. As in so many things concerning China, Pakistan's relationship with that country and its very far-reaching effects on the whole power structure in the Indian Ocean area seems to be unique. It is certainly not just a medium-power relationship. In this case China is in the position of a sponsoring superpower and India sees her as such.

PART TWO:

TOOLS OF THE TRADE: CONCEPTS AND MATERIEL

5 GENERAL CONCEPTS

Theorists of sea power are often accused, not least by other theorists of sea power, of forming grand abstractions rather than workable strategies.[1] On many counts the charge sticks. The first systematic study of sea power was made against the background of a simpler age, an age that lent itself to slogans; and Mahan was a handy man with a slogan. When lesser men came to apply them a generation or more later, in a much more complex world, it was no wonder they appeared stale and unprofitable. And though attempts were made to regenerate and modify them, they seemed rather pale aphorisms in contrast to the confident assertions of earlier writers, hedged about with qualifications and of doubtful general validity. The more clear-cut they were, the more they appeared to be labelled 'for superpowers only'; medium powers were left with ever more dubious theoretical bases for planning.[2]

It is absolutely right that strategies should be appropriate to the present reality and the future contingency. They must take full account of interests, threats and resources, must balance and compound them for national security and well-being. But there are limits to pragmatism. Trying to derive a strategy from a bottom-up survey of the total situation, without using any of the conceptual tools which are at hand, is as cumbersome as trying to derive a theoretical model divorced from the facts is dangerous. Some concepts exist which do help the medium power to shape the maritime side of its strategy. It is these — along with some less useful or misleading ones, which must be used with caution or rejected — that will be studied in this chapter.

Deterrence

Deterrence, as a strategic idea, is now commonplace. It is in general use not only by Western writers on defence but by those in non-aligned countries, and more and more examples of it appear in Soviet literature although it is not central to Soviet military doctrine.

The words deterrence and deterrent (as a noun) seem to be of comparatively recent origin,[3] though deterrent was used adjectivally, in the context of strategy, in the 1930s.[4] The idea is as old as strategy itself: by making military preparation, to convince a potential opponent that military action will be unprofitable for him. But the advent of the atomic bomb, with its threat of very widespread destruction of life and property as well as unpredictable after-effects, greatly enhanced in the eyes of some statesmen and strategists the feasibility of the idea's general application. Thus in the late 1940s the speeches of Baruch and Churchill, and the work of writers such as Slessor, laid down new foundations in new language.

Inevitably, over the next 40 years, complications crept in. First, great confusion was caused by the application of the noun deterrent to the means of nuclear bombardment alone. Frequently the atomic weapon and its means of delivery were referrred to as *the* deterrent, and this led to many distortions and errors of emphasis, not least in organisations and budgets. Theories such as massive retaliation, and the Sandys aberration in the 1957 British Defence White Paper, gave nuclear bombardment a deterrent function over too wide a range of issues, a function it could not credibly sustain. The misconception is inclined to survive in the more simplistic French attitudes to nuclear retaliation in response to any attack on metropolitan France.

Second, at the other end of the scale, the notion of deterrent preparations, of whatever scale and complexity is necessary, as a means of dissuading *all* potential opponents from *any* military action may, for all but the greatest superpowers, be a chimera. Britain, for example, cannot credibly deter China from a military assault on Hong Kong by any military means. Brazil in her present state of development can only consider the possibility of deterring relatively local and conventional attacks. Thus, although deterrence is an all-arms affair, does operate at all levels of potential conflict, and must be planned and seen to do so, the 'seamless-robe' theory of comprehensive deterrence is likely, for medium powers, to be an aspiration rather than a reality.

Finally, and most importantly, the theory is so commonplace as to be stale — and therefore too often forgotten. In strategic debate, particularly among laymen, there is a tendency to discuss military organisation, weapons and systems in fighting and even scenario terms without reading back into their deterrent effect. Of course fighting effectiveness and the ability to exact unacceptable penalty is the rockbed of deterrence, but it is always necessary to view it through the eyes of the opponent, and to take account of his other preoccupations, to assess what it will do.

Sea Command and Sea Control

Command of the sea is a heavily worn phrase. Its use has been well analysed by Till and there is no need to reiterate the analysis here.[5] It can be summarised by saying that, in the view of all the more thoughtful writers on maritime power, command of the sea is relative and partial rather than absolute and general.

The reasons lie deep in the scale and nature of world relationships at sea. The sea is very large compared with either a ship or a fleet; coastlines are similarly long. Maritime units are numerous and varied in size, strength and manoeuvrability. Nations are many, adversary conditions and confrontations diverse. It is therefore beyond the bounds of possibility that at all times and in all places any power could be in a position comprehensively to impose its will on all that goes on at sea. This was true in the days of sailing ships, which were limited by their speed, the scope of their horizon, the range of their guns, and their numbers; they could blockade strategic ports, control key straits, protect important shipping, and threaten isolated descents on the enemy coast, but their writ was not universal. For different reasons it is equally true today, where threat and conflict at sea have spread into four media: the surface, the sub-surface, the air and outer space.[6] While the resources available in these media, linked and co-ordinated by modern communications, give greatly enhanced options for the application of power by sea, they also give much bigger and more diverse opportunities to the opposition. Absolute and comprehensive command, therefore, is further off than ever.

Consequently, emphasis has shifted to a more limited concept; that of sea control. This has been a largely American development, a rebuttal perhaps of those who regard American strategic thought as proceeding in too absolutist a way. Admirals Eccles and Stansfield Turner led the way, the former putting forward the best practical case as 'the ability to operate with a high degree of freedom' and the latter defining control as being 'in limited areas and for limited periods of time'.[7]

The limited areas referred to can, of course, be moving ones.[8]

'Control' can then be sought in that area round a battle group, amphibious force or convoy where a threat could be expected to exist. Equally, areas can be geographically fixed; many medium or small powers would expect to exert control in coastal waters, at least over the surface and air spaces, by the use of quite limited resources aided by propinquity. It has many times been said that the Russians regard the Barents and now perhaps the Norwegian Sea as a 'bastion' over which they seek to exercise control, mainly for the unchecked deployment of ballistic missile submarines.

Medium powers will no doubt have welcomed the passing of the concept of, and any aspirations by anyone to, sea command. The more fluid and flexible idea of sea control they can live with, as an operational and deterrent basis for something that lies at the heart of maritime power: sea use.

Sea Use

'The ability to use the sea' is one definition of maritime power, and in the writer's view by no means the worst.[9] As was demonstrated in Chapter 3, sea use in normal conditions can result in great economic gain, and great advantages in the intercourse of states. In time of confrontation or conflict values become harsher, the prizes for success more precious and the penalties of failure more acute. From the Peloponnesian wars to the Falklands, the ability to use the sea has been a common though not universal characteristic of successful campaigns. It confers mobility, initiative, the ability to choose new axes and to complicate the opponent's problems; it allows those entities (nations, garrisons, expeditionary forces) that are not self-sufficient to be sustained; it is an important vehicle for maintaining the territorial integrity of the more vulnerable participants.

The economic uses of the sea consist of trade and commerce on its surface, and exploitation of resources in its depths and subsoil.[10] A notable characteristic of sea resource exploitation is that, although it occurs beneath the surface, it is almost always dependent on surface-borne agents for its effectiveness. The fishing boat is a surface craft. The oil rig is a structure at the sea's surface. Very few people who carry out either fishing or extractive operations go beneath the surface, and then only for brief spaces of time. Effectively, therefore, the economic exploitation of sea resources is done from the surface.

The same goes for the most ancient of economic sea uses, trade between nations or along coasts. A decade and a half ago there was much talk of submarine cargo vessels and many ingenious ideas and designs were produced. All so far have turned out to be hopelessly uneconomic compared with the plodding surface-borne monohull. Projections suggest that it will remain so.

Turning to the use of the sea for military purposes in their broadest sense, the surface again assumes primary importance. Large formations of troops, ready for combat and logistically supported, can only be carried on the surface of the sea; airlift can manage relatively large numbers of men but few heavy stores, submarines can handle only very small parties. Blockade or control of shipping operations have their *point d'appui* in surface craft; the more of the total process that can take place on the surface, the more economical it will be. And the sustaining of nations, stations and forces that are not self-sufficient in times of conflict must be done by surface means except in those rare cases where airdrop or submarine supply, both inherently very limited, are sufficient.

Thus it turns out that sea use is, overwhelmingly, use of the sea's surface. It is unsurprising, since man is himself a creature of the interface. But it raises considerable problems, because sea use is vulnerable to sea denial.

Sea Denial

Denial of the sea to one's adversary has often been regarded as the obverse of sea control for one's own use, as in Roskill's classic definition.[11] Yet history and geography combine to assert that this is an oversimplification. Whether one subscribes fully to Mackinderish notions of geopolitics, of heartlands and rim lands, it is clear that the curtailment or deprivation of sea use will affect quite differently the respective combatants in any geographically realistic conflict or confrontation. Germany versus Britain, Russia versus America, India versus Pakistan, Syracuse versus Athens, the examples from both historical and projected events are endless; even the most balanced recent example one can think of, the Iran/Iraq war where both sides have an interest in sea use and some capacity for sea denial, still shows marked imbalances that make Iran's sea-dependence a good deal more critical than Iraq's. The fact that this has apparently had the effect of damping down the conflict at sea to levels where it is still managed within a small area in the northwest of the Gulf is not, here, relevant.[12] But the asymmetries of the need for use and denial are plain.

Sea denial, then, may be a policy embarked upon by any national actor at any stage of a dispute and does not depend on a complementary need for sea use or control. It may be used as a means of helping to secure sea use, either in the same geographical area or elsewhere; a sunk enemy cannot any longer threaten. Viewed in this light, the sinking of the *General Belgrano* in the South Atlantic campaign was a sea denial operation outside the Exclusion Zone declared by the British Government in order to secure sea use within it. But in general the notion of using sea denial as a means of sweeping the sea clear of enemies, so that unbridled sea use may take place, has not worked well against a determined and resourceful opponent. The failure of 'offensive' anti-submarine operations, in both World Wars, is a particularly cogent example.[13] Sea denial, therefore, tends to be the policy of the power less dependent on the sea, and of the inferior naval power.

But in these days that is a generalisation that needs qualifying. The advent since the beginning of the century of the aircraft and the submarine, and in the last four decades of the aerodynamic homing missile, has meant that units on the surface of the sea are now subject to assault from both sides of the interface between sea and sky, as well as from their own kind. This sharply complicates the problem of preserving them for sea use. In particular areas or at certain times it can make nonsense of the idea of 'inferior' or 'superior' naval power, and it increases the utility of sea denial, particularly in conflicts that are latent or limited.

For medium powers these developments cut both ways. On the positive side, the possibility of exerting sea denial against an intrinsically stronger power, in favourable circumstances of one's own planning or choosing, may be attractive in a variety of conditions from deterrence to limited conflict. On the negative side, powers weaker (often much weaker) than oneself may be guided by exactly the same considerations and embark on policies aimed at denying the sea to one's use. The three so-called Cod Wars of 1958–60, 1972–3 and 1975–6 in which Iceland successively and successfully denied to British trawlers ever larger areas of fishing grounds, are the classic example in recent times of such David-and-Goliath tactics.[14]

There are two considerations that qualify the attraction of sea-denial operations. First, the penalties for getting it wrong may be quite severe. It may be that the Argentine services were confident of their ability to deny the sea to the British task force in 1982, or, at least, confident that the risk to sea use was enough to deter the British from trying. For this misconception they paid dearly. Second — and like so many considerations about maritime power, the point is linked with its predecessor — there will in most medium-power conflicts and disputes be a whole raft of concomitant factors concerning other actors and other forms of power. Again the Cod Wars are instructive. As Cable points out, Iceland was an ally of Britain, accommodated a large US base at Keflavik, and occupied a strategic position on a much larger canvas than a mere fishing dispute; but these were considerations that weighed much more heavily with Britain than with Iceland, and this strengthened Iceland's position in its sea-denial efforts.[15] On the other hand, strait-bordering states such as Spain, Malaysia and Indonesia, though often claiming rights more extensive than those generally accorded, have not carried their claims so far as to attempt sea denial, for a variety of reasons ranging from the state of international law negotiations to Spain's desire to join NATO.[16]

Levels of Conflict

Of all the conceptual tools available to a medium power planning the maritime side of its strategy, Levels of Conflict is probably the most important. More than any of the rather general and abstract ideas that have gone before, it helps to set limits on what a medium power needs to be able to do on its own; or, conversely, on what a medium power will be able to do on its own with the resources it can provide.

There is nothing new about the idea of levels of conflict. From the earliest Chinese strategic writings, through Greek and Roman historians, Clausewitz, Corbett, Liddell Hart, and Kahn, to writers as newly emerged as Moineville, a central thread is the Aim of Conflict and limitation of means to attain that Aim. Such limitation is also the foundation of the laws of war. Even in the most unbridled conflicts such as the First and Second World Wars, there were many voices questioning whether totality, demands for victory, insistence on unconditional surrender, were rational; with hindsight, the voices are louder. It is safe to say that the general pattern of conflict is limited, its intensity less than absolute, and that it is subject to gradations.

These gradations are more readily identifiable at sea than on land. The main unit on land is the individual; freely moving, autonomous, very numerous, relatively easily concealed, not always predictable. Large military formations, particularly if they include armour or artillery, are of course more readily identifiable and their actions can more easily be judged. But by and large the fog of a land battlefield is going to be thick and the level of conflict not easy to determine. At sea, units are much larger, discrete and under strict control — certainly of themselves, often from higher command. The position and movement of surface and air units is more readily observable than ever before; their actions are similarly often observable. Subsurface units are not so easily detected and localised and often constitute a factor of uncertainty. But generally, the level and intensity of a conflict at sea is assessable both in the event, and long before in the planning stages.

It is tempting to seek, from the examples that history, including recent history, has to offer, a minutely ascending staircase of conflict levels, tidy and satisfying. But such a classification would be subject to the same defects as Khan's over-runged ladders of escalation; in the real world, the appropriate position of each rung depends to some degree on the surrounding circumstances, whatever theory may say.[17] It is therefore best to assess the level of a conflict, historical or projected, by its general characteristics and allocate it to a group of conflicts of similar nature, in order to extract the maximum planning value from it.

On the other hand, the number of levels must not be too small or the method loses its utility. NATO has traditionally divided levels of operation into peace, tension and war. This categorisation leads planners to ignore the condition of low-tension not-quite-peace that is the norm at sea in many areas today; of sporadic warlike operations in times of crisis that have not reached the stage of war; and, perhaps most important of all, of limited warlike operations once crisis has sharpened to the point where a military, as well as a political, aim has had to be established. Such lack of sophistication in strategic thought has led to a good deal of naïve planning and overprovision.

The levels of conflict which this book will consider, therefore, are four, and they will form the subject matter of the next four chapters. They are, respectively, Normal Conditions; Low Intensity Operations; Operations at the Higher Level; and General War.

Reach

Finally, a concept which cuts across all others is that of Reach: the distance from the home base at which it is necessary to be able to carry out operations of various descriptions. In some ways it is the most decisive of all in the force structure of a medium maritime power; and the limitations it can impose may powerfully influence strategy. It too will be given a chapter to itself.

Notes

1. G. Till, *Maritime Strategy and the Nuclear Age* (Macmillan, London, 1984), p. 90; J. Cable, *Britain's Naval Future* (Naval Institute Press, Annapolis, 1983), p. 43.
2. P. M. Kennedy, *The Rise and Fall of British Naval Mastery* (Allen Lane, London, 1976), pp. 337ff.
3. *Oxford English Dictionary Supplement* (1972), p. 784.
4. C. Barnett, *The Collapse of British Power* (Methuen, London, 1972), p. 473.
5. Till, *Maritime Strategy and the Nuclear Age*, pp. 128–32.
6. Vice Admiral Pierre Lacoste, in *Stratégie Navale* (Nathan, Paris, 1981), pp. 65–79, calls these 'dimensions', and it is a pity that the word has a more restrictive application in English.
7. Quoted in Till, *Maritime Strategy and the Nuclear Age*, p. 189.
8. Rear Admiral M. LaT. Wemyss, 'Submarine and Anti-Submarine Operations for the Uninitiated', RUSI, *Journal*, September 1981, p. 26.
9. J. R. Hill, *British Sea Power in the 1980s* (Ian Allan, Shepperton, 1985), p. 1.
10. Air traffic above the sea is, of course, important. But it is subject to a complex of control and regulation that, although governed by international law as regards territoriality, in practice transcends the distinctions between overland and oversea airspace. It is not therefore included in this section.
11. 'The function of maritime power is to win and keep control of the sea for one's own use, and to deny such control to one's adversaries': S. W. Roskill, *The Strategy of Sea Power* (Collins, London, 1962), p. 15.
12. *Strategic Survey, 1983–84*, p. 81.
13. D. W. Waters, 'Seamen Scientists Historians and Strategy', Presidential Address to the British Society for the History of Science, 1978.
14. Cable, *Gunboat Diplomacy*, pp. 23–4 and Appendix 1. A longer analysis of the 1958–60 operations is in J. R. Hill, *The Rule of Law at Sea*, Annex B.
15. Cable, *Gunboat Diplomacy*, pp. 23–4.
16. Buzan, *A Sea of Troubles?*, pp. 28 and 41.
17. Herman Kahn, *On Escalation* (Praeger, New York, 1965), p. 40.

6 NORMAL CONDITIONS

'In fact,' says Hubert Moineville, 'in the state of the world today, and in that unprotected space that is the sea, peace does not really exist. The word is used, mainly as a linguistic convenience, to describe the permanent state of tension in which we live.'[1] It is necessary to add to this admirable statement (which could, one suspects, have been applied to most periods of history as well as our own) that almost by definition, in normal conditions the tensions must be compensated. That is to say, changes in the international situation occur in a controlled way aided by processes of negotiation; no use of force is taking place except at internationally accepted constabulary level; and threats of force are confined to the normal processes of deterrence.

In our power-directed world the maintenance of this state of equilibrium demands carefully-judged provision and management of power, including military power, by a multiplicity of actors. The watchword for all, including medium powers, must be readiness.

Readiness

There are two reasons for this. First, deterrence, which is the philosophical basis of the equilibrium, demands that forces should be capable of credibly effective action directly related to any military action against vital interests. If the action has, through insufficient preparedness, to wait some considerable lapse of time its threat is much less likely to deter. The unreadiness of French and British forces in the years before and including 1939, and in 1956 before the Egyptian take-over of the Suez Canal, were both arguably critical factors in the decisions of Hitler and Nasser to make the moves they did. At the strategic nuclear end of the scale, India, although she almost certainly could produce a nuclear weapon, is not at present regarded as having a strategic deterrent because she has no such weapon at operational readiness.[2]

Second, the nature of modern warfare is such that forces are inherently able to strike quickly and with great weight. In this generation projectiles of all kinds — shells, aerodynamic missiles, aircraft-carried bombs, charges and rockets, torpedoes, ballistic missiles — can be armed and despatched in a matter of minutes, an interval which in strategic terms is instantaneous. True, campaigns may take longer to mount, but the history of operations since 1945 suggests that preparations are more easily detectable in hindsight than at the time. Therefore readiness is at a premium. At sea, it need not always take the form of deployed readiness; the mobility of maritime units may in many situations allow them to remain in being, away from immediate likelihood of contact with a potential opponent, provided that their capacity for effective action is known.

Effectiveness

Effectiveness is the product of sound planning, material efficiency and adequate training and organisation. Since planning, particularly strategic planning, is the end-theme of this book it must await a few more chapters before being addressed in detail, but the other factors have a place here.

Material Efficiency

As a critical component of naval effectiveness, material efficiency probably reached its zenith in the public mind at the turn of the nineteenth century. Battleship design was a matter of intense public debate, not only in Britain but round the world; armour, shell penetration, fighting ranges, gunnery control, were all discussed with fervour in a great range of milieux. The Battle of Tsushima in 1904, where Japanese technical mastery was held to have been the deciding issue in Togo's victory over Rodzhestvensky, increased the materialists' case.

A similar situation obtains today, though the debate no longer rages through fashionable drawing rooms. The exceptional number of technical means available to solve any tactical problem does undoubtedly mean that choosing the better one may make all the difference in the event; but whether the better one is that which is cheaper, or more reliable, or of longer range, or lighter, or more agile, or cleverer, is a matter for endless debate, taking in all too many assumptions about the nature of the opposition and relying all too much on technical predictions of performance which may or may not be fulfilled.

One or two generalisations are not out of place, however. Materiel must be within the capacity of the owner state as regards not only initial cost but ability to maintain. Thus, if complex equipments are held to be necessary, there is a need also for a reliable maintenance and repair service of matching sophistication. Recalling the medium power's aspirations to autonomy, it is unlikely that a satisfactory service of this kind can be placed outside the medium power itself. This may mean that medium powers are reluctant to procure from foreign sources equipments that depend on subsequent foreign maintenance support. It means, moreover, that they are certain to require at least one indigenous maritime base at which the critical maintenance operations can be carried out.

The same considerations apply to stocks: not only of spare parts, which vitally affect the efficiency of maintenance, but of stores, fuel and ammunition. Readiness against a conflict that may take only a short time a-brewing implies also the ability to sustain that conflict until necessary resupply can be arranged. A characteristic of conflict over the past 15 years has been the unexpectedly high usage of all kinds of store, and for medium powers who look for maximum operational freedom of action this is a considerable logistic headache.[3] The maintenance in the country of sufficient stocks is expensive at the best of times and when a variety of systems, of diverse age and provenance, is held it can be crippling.

Training

However good the material state of a fighting force may be, it will be of little value if those manning it are poorly trained in its use. Even the advent of fire-and-forget weapons, which arrive on board in a capsule, need only the minimum of user checks and target indication, and are autonomous throughout their trajectory, has not altered the need to bring them into action and use them to the best tactical advantage.[4] All systems, in fact, demand skilled and dedicated operation. Platforms must be able to perform at their optimum; this goes for aircraft, ships and submarines, and requires from those who tend them a 'feel' for machinery and equipment that is little less than it was in the days of the steam reciprocating engine, and is at its best a combination of intelligence, application and experience. The same goes for equipments, both sensors and weapons. Knowing how to get the best out of radars, sonars, intercept and communications equipments; what their limitations are; when they are underperforming: all these can come only from long and rigorous training both ashore and at sea or in the air.

The ability to keep the sea stems as much from good logistic organisation on board as ashore; cooks, storemen, medical staff, canteen staff are key figures. Amphibious forces are of diminished utility if the soldiers have been seasick an hour before landing: training has to take account of this and forces acclimatised as far as possible.

Finally, and most important of all, the necessary leadership and co-ordination can only be provided by officers and senior ratings and NCOs who are intelligent, highly motivated, seasoned and mindful of the needs of their men. To them is given the task not only of operating the ship or aircraft and fighting it if need be, but of drawing together the organisation into a team and thereby turning individual effort towards a single objective.

Training of this kind is not an implicit characteristic of maritime forces. It is quite possible to get ships to sea, to steam after a fashion, and to fire guns in a desultory sort of way, without much fighting potential as an end result. Even aircraft can be flown similarly, with enough skill to get them up and down safely and enough ground control to ensure that they usually land at their base, but scarcely any of the tactical skills that would avail in conflict. What is more, such forces will always have *some* utility; they may appear in foreign intelligence assessments as 'of low efficiency' or 'at a poor standard of training' but the order of battle will still be there and cannot be ignored.[5] But the medium power, if it ever believes its maritime forces to be in such a state, will be uneasily aware that they could all too readily be brushed aside: not the ideal conditions for deterrence.

Organisation

Really good individuals, working towards a common end, well-trained and with decent materiel, can probably make any organisation work. But even the Great Duke said 'I am but a man'; and most men and women do best in an organisational framework that is straightforward, unambiguous, and endowed with reasonable communication facilities.

It is much easier said than done. Maritime forces require, for their proper operation, to be responsive to political direction, controlled to an appropriate degree by the higher command, co-ordinated to the best advantage for the operation in hand, and supported by a variety of things from public relations to potatoes. This means a complex of civilian and military agencies, often spanning two or more military services (typically a Navy and an Air Force, sometimes a Coastguard, a Marine Corps and an Army as well) and several Ministries. The organisation of the Argentine effort in the Falklands campaign has been criticised as one of the principal reasons for failure; similarly, the British was apparent cause for self-congratulation.[6]

It seems certain that organisation is a highly important factor in military success, and therefore in military potential. However, it is not too easy for a prospective opponent to assess its efficiency. Sometimes, as in the Israeli descent upon Entebbe or some of its counter-terrorist actions, it is shown to be formidable and no doubt this adds weight to deterrence; sometimes, as perhaps before the Turkish occupation of Northern Cyprus in 1974, opposing forces can be assessed as insufficiently organised for reaction. But generally, the internal organisation of a medium power for maritime operations is Byzantine enough (even to its own practitioners) to be something of a mystery to foreign intelligence departments, and therefore the least clear of its characteristics in deterrent terms.

Intelligence Gathering and Surveillance

Intelligence can act in the most direct way possible on deterrence under normal conditions. From all accounts, timely intelligence in 1977 about Argentine intentions towards the Falklands allowed the British Government to make a deterrent deployment of two frigates and a nuclear-powered submarine whose presence could have been officially revealed at an appropriate moment. The same use of intelligence was either not available, or was not made, in early 1982.

Operational intelligence of this sort is expensive. The means of procuring it are numerous: diplomatic sources; agents in place; surveillance by units under the sea, on the sea, in the air and in space; communications intercept, decryption and analysis. None of these is cheap, and if the information is to be for immediate or very short-term analysis and use, the means become correspondingly dearer. A medium power will need to assess its priorities for this kind of intelligence carefully and link it particularly closely to its own vital interests.

The great bulk of intelligence gathering, however, is not so much to provide indicators of immediate coming danger as to build up a picture of potential opponents. In the maritime field this will of course include their maritime forces or all those forces that could have a bearing on maritime matters: their composition, material state, organisation, state of training and operational methods. Such knowledge, if reasonably complete, can be a force multiplier of great power for its possessor. Lack of it can lead to quite unnecessary losses in the event of conflict.

The expense of gathering this longer-term intelligence is not so extreme as that required for short-term indicators. It can depend far more on exchanges with intelligence services of friendly powers who may be better placed for economical gathering of certain elements. Its more salient aspects will be available in the open press and from the published work of numerous analysis agencies. Nevertheless it will need a structure of procurement and analysis that will never be cheap and will become sharply more expensive if much gathering and processing of raw information is involved. The trouble is that it is just this raw information, especially if it is from a well-placed source which can provide data that an opponent wishes to keep secret, that is most tradeworthy. Once more, the medium power will need carefully to judge its priorities and its partners.

Surveillance

This can be viewed as a subset of intelligence gathering. In the maritime environment, it means the systematic observation of activities with the object of providing indicators of impending conflict or crisis, or of increasing the stock of intelligence. Some surveillance operations may answer both objectives.

A wide range of surveillance methods is available even to the medium power, which for reasons of expense will probably be unable independently to make use of outer space with its rich potential in the maritime field. It must, therefore, carefully judge what events it needs to survey, how often and in what depth; and how much reserve capacity is needed for special circumstances.

The events to be surveyed are, primarily, those which have the potential to damage state interests and those which will critically improve its intelligence stock. The area of interest is therefore bound to include all zones under jurisdiction, with particular emphasis on those where economic activity is taking place. Threats to such activity will mostly be spasmodic: the poaching fishing vessel, the collision, the derelict, the saboteur. Surveillance can have a deterrent effect on those that are deliberate, but not on those that are fortuitous; for the latter, it will simply be of utility in reporting what has occurred. The frequency of surveillance will be subject to diminishing returns; from a deterrent point of view, 10 per cent cover of an area is likely to deter all but the boldest, and if its system and programme has a high apparent randomness, it will be more effective. Moreover, fortuitous events are likely to be quickly reported by the normal emergency radio procedures.

Generalised patrolling or survey to protect the marine environment — what might cynically be called 'looking for oil slicks' — is most unlikely to have any worthwhile product. The environment is better protected by careful monitoring and sampling over a long term by scientific means and subsequent analysis, and this scarcely comes within the category of surveillance. Naturally patrols with other objectives must be alert to immediate environmental threats and report them as a matter of course.

Some medium powers may apprehend a threat to their security from incursions by foreign warships or auxiliaries into their jurisdiction. They will, in any case, wish to exercise some surveillance over such units simply to increase their intelligence stock. States such as Denmark, Turkey, Spain and Indonesia are bound to make a considerable surveillance effort over naval activities in the straits which they border, as indeed Britain and France do over the Channel. The lack of any requirement in international law for notification of passage does not preclude much less forbid the surveillance of warships, auxiliaries or even merchant vessels of foreign powers.

This surveillance can extend well beyond the jurisdiction of the surveying state. The activities of foreign maritime forces, in all areas but their own territorial seas, are fair game so long as safety is preserved. This is not always easy, since the manoeuvres of other people's units are not necessarily predictable, and a series of incidents in the 1960s between the superpowers' navies and surveillance forces resulted in an agreement between them to observe certain rules.[7] Medium powers, when they wish to conduct such activities, need to be correspondingly careful.

Covert surveillance is clearly the kind which is most likely to achieve intelligence dividends. It is also that which could lead to most embarrassment if discovered. However, observing the general known level of surveillance and intelligence gathering world-wide, such embarrassment is unlikely either to be crippling to relations or to lead to conflict unless gross misjudgements have been made.

In summary, therefore, surveillance is likely to be most effective when it is systematic; when its system is not well known to the victim; when it is directed rather than aimless; and when it chooses appropriate means. Within these guidelines the medium power can continue to seek economy in a field that can be very expensive.

Counter-intelligence

It is not easy to safeguard maritime materiel or activities from foreign intelligence, particularly under normal conditions when observation often cannot be opposed. The means of gathering intelligence are so diverse, and their possible scope so widespread, that deployed surface and air units are bound to come under the scrutiny of anyone who makes a serious effort to scrutinise them. Even units in harbour or on airfields are liable to surveillance from sophisticated technical means, though it is their presence rather than their activities that may be most readily identified.

Clearly this exposure is a matter of degree. First, subsurface forces are much less easy to localise and track than are surface or air units. The resources required are much more expensive. Second, exposure in the short term will not always yield useful dividends to a potential opponent whose resources are limited and who therefore cannot afford frequent surveillance or widespread human intelligence effort. It seems likely that the surprise achieved by Turkish amphibious forces in their invasion of Cyprus in 1974 owed much to Greek inability to penetrate their preparations, as well as Greek unreadiness to react quickly enough when those preparations became at length apparent.[8] It is almost certain that the low priority given to British intelligence against Argentina allowed Argentine preparations in March 1982, and probably earlier, to go undetected.[9] Third, some key elements of fighting ability are easier to conceal than others. For example, codes, cyphers and radio frequencies for use in hostilities need not be the same as those in normal conditions, and when they do come into use can give valuable security; however, unfamiliarity may throw the operator as well as the observer and, moreover, a sudden changeover can alert the opponent to the fact that conflict is about to begin. And some weapons — though in these days of closely observed tests, not many — can hold nasty surprises for the opponent when put into operation.

In the upshot, the opportunities for concealment of capability are, for the medium power in the maritime field, very limited, and the more active it is at sea the more limited they become. Concealment of intention in less difficult, but, given the close links that most medium powers must perforce forge with other states, and the open nature of most medium-power societies, it still needs the utmost care. In consequence, a medium power in particular must be careful to sort out what it needs secrecy for, and in what fields that secrecy is essential. However embarrassing it may be in the short term, to operators and functionaries as well as to governments, publicity generally turns out to the advantage of the publicised, and in normal conditions the demonstration of both ability and intention in the maritime field is more beneficial than its concealment.

Presence

Nowhere is this ascendancy of openness over concealment more apparent than in the so-called presence role. It is a curious fact that the term presence is much more used by naval officers than by academics, who prefer more specific, activity-based terms like 'naval diplomacy' and 'constabulary duties'.[10] This is not necessarily due to naval vagueness and academic precision. Academics are used to analysing, in depth but also in hindsight, the consequences as well as the objectives of specific activities. Naval officers are used, at first hand, to the experience of simply Being There.

For, much of the time, that is what presence consists of, and the benefits it confers are often both difficult to express and impossible to quantify. At the very least, it indicates some kind of stake in the area of presence, even if the stake is only passage for the purpose of getting to somewhere more interesting. Moreover, it always carries the potential for action within the scope and reach of the unit concerned; the work of HMS *Fife* after a hurricane in Dominica in 1979 is a typical example of presence potential being turned into action.[11] At a somewhat more directed level, presence is a clear expression of interest. French ships based on Djibouti indicate some potential to support that country and to become involved in the power balance of the Red Sea approaches.

There is a distinction, though it can be overdone, between permanent and intermittent maritime presence. In general, the French pattern in recent years has been to maintain rather low-capability forces permanently in such areas as Djibouti and the southern Indian Ocean, while the British have deployed balanced forces of several powerful warships about once a year on peripatetic tours of the Indian Ocean and Far East.[12] The French system has the advantage of permanence, of clear readiness; but it may be the permanence of weakness, an invitation to pre-emption. The British system is more overtly a flag-showing parade, demonstrating ready power, and it has the advantage of being capable while in an area of significant impact in a variety of ways from children's parties through flood relief to deterrent effects; but when it is not there it isn't, and out of sight may be out of mind.

One of the functions of presence, particularly in distant waters, is to allow maritime forces to become familiar with new seas and new climates. It also permits, if the forces are of sufficient operational scope (here the British system has a distinct advantage over the French), operational exercises over a protracted period in a relatively uncluttered environment. All these advantages were exploited anew by the Russian Navy, after a long period of confinement to local waters, when it took to the oceans in the early 1960s. It has kept substantial presence forces at sea ever since, though one is bound to say that it does not exercise as frequently or as intensively as it might, and Being There is what it does most of the time.[13] Even its port visits are, by the standards of other deploying nations, not numerous.[14]

Port Visits

Diplomatic activity as typified by port visits is a subset of presence. No writer on seapower of modern times has neglected this aspect and some (including Gorshkov) may have tended to overemphasise it.[15] Certainly, although port visits and maritime embassies are as old as sea use itself, the phenomenon has become widespread in the twentieth century, the more so as the travelling range of maritime units has increased. The ubiquity of liquid fuel stocks, in particular, has made the necessary mobility available to maritime forces that would not previously have possessed it. Thus any medium power with ocean-going ships or submarines can consider visits to foreign ports as part of its maritime effort under normal conditions.

The objectives can be as diverse as any that are offered by the full range of international intercourse: to foster goodwill, to inform, to gain information, to demonstrate a way of life or ideology, to impress, to deter by demonstrating power, to support or facilitate negotiation, to support the activities of economic power.[16]

All these visits are state objectives and can be aimed at in a port visit, much more directly than in most forms of international exchange, because the units involved are so discrete and so patently under state command. They are parcels of national sovereignty; however trite it may be to say so, they are a kind of floating embassy. While the ships are there, a high proportion of at least the people in the port, and often much further afield, is significantly aware of the visiting nation.

The more familiar the host country is to the visiting nation, the more special and highly-geared the visit will have to be to make a significant impact; nevertheless, the continuity imparted by regular visits is an economical way of, for instance, keeping an alliance warm. Visits by unfamiliar maritime forces, particularly if the units involved are large or numerous, tend to generate more interest, though the difference may be more apparent in the capital than in the port visited itself.

For a great deal of the impact of a port visit is diffuse and unquantifiable, simply because it depends on the activities of many individuals, the crews of the visiting units and the citizens whom they meet. Traditionally, among maritime forces of the Western hemisphere, these activities have been relatively free of the trammels of military discipline; a *Punch* joke of uncertain date, showing a Commanding Officer addressing his Ship's Company with the words 'Since this is a goodwill visit, there's no question of any shore leave for you men', is fortunately far-fetched enough to be funny. And while some Eastern navies, particularly the Soviet, have been criticised for allowing sailors ashore only in supervised parties, it is probably due as much to Russian *mores* as to Soviet fear of defections or misbehaviour. Nevertheless, the free and easy sailor is likely to be the better ambassador in most cases.

It goes without saying that the visibility (and indeed visitability, for 'ship open to visitors' is a most significant part of any port call of any length) of the units involved is highly important. The beautiful Italian three-decked sail training ship *Amerigo Vespucci*, one of the most eye-catching craft afloat, has much to say in any tall ships' assembly about Italian seafaring and style. At the other end of the scale, a submarine is undeniably a low-profile craft, and a nuclear-powered submarine may in addition — however unjustly — carry protest on its humped back. Large, land based maritime aircraft are perforce landed at host-country bases which are usually far from cities, and the 'port-visit' capacity is therefore almost nil. In consequence, the brunt of port-visit responsibility falls on surface vessels.

Constabulary Duties

The rights and responsibilities of a state in the waters off its coast can usefully be divided into sovereignty, good order and resource enjoyment.[17] Sovereignty, which extends only to the territorial sea, is a highly emotive concept though not, at sea, an entirely precise one since it is qualified by the rights of other users. Although safeguarding it is a function of maritime forces, it is unlikely to be a major preoccupation of a medium power under normal conditions. The preservation of good order in the territorial sea and, to a limited extent, in zones further offshore is quite as much a responsibility as a right. It entails creating the conditions in which the peaceful use of the sea can equitably and safely be carried on. Finally, resource enjoyment demands a variety of regulating institutions and skills to allow optimum exploitation by those entitled, the exclusion of those not entitled, the preservation of the marine environment and proper exercise of rights by other sea users.

The Framework of Municipal Law

Any state desiring an orderly basis for its maritime constabulary has to evolve a framework of municipal law within which it can operate. The scope of this law must be limited to that allowed by the international law of the sea, whose prime function — purists might say, only function — is to allot and define jurisdiction as between states. But in the present state of international law, even given the detail of the 1982 Convention, the room for interpretation is wide. Some states will agonise over this in order to frame their laws correctly, most will welcome it as a means of framing municipal law to their maximum advantage.

The framework of state law can cover all three of the basic rights and responsibilities. For example, the Soviet Union Regulations of 1960, in a section headed 'Regime of the State Frontier', asserted that the passage of foreign warships through its territorial waters was subject to prior authorisation.[18] This was clearly municipal law framed to safeguard sovereignty; that it was contentious then, in face of the 1958 Convention which made no provision for coastal-state authorisation of the passage of warships, and is even more contentious now in the face of the 1982 Convention with its continued silence on the matter, is something which no doubt the Soviet authorities took and take into account in their deliberations.

So far as resource enjoyment is concerned, most states have now formulated basic laws declaring exclusive economic zones in accordance with the 1982 Convention and many have in addition detailed laws concerning various forms of exploitation and exploration covering living and non-living resources. Some medium powers, the younger ones, will have had the advantage of building this legislation from the keel up, so to speak. For the majority, it will be a matter of reconciling and amending existing legislation with the emerging needs. Western European nations in particular have whole rafts of law that need rebuilding or modifying as community law evolves, particularly with regard to fishing.

Finally, legislation concerning good order may be closely linked with the laws on resource enjoyment. For example, the basic continental shelf exploitation rights in the UK were enshrined in an Act of 1964, and this enabled the establishment by Orders in Council, for good-order purposes, of prohibited areas round oil and gas installations.[19] However, good-order legislation will not be confined to safeguarding resource enjoyment and its appropriate machinery. It will also be concerned with the preservation of the marine environment, and therefore with the accidental or deliberate discharge or dumping of pollutants; and it will be concerned with the safe and efficient conduct of maritime traffic, as for example in the operation of traffic separation schemes in busy places and the orderly conduct of port approaches. Most states, old or new, will expect to build up a body of municipal law on these matters. The sensitivity of public opinion to disorder or danger round the coast of any sort is acute, and can rise to near-hysterical levels in cases of massive oil pollution.[20] Medium maritime powers, almost by definition, cannot afford to ignore the need for such laws; and their enforcement will be the duty of the constabulary forces of the state.

Information

The first and most pressing requirement for the proper conduct of maritime affairs by a coastal state in its offshore waters is information. The state, through its appropriate agencies, must know the patterns of sea use in the waters under its jurisdiction so that it can make proper arrangements, that are neither unnecessarily restrictive nor unduly lax; it must also have warning whenever possible of the development of dangerous or unlawful situations; if such warning has not been forthcoming it must at least have speedy information when such situations actually occur so that it can react appropriately. Equally, other sea users must know at least the coastal-state regulations that immediately concern them, and must be capable of being informed further in real time as they continue their use of the offshore waters whether it be for passage, entry into port, or licensed resource use.

An information network covering all these needs is a formidable undertaking for a state with a long coastline. It demands both long-term and short-term intelligence gathering and collation about a variety of subjects: merchant shipping traffic, fishing vessels, oil and gas drilling and production platforms, foreign warships and auxiliaries including those beneath the surface, and not least the state's own constabulary forces. It demands also efficient regular communication with a large proportion of these entities, and ability to communicate in emergency with all of them.

There is only one consolation for the coastal state. Most of the users will be, if not exactly falling over themselves to help, at least not actively uncooperative. Most will not deliberately flout state law, though some foreign fishermen are always an exception. Thus an intelligence operation which would, against a hostile or potentially hostile power, be truly daunting, comes at least within the bounds of manageability. It will be no good expecting perfection, and only landsmen of some ignorance, which category regrettably often seems to include Western media reporters, will demand it. But a medium power should expect to command resources which will acquire, collate and discriminate enough relevant information to preserve good order in sea areas under its jurisdiction.

Instructions and Orders

If the extent of information that needs to be given and received by a coastal state is relatively uncontentious, the same does not go for the extent to which it ought to give instructions and orders to sea users within its jurisdiction. This has been a matter for warm debate for over two decades. Extreme positions include at one end a virtual free-for-all and at the other a full, internationally instituted sea traffic control system as rigorous as Air Traffic Control under ICAO rules.[21] Neither extreme is likely to prevail. This is fortunate since, on the one hand, a free-for-all has consistently been shown to be more dangerous than a moderately regulated pattern; and on the other, over-tight control particularly from the shore of unwieldy craft in uncertain sea and wind conditions is, as any mariner or port pilot will be quick to point out, a recipe for man-made disasters.

A medium power, with a stake in international maritime trade and resource enjoyment, will generally want to see all connected operations off its shores conducted expeditiously as well as safely. If it is wise, it will also want to see them conducted without discrimination, for its own foreign-going maritime interests will be vulnerable if it gets a reputation for partiality. In consequence, the times when orders and instructions need to be given to passing traffic, and to authorised resource-enjoyment users, are relatively few. They are, by and large, confined to incidents of potential or actual transgression of state laws, and of accident or breakdown.

But when there is a need to pass orders to such users, they must be given unequivocally by an authorised agent of the state. If full two-way communication is already established between, say, a shore station and a merchantman exercising innocent passage through the territorial sea, the problem is simply solved. Frequently, however, that desirable state of affairs does not exist. Transgressing merchant ships are, typically, vessels substandard both in operation and in equipment; the blunderer in the wrong traffic lane may well be the same ship that is lax in setting radio watch and whose VHF set turns out to be defective. Consequently it may be necessary physically to go out and tell a transgressor the error of his ways. This demands the right craft in the right place: provision will be neither cheap nor easy.

Transgressions of state law in the field of resource enjoyment are confined mostly to fisheries, though they frequently extend to fisheries such as crustacea which are generally regarded as a sedentary, that is a continental shelf, resource. With a world catch of 70 million tonnes, an enormous complex of fish stocks, still-emerging international law, and a history of fishing practice going back in many cases over a thousand years, it is no wonder that fisheries law in most countries or groups of countries is in a considerable muddle. It is difficult to enforce partly because it is difficult to understand. Nowhere is it more complicated, either in its provisions or its enforcement machinery, than in the northeast Atlantic, where several medium maritime powers congregate in the European fishpond; but many other areas exist round the world that are either disputed or under uneasy and contentious regulation.

Fisheries regulation in general demands not only a great deal of information, from deep statistical research to on-the-spot surveillance, but agents in the main concentrations of fishing vessels to ensure that the law is obeyed. Remote control is not effective; fishermen are too accustomed to bending rules to be amenable to instructions from afar.

So far as exploration or exploitation of other resources is concerned, actual transgressions by mineral concerns, in the sense of illegal drilling or extraction, are relatively rare. They are large and easily detectable operations and, once detected, escalate rapidly into international incidents.[22] Small powers with few other offshore interests may find it necessary to make special provision to deter such activities. Medium powers are likely to find, from among their resources provided in support of the offshore task in general, enough capacity to deter, and to deal with such cases as occur.

Naturally, detailed orders and instructions are delivered by the agents of the coastal state to a much greater extent close inshore and particularly in the approaches to the ports. Here one of the most important agents can be the pilot. He is a link with the shore, an adviser to the command and an interpreter of the rules. Command quite rightly rests with the master of the ship: if it did not, her officers and crew would be in an impossible position. Other port authorities, customs officials and health officers are further agents who play an important part in the efficiency, or otherwise, of the machinery of access to the shore.

Inspection

Coastal states may find it necessary to inspect foreign vessels in four sets of circumstances: as a matter of routine, to ensure that laid-down standards are being complied with; where there is evidence that such standards are not being complied with; where it appears that the vessel's condition or conduct threaten the good order and security of the coastal state; and where significant pollution of the marine environment is being or has been caused by the vessel concerned.

Broadly speaking, so far as merchant vessels are concerned the first two kinds of action take place in internal waters where the coastal state has full jurisdiction. This being so, there is no need for the coastal state to confine itself to internationally agreed standards for equipment, certification and operation. However, most medium powers, having at the back of their minds an inevitable *tu quoque* to their own merchant marine if they take too draconian a line, will set their standards of in-port inspection in accordance with internationally agreed rules, in the framing of which the International Maritime Organisation (IMO) has taken a leading part. In the majority of vessels, random or relatively cursory inspections, backed up by activities of registration societies, suffice; sub-standard ships, fairly detectable to the trained eye, require more rigorous inspection. This may be an expensive commitment for a medium power with a long coastline and many small ports.

Inspections in the case of violations of good order are most likely to occur in the territorial sea or when under way in internal waters. They may spring from a variety of causes: an underworld tip-off about narcotics smuggling, a pattern of illegal immigration, a 'rogue' tanker in the wrong traffic lane. Some will encounter co-operation on the part of the craft to be inspected, many will not. They therefore require a quite different approach from the in-port inspections; certainly different means of boarding and probably, at least in part, different personnel, some of whom may need to be armed.

The fourth category of inspection may extend far out to sea, since the Law of the Sea Convention allows such inspections, in the circumstances described, in the Exclusive Economic Zone.[23] Such inspections depend, of course, on prima facie evidence that serious damage has been caused by the vessel concerned, and this itself may be hard to come by. Boarding for the purpose of inspection may be far more so, requiring extensive resources.

It is no doubt partly because of the likely difficulty of such actions that the notion of Port State Jurisdiction has been introduced.[24] Under this concept a ship suspected of having caused damage to the marine environment may be investigated by the port state in its next port of call; in a sense the port state is acting as an international agent on behalf of the state whose marine environment has been violated.

Fishery protection is a special case of all the categories of inspection already mentioned. It differs somewhat in that in all areas of coastal-state fishery jurisdiction, inspections may take place for the purpose of checking laid-down standards; these are particularly important in matters like the mesh of nets, type of gear and nature of catch. Lucky is the medium power that has a straightforward set of rules to administer; the complexity of rules, restriction on policing and consequent lack of control over the fisheries of the European Community is a matter for deep concern.[25]

Inspection, then, is a multi-headed business, demanding of a medium power resources not only of considerable size but also some variety. The personnel need many sets of skills and knowledge; a fisheries inspector cannot well be the same person as a customs officer. (Naval or coastguard officers may sometimes have to act as either, but they have always been infinitely adaptable, or very good purveyors of flannel, according to one's view.) The means, again, need to be various: a gangway will suffice for port inspection, but for boarding at sea boats from ship and shore, helicopters, and sometimes even ships themselves are required. Broadly speaking, the more uncooperative the vessels to be inspected, the faster, more agile and stouter the boarding craft must be.

Detention

In cases where legal process is to be initiated by or in the coastal state against the vessel concerned, the vessel must be detained by the state's officers. In port this is relatively easy; writs still are nailed to the mast, and ships cannot generally slip away without the consent of the port authorities. At sea, if the detention has arisen out of inspection, the process ought not to be too difficult, since by definition a foothold has been established. However, those tempted to use no more than token boarding parties may well recall the case of the *Red Crusader*, where a Scottish fishing captain locked up the Danish boarding party of a lieutenant and one seaman in his cabin and set off for Aberdeen.[26]

When inspection has not occurred, either because it was opposed, impossible or unnecessary in the face of overwhelming prima facie evidence of transgression, detention may be a stern business. 'Angry boarding' of alleged transgressors is not uncommon in coastal waters round the world, and many states give their navies and coastguards considerable latitude in their municipal law.[27] Force must be confined however to what is necessary and proportionate. A classical example is that of the British coastal minesweeper which, frustrated in its attempts to inspect a known Belgian poacher fishing within British national limits, conducted a carefully planned night boarding: it approached with Wagnerian menace, firing blank 40mm Bofors furiously on the disengaged bow and directing a single large King Edward potato through the trawler's bridge window. Surrender was instantaneous.

Disaster Control

A duty is laid on all states to require seafarers flying their flag to go to the assistance of those who are in distress at sea.[28] Oddly, none is laid on the authorities of a coastal state to do likewise. However, most maritime powers do in fact pay attention to the need for life-saving round their coasts and many dedicate resources to it. For example, the first six of the Lynx helicopters ordered by the Royal Netherlands Navy and delivered in 1977 were configured to the Search and Rescue Task.

Efficient search and rescue demands arrangements for information flow that can be rapidly stepped up in emergency; shore, sea-going and flying resources that can react in time along any part of the coastline; and command and control facilities and personnel which can effectively and economically direct the assets available. For a state with a long coastline and limited resources this may be a prohibitively expensive undertaking and some medium powers, even, will have to concentrate their effort in the more likely areas of disaster. In the remoter areas, the general purpose maritime forces of the state may be able, on receipt of distress messages, to help but dedicated resources will not be available.

Salvage is the rescue or recovery of materiel and is a quite different matter. It is one of the most blatantly entrepreneurial activities of the modern world. The Lloyds standard salvage form, with the legend 'No Cure — No Pay' at the top of it, sets the pattern. In capitalist and mixed economies, by far the greater part of salvage potential is privately owned and subject to the operations of the market, while the salvage effort of centrally directed economies is confined to their own coastal areas, or, occasionally, vessels of their own flag further afield.

This commercial basis for operations which often affect both individual lives and the environment can have unfortunate results.

In the case of the *Amoco Cadiz*, the stranding of a large laden tanker with consequent extensive pollution might have been averted had the master not been reluctant to take a tow and thereby to lay his owners open to a massive salvage claim. The disaster, with subsequent very strong public reaction, has led to traffic control measures designed to keep such vessels further off the Brittany coast when on passage; but some authorities believe these measures will increase the risk of collision.[29] Thus the consequences of inefficient salvage may spread far beyond a particular incident. It may be that medium maritime powers, which characteristically are concerned with areas of high concentration of maritime activity, have a particular interest in taming the more jungly parts of salvage law and organisation, and in considering whether the salvage services of the state can and should be improved.

For state resources do take part in both salvage and more generally in disaster control. Often these actions are *ad hoc*, using whatever assets are to hand. In British waters, for example, up to half a dozen non-commercial organisations can be involved in the practical business of controlling a disaster: the Royal National Lifeboat Institute, HM Coastguard, the Royal Navy, the Royal Air Force, Trinity House and the Police. Many more agencies and organisations can be involved ashore. In Japan, on the other hand, the Maritime Safety Agency exercises a co-ordination function and generally provides most of the resources. They seem to be well used; between 1973 and 1980, 70 vessels involved in collision or grounding incidents required assistance in Tokyo Bay alone.[30]

The control of oil spills once they have occurred is a matter of high visibility and immediate public concern and therefore has occupied a disproportionately prominent position in discussion on disaster control at sea. The problems that can arise are very varied and require for their quick solution a rich mix of resources and a flexible organisation. Unfortunately, however good may be the measures taken to avoid the occurrence of disasters in the first place, the medium power must have some such residual capacity for their control if they do occur.

Strategic Deterrent Patrols

The notion of seaborne strategic deterrence is not subscribed to by many medium powers. Moreover, its objective is not specifically maritime. Nevertheless, it must be mentioned here because some medium powers practise it, it is a maritime activity, and it significantly affects the allocation of resources and the deployment of maritime assets.

While deterrence is a process that operates at all levels of conflict, it is seen at its sharpest in the capacity to inflict massive, unacceptable damage on the heartland of an opponent, or as a British document has it 'key aspects of state power'.[31] For the past two decades the most secure method of deploying such deterrent means has been the nuclear-headed ballistic missile at sea in a nuclear-propelled submarine. The submarine's independence of the surface, its relative undetectability when submerged and operating in the optimum manner to avoid detection, its ability to remain on patrol for periods of up to two months and its swift reaction to a signal to fire its missiles, are all great advantages when compared with any other method of basing.[32]

At present, submarine-based ballistic missiles are not accurate enough to neutralise point targets on land such as missile silos. But this is not really a disadvantage for medium powers since for them strategic weapons are indeed weapons of last resort; unquestionably they would not be employed in a first strike against a vastly more powerful enemy, for this would invite obliteration of the homeland. The fact that they would be used only if deterrence had failed does not in any way invalidate the theory or purpose of deterrence.

In order to preserve the continuity and credibility of sea-based deterrence it is necessary to keep on patrol, and ready to fire, enough submarines to inflict unacceptable damage on an enemy. This implies in its turn safe and timely access to and from bases, the ability to slip away from any units that may attempt to detect and track them, secure and constant communication from shore to submarine, effective logistic and training support organisation ashore, facilities for adequate and timely refits, and trained and sufficient crews. The whole must be backed by a national nuclear industry for both warheads and propulsion. The undertaking is a very large and expensive one by any standards. It has been said that the French spend over 20 per cent of their defence budget on nuclear deterrence, although this has some land-based aspects as well as maritime ones. The British spend a lower proportion, even in peak years amounting to well under 10 per cent, but they do this by technical reliance for missiles on the United States, which introduces as Lawrence Freedman says 'a curiosity in such a vital national programme depending for its materiel on the largesse of the United States while depending for its rationale on a distrust of the United States'.[33]

The Care of Alliances

Strategic nuclear deterrence demonstrates in extreme form the dilemma of the medium power: how far, and against what threats, it is necessary to depend on allies. Freedman's word 'distrust' may be a trifle stark; usually medium-power planners have to consider degrees of trust, and degrees of risk; they are players of percentages. Normal conditions give them time to reflect on these factors and to nurture alliances as may be necessary for harsher situations. In normal conditions most operations, deployments, programmes and plans will be national, but planning and exercising with allies is an integral part of strategic activity at this level. Even in the case of loose alliances such as those between the United States and the South American States, there is a good deal of evidence of common procedures and combined exercises at sea such as the UNITAS series.[34] In tighter and more structured alliances like NATO and the Warsaw Pact, such exercises are a commonplace of normal conditions.

Notes

1. H. Moineville, *Naval Warfare Today and Tomorrow* (Blackwell, Oxford, 1983), p. 9.
2. G. S. Bhargava, *India's Security in the 1980s* (International Institute for Strategic Studies, London, 1976), p. 22.
3. Cmnd. 8758 (HMSO, London), p. 25. There were similar experiences in the Yom Kippur War of 1973 and the Indo-Pakistan War of 1971.
4. J. Ethell and A. Price, in *Air War South Atlantic* (Sidgwick and Jackson, London, 1983), p. 75, recount how an Argentine Super Etendard strike with Exocet missiles was aborted on 2 May 1982 because in-flight refuelling did not take place; and on p. 95 a strike where no target was found.
5. Arthur J. Marder, *The Anatomy of British Sea Power* (Frank Cass, London, 1964), pp. 261, 277.
6. Cmnd. 8758, p. 16.
7. USA and USSR, Treaty on the Prevention of Incidents on and over the High Seas, 1972.
8. *Keesing's Contemporary Archives* (Longmans, London), Nos. 26661A and 26669; Thanos Veremis, *Greek Security: Issues and Politics* (International Institute

for Strategic Studies, Adelphi Paper No. 179, 1982), p. 12.

9. Cmnd. 8787, para 318.

10. For the naval officers, Vice Admiral Sir Peter Stanford, 'The Current Position of the Royal Navy', *The Future of British Sea Power*, ed. Till, p. 33; Moineville, *Naval Warfare Today and Tomorrow*, p. 34; Hill, *The Royal Navy Today and Tomorrow*, p. 24; Ferreira, *The Navy of Brazil*, p. 38. For the academics, Luttwak, *The Political Uses of Sea Power*, pp. 30–3; Booth, *Navies and Foreign Policy*, pp. 17–18; Till, *Maritime Strategy and the Nuclear Age*, pp. 209–15.

11. Cmnd. 7826-1, p. 46.

12. *The Military Balance, 1984–85*, p. 39; Leenhardt, 'The Role of the French Navy in the National External Action Policy', p. 40; Cmnd. 9227-1, p. 32.

13. B. M. Ranft and Geoffrey Till, *The Sea in Soviet Strategy* (Macmillan, London, 1983), pp. 197–8.

14. Ibid., p. 195.

15. Luttwak, *The Political Uses of Sea Power*, pp. 30–3; Booth, *Navies and Foreign Policy*, pp. 18–19 and 44–50; L. W. Martin, *The Sea in Modern Strategy* (Chatto and Windus, London, 1967), p. 139; Hill, 'The Role of Navies', p. 104; Till, *Maritime Strategy and the Nuclear Age*, pp. 109–15.

16. This final category refers to ship visits directly in support of such activities as Trade Fairs. The writer has been closely involved in two such visits; they certainly added a further dimension to the fairs' impact.

17. Booth, *Navies and Foreign Policy*, p. 17.

18. Act of the Union of the Soviet Socialist Republics, 22 December 1960, Art. 16, quoted in UNST/LEG/SER.B/15, p. 213.

19. Continental Shelf Act, 1964 (1964 Ch. 29, 15 April 1964) and, for example, Continental Shelf (Protection of Installations) (No. 2), Order (SI No. 323 of 1968).

20. The case of the *Amoco Cadiz*, an admittedly shocking grounding of a laden tanker on the Brittany coast in 1978, led to French legislation of great severity.

21. The controversy can be traced through, *inter alia*, the *Journal of Navigation*; the latest round at the time of writing is in *Journal of Navigation*, Vol. 38 (1985) at pp. 71–84.

22. For example, the Abu Musa incident, 1970, reported in *The Times*, 29 May-6 June 1970 and analysed in Hill, *The Rule of Law at Sea*, p. 85.

23. Law of the Sea Convention, 1982, Art. 220(5).

24. Ibid., Art. 218.

25. Peter Hjul, in Till (ed.), *The Future of British Sea Power*, p. 66.

26. *International Law Reports*, Vol. 35, p. 485.

27. US Code Title 14 para 637(a), for example, gives US Coast Guard vessels statutory permission to fire, after a warning shot, at craft that do not bring to.

28. Law of the Sea Convention, 1982, Art. 98.

29. A. N. Cockcroft, 'Development of Routing in Coastal Waters', *Journal of Navigation*, Vol. 38 (1985), p. 78.

30. Y. Fujii, 'Recent Trends in Traffic Accidents in Japanese Waters', *Journal of Navigation*, Vol. 35 (1982), p. 91.

31. United Kingdom Defence Open Government Document 80/23, p. 6.

32. A description of patrol cycles and the operation of a strategic deterrent patrol appears in Lacoste, *Stratégie Navale*, pp. 42–50.

33. L. Freedman, 'The Future of the British Strategic Nuclear Deterrent', in G. Till (ed.), *The Future of British Sea Power*, p. 120.

34. Robert L. Scheina, 'The Malvinas Campaign', in *US Naval Institute Proceedings*, Vol. 109 (May 1983), p. 116.

7 LOW INTENSITY OPERATIONS

The phrase 'Low intensity operations' first came into prominence as a result of work in the late 1960s by Brigadier (now General Sir) Frank Kitson.[1] As the title of his subsequent book implied, this work concerned mainly land operations in the counter-insurgency or counter-terrorist roles, and peacekeeping in a mainly national rather than United Nations setting.

However, the concept is readily transferable to the maritime scene, with the proviso that the main actors on both sides will generally, though not always, be the organised forces of sovereign states under governmental control. In this aspect at least, the structure and aims of the conflict are likely to be more clear-cut than on land, where many sub-national organisations often at loggerheads with each other may be involved; the factional situations in both Lebanon and Northern Ireland are obvious examples, and could scarcely be reproduced at sea.

Low intensity operations never merit the title of war, are limited in aim, scope and area, and are subject to the international law of self-defence. In practice they may include sporadic acts of violence on both sides.

Limitation of Aim

Properly speaking, there is no such thing as a purely political or a purely military aim to any conflict. All have some political and some military element, but the proportions can vary considerably. Analysis of low intensity operations at sea since 1946 suggests overwhelmingly that the aims of such operations are much more political than military. The Beira Patrol, for example, had the immediate objective of stopping oil supplies to Rhodesia through the port of Beira and the means to be used were military; but its ultimate objective was to help bring down the illegal regime in Rhodesia. It succeeded in the immediate, but not the ultimate objective. The political side of the aim may be, often is, economic in its genesis; Iceland's objective in the cod disputes was to create conditions in which British fishing vessels were excluded from fishing grounds off Iceland so that Icelandic fishermen could benefit from the removal of competition for a limited catch.

More than anything else, however, the aim in low intensity operations at sea is likely to be confined within quite narrow limits. It may even be definable by the higher organs of government. It is usually possible, through care, to avoid its overlapping into other aspects of state power or interest. If indeed it cannot be stated and limited in this way it, and the operations to which it gives rise, will need careful re-examination. British excursions in support of Belize against Guatemalan threats, in the 1970s, were good examples of timely, limited-aim operations that were successful in their deterrent objective.[2] But, as already suggested, the Beira patrol suffered from a certain woolliness and over-extension of aim that made it, in the ultimate, ineffective.

A common and unsurprising fact about the aims of low intensity operations is that one side or the other generally has the objective of preserving the *status quo*. If it is not quick enough off the mark, of course, this turns into the job of restoring the *status quo ante*, which tends to be more difficult and may even involve escalation to another level of conflict. *Status quo* at sea is unusual in that in many cases it has no permanently observable features; sea with a right of passage through it is not distinguishable from other sorts of sea, but it has a status which men have died to demonstrate.[3]

Limitation in Scope

A central characteristic of low intensity operations is that the violence involved, if it is involved at all, should be sporadic and contained.

This springs partly from the limitation of aim. It is a fundamental maxim of strategy that means should be no more than are appropriate and necessary to achieve the aim, and economy of force is one of the principles of war to which Western staff colleges, at any rate, subscribe. But limitation of scope has many other roots.

The first is the law. In low intensity operations on land the state's laws against violence have to be modified or interpreted for those taking part on behalf of the state; if they are operating in another country, *ad hoc* rules based on the international law of self-defence have to be framed.[4] At sea, the waters may or may not be under national jurisdiction; or the jurisdiction may itself be in dispute; in any event the sway of municipal law will not be so complete as on land. Moreover, the units involved are generally larger, more discrete and can be more tightly controlled. In consequence, low intensity operations in the maritime field require much more account to be taken of the international law of armed conflict and the use of force, and in particular the law concerning self-defence.

The right of self-defence is accepted internationally not only for individuals but for states and is enshrined in Article 51 of the United Nations Charter, where it is treated as overriding: 'Nothing in the present Charter shall impair the inherent right of individual or collective self-defence . . .' Some questions of interpretation arise nevertheless.

The two great principles governing self-defence are necessity and proportionality. They were first stated in a case, significantly one that involved violence by water, of 1839. The colony of Canada was under threat from armed bands based in the United States, who raided and terrorised the province of Quebec from bases across the Erie River. One night a party from Canada crossed the river and cut out the American supply vessel, the *Caroline*, with some loss of life. Then they set her on fire, cast off her mooring ropes, and allowed her to drift over Niagara Falls. The American Secretary of State, Webster, protested to Britain through Ambassador Fox, requiring Britain to show a need 'immediate, overwhelming, leaving no choice of means and no moment for deliberation', and that the raiders 'did nothing unreasonable or excessive; since the act, justified by the necessity of self-defence, must be limited by that necessity and kept clearly within it'. In a subsequent exchange of letters it was accepted that these requirements had been met.

The *Caroline* principles require, then, that acts in self-defence must be limited to those necessary to cause the assault or aggression to cease. By extension, it is possible to argue that if acts of assault or aggression are widespread and systematic, then similar acts, not necessarily directly related, are required in self-defence. This is no doubt the attempted justification in self-defence terms, for example, of the Chinese incursions into Vietnam in the early 1980s with the aim of 'teaching Vietnam a lesson'. But in general, at sea, evidence of system needs to be accumulated before any general riposte is appropriate; and by then, operations may have reached the higher level anyway. At low intensity, incidents tend to be encapsulated and their sequence is clearly traceable. Not only necessity but proportionality, therefore, become of great importance. The use of excessive force to counter even an assault is, by the *Caroline* principles, unlawful; if for instance a British frigate, in the Cod dispute of the mid-1970s, had countered an Icelandic gunboat's trawl-cutting assault by sinking it with gunfire, which could easily have been done, the law would have been heavily on Iceland's side.[5] Britain's only possible defence would have been that by a single disproportionate act it had reduced the total level of potential violence. But such arguments generally do not hold water in low intensity operations. It goes without saying that against non-violent violations of state law, such as may occur at sea and which are sometimes the trigger for low intensity conflict, proportionality and necessity are also essential principles. Again the Cod dispute is instructive: Icelandic gunboats went to great lengths not to use guns against trawlers.

There remains the question of anticipatory self-defence. Arguments about this are as old as the notion of self-defence itself and are not helped by the well-known discrepancy between the English and French texts of the United Nations Charter.[6] The *Caroline* case itself was in part a matter of anticipatory self-defence, since no American raid was in progress at the time and the *Caroline* was a supply, not an assault, vessel. Many cogent arguments have been advanced that in modern conditions, with the speed of reaction and short preparation time of weapon systems, anticipatory self-defence is a matter of necessity once hostile intent is established. American practice particularly tends to this view.[7] Nevertheless — and probably this applies specially to medium powers who must maintain an image squarely between the bully and the whipping-boy — anticipatory self-defence, before any shot has been fired in a particular confrontation, is a matter that needs very careful consideration, if possible before the event.

Limitation in Area

The limits of the area of low intensity operations may very well be defined by the aim. If, for example, the dispute concerns exclusion from a fishery the aims of both sides will centre on establishing rights of a certain kind in a certain geographical area, and it is rather unlikely that any incident will take place outside it unless one side or the other deliberately extends the conflict. Similarly, if there is dispute concerning claims to jurisdiction by neighbours over a particular piece of water, operations initially at any rate will be confined to that area.

In other, less territorially-based disputes or operations, such as the demonstrations of resolve conducted since 1980 by United States, United Kingdom and French patrols in the northwest Indian Ocean in connection with the Gulf War, some limitation of area is still apparent but in this case is governed by a variety of military as well as legal and political factors. Desire not unnecessarily to expose maritime forces to sudden attack will tend to put their operating area beyond the range of shore-based aircraft and of missile-boat sorties; militating against this will be the need to react quickly closer inshore if that is where a test of resolve should occur.

It is tempting to any government seeking precision in low intensity operations to declare the limits within which it regards the conflict as taking place. This is held to demonstrate a desire to keep the conflict at a manageable level; to avoid ambiguities and escalatory incidents; and to score propaganda success. Such a course might recommend itself particularly to a medium power in dispute with a small power. But it also has grave disadvantages. It can gratuitously imply that a pattern of conflict has been established and thereby be escalatory in itself; it can give valuable hostages to the opponent in negotiation, either concurrent with or subsequent to the conflict; and most important of all, it exposes the declarer to outflanking if the opponent decides on escalation.

None of this is to say that the limits of the area of conflict should not be carefully defined for one's own forces. This is necessary for their proper deployment and disposition by the fleet and local commanders, the focusing of intelligence effort, and the drafting of Rules of Engagement which may differ markedly between the area of low intensity operations and the area of normal conditions that, by definition, borders it.

Types of Low Intensity Operation

Demonstrations of Right

Rights under international law account for a substantial proportion of disputes leading to low intensity operations.[8] Of these, in turn the majority concern fisheries and characteristically are closely contained by the limits of aim, scope and area that both sides apply, though they tend to be very drawn-out and some, such as those between Spain and Morocco and Japan and the USSR, have gone on for decades.[9] Less frequent, but more sensitive and liable to escalation, are questions over rights of passage. These rights are of course demonstrated by the thousand daily throughout the world, even where coastal or straits states claim rights in excess of those which the passage-makers would concede and vice versa. Acquiescence in these cases ensures that no actual low intensity operation is involved. But when dispute flares up it may do so quite suddenly and acutely. By no means does it always concern warships, although for instance in the Indonesian Straits in the 1950s and 1960s it was the rights of warships to make passage that were in dispute.[10] On the other hand, the Egyptian closure of the Strait of Tiran in 1967 applied to all vessels.[11] Finally, many disputes exist over demarcation of jurisdiction under international law, ranging from the contention over sovereign waters in the Bay of Gibraltar (or, as Spain would have it, Algeciras)[12] to the Russian-Norwegian controversy in the area north of North Cape.[13] Often these remain at the level of negotiation, but they can break out into confrontation or flare into incident, and demonstrative forces may play a part as much in keeping them damped as in stoking the fires if anything goes wrong.[14]

Crucially, demonstrations of right can often be achieved simply by Being There, and always by both Being There and Doing Something. The Something will hardly ever involve the firing of weapons; the only case where this would not apply is the demonstration by war vessels or aircraft of a high-seas right to carry out weapon practices in an area where some other state claimed that this right did not exist. Such practices do no doubt occur, but are rarely contested at present; it is possible that sensitivity over economic zones (where the right appears to exist under the Convention) may cause coastal states to protest more frequently in future. But that, as has been pointed out, is an exception. Generally demonstrations of right are demonstrations of the right of peaceable, overwhelmingly civilian, units to carry out peaceable activities. The principal actor, fishing vessel or merchant ship, goes on fishing or making passage until an opponent attempts to stop it.

In an initial encounter, such attempts are unlikely to involve the immediate use of weapons. They will go through the gamut of the constabulary techniques of regulation: radio warning messages, instructions by radio or visual signal or loudhailer, manoeuvres by aircraft or ships, attempted boarding. But, particularly in the case of states sensitive over their sovereign rights, the sequence may be a rapid one. (The sea has however this advantage over the air, that situations take hours rather than seconds to develop and that catastrophic incidents like that of the Korean airliner shot down over Soviet airspace in 1983 are less inherently likely even when the protagonists are trigger-happy.)

The first intimation that rights will be contested comes often from an encounter of this kind, when no support from the forces of the molested state is available. On the other hand there may have been warning from diplomatic or intelligence sources that rights will be contested, in which case it is possible to make predispositions. The Strait of Tiran affords examples of both situations: in 1962 the British auxiliary *Empire Roach* was detained by Egyptian forces at Sharm el Shaikh, which commands the Strait, when no British warships were about; in 1967 the Egyptian ejection of United Nations forces gave a clear signal that passage of Western vessels to Eilat was bound to be opposed, and elaborate plans — lamely pursued and subsequently swept into the furnace of the Six Day War — were made to support a demonstrative passage through the Strait.[15]

However the intimation that rights will be opposed is received, the upshot, if it is intended to uphold them in a practical way, is the same: support from the forces of the state seeking to demonstrate the right. It is very pertinent to medium-power strategies that there are hardly any examples in low intensity operations of one state's forces protecting the rights of other states' vessels.[16]

The forces involved need to be very carefully judged as to scale and capability. There are proponents of the 'superior-fleet' philosophy:[17] the deployment of as powerful a force as possible in order to overawe an opponent and deter any further contesting of the right. But this has two severe disadvantages for a medium power. First, it is expensive to mount and even more expensive to maintain, and by their nature contested rights are not short-term problems. Second, it carries particularly if applied to small-power opponents a clear public image of bullying, and while some medium powers may feel themselves impervious to such charges, many will not. There are, therefore, cases where demonstrations will be best supported by relatively massive shows of force, but the much more appropriate response in most cases will be the small unit, perhaps no more than a single vessel, in the area of dispute.

The characteristics of forces for this forward role are not unlike those required for regulation itself. The situation is one of self-defence (which of course includes the defence of civilian craft under one's flag) and the rules of necessity and proportionality apply. Moreover, it is in the interest of all that situations should not be exacerbated by unnecessary escalation, and that is more likely to be risked by the use of inappropriately heavy weapons than any other cause. It will be no bad thing, indeed, if a number of options that do not involve weapons at all are available to the forces involved. The games of boomps-a-daisy indulged in by British frigates and Icelandic gunboats in the 1976 Cod dispute were undignified and sometimes unpleasant, but they were better in demonstrative terms than shooting, killing and maiming.

The general concept of such operations, then, calls up a variety of requirements in the units that carry them out. They must, first, be very responsive to changes both in the situation and in the political directives from their governments. This means that their systems for both data acquisition and communication must be effective and capable of continuous operation. It is also desirable that the units should be visible: this may of course increase their vulnerability to surprise attack but that is outweighed, in these operations of primarily political intent, by the need to indicate (not least to the prime actor in a demonstration of right, the merchant or fishing vessel) the involvement of state power in the affair. They must possess a variety of weapon systems at least some of which must be capable of fine discrimination in their application. It is perhaps a bit fanciful to suggest that the bottom end of the scale is the Officer of the Guard with his ceremonial sword, but such weapons have been seen in the Bay of Algeciras/Gibraltar, and on one occasion a large shaggy dog too.[18] At the other extreme, at least some ship-disabling weapons are highly desirable; they may not be used, it is to be hoped they will not be used, but there must be some sanction. Again, the craft in these exposed forward positions ought ideally to be able to look after themselves in case of a sudden escalation; this may entail sophisticated and extensive self-defence capabilities. Finally, the characteristics of forces supporting demonstrations of right include sufficient endurance, sea- or air-worthiness, handling qualities and manning; what is sufficient for each operation will depend on the situation at that time and place.

Demonstrations of Resolve

If demonstrations of right are very closely linked to the process of claim and counterclaim that is an integral part of the operation of international law, demonstrations of resolve are similarly linked to the countervailing tensions of international power. It goes without saying that the two are often inextricably mixed; the Armilla Patrol off the Strait of Hormuz from 1980 to 1985 is, for example, a demonstration of resolve that could if need arose provide ready forces to support a demonstration of right.

Clearly also they share many common characteristics. The principles of self-defence apply no less severely. The image that forces present to the international public must be no less carefully judged. Considerations about rules of engagement, communication and data acquisition, staying-power and ability to cope with escalation, are of similar weight.

But there are, potentially, quite important differences. Many of the situations calling for a demonstration of resolve will be less geographically focused than those involving demonstrations of right, and this gives an opportunity to station forces further from the most likely points of confrontation or escalation. Neither may they be so tied to any specific activity by civilian craft, and with no vulnerable units of this kind to protect maritime forces can be in a more operational formation. The level of forces too can be more flexibly judged. The demonstration of resolve which, according to Dr David Owen, deterred Argentine attack on the Falklands in 1977 was carried out by a small force of frigates and a nuclear-powered submarine. Such a force might not have appeared appropriate had a demonstration of right been involved. Nevertheless the deployment of too much power is probably to be avoided; the United States' excursion to the Indian Ocean at the time of the Indo-Pakistan War of 1971 was universally condemned in India and the suggestion that the United States was endeavouring to bully by the presentation of overbearing power, at a time so sensitive to Indian pride, was probably an important factor in its failure to achieve whatever purpose it was sent for.[19]

From the foregoing it might be thought that demonstrations of resolve are less arduous, dangerous and acute than demonstrations of right. There is a good deal of evidence for this as a general rule. For example, the ships on the Indian Ocean (Armilla) Patrol were reported in 1984 as hoping 'to be alongside at Christmas',[20] and their predecessors paid a port visit to Muscat earlier in the year.[21]

The guardship at Gibraltar in the 1970s spent much of its time alongside in that pleasant, if gently beleaguered, colony. On the other hand, demonstrations of resolve can involve uncomfortable situations at close quarters for long periods of time; in 1951 the author spent a couple of weeks in a ship on the Iraqi bank of the Shatt-al-Arab opposite the Iranian port of Abadan during the crisis there. Distances were so close that even with the weaponry of the time any use of arms on either side would have resulted in considerable damage and casualties. The *Amethyst* incidents in China in that and the previous year were another example of such a close-quarter situation that had more to do with resolve than anything else. Moreover, demonstrations of resolve are sometimes long-drawn-out and exceptionally arduous; French naval deployments in support of nuclear tests in the Pacific can go on for months at a time and Soviet 'marking' of US naval units in the Mediterranean must be an equally tedious task.

Amphibious Landings by Invitation

While the landing of troops to support a government that regards itself as under threat, and has asked for help, may be viewed as a special sort of demonstration of resolve, it has characteristics of its own that merit separate treatment here. Operations of this kind were thought, certainly in Britain, to have been outlived after a spate of them in the early 1960s had run its course. The check to Iraqi designs against Kuwait in 1962, and the restoration of the Tanganyikan government in 1964, were highly successful operations but — partly no doubt because the regimes that had been preserved behaved less than graciously towards Britain in the years that followed — it was unfashionable to say so, or even to talk about them much, in Whitehall.[22]

A more reasonable ground for loss of interest in this kind of operation as a maritime function is the growth of air transport and particularly of ground facilities for aircraft in countries that may need, and request, this kind of assistance. The landing of contingents in the condominium of the New Hebrides, now Vanuatu, to smooth progress to independence in 1980 was done by air; 20 years before it would probably have been necessary to do it by sea or, more hazardously, by parachute.[23]

Because even by-invitation landings must take place in a reasonably operational posture, conducted by units familiar with the task and inherently well-trained in independent operations, they represent a considerable specialised commitment and may demand resources that could otherwise be released for other purposes, military or non-military. Medium powers will have to view carefully the requirement for this kind of operation, though the capacity for it may be implicit in the provision that is made for sterner operations at the higher level.[24]

Evacuation of Nationals

The hostage is not a recent phenomenon, any more than is the political assassination. Expatriates from the more travelled countries of the globe, which tend to include most medium powers, are more numerous and mobile, however, than they have ever been before, and it is probable that they are less cautious too in the sense that fewer of them ensure that a line of retreat to their own country is open in emergency. Many of them work for large, often multinational corporations whose paternalism may or may not extend to such lines of retreat.

At the same time, nations subject to instability, at least to the extent of endangering a proportion of foreign nationals and threatening some with captivity, are no fewer than they were. In one or two maverick states, indeed, governments themselves may consider putting such indignities on expatriates; in many more it is terrorist organisations or the simpler processes of the mob that cause the danger. But wherever the threat comes from, it is certain that the intervention of the forces of another state, in order to succour its nationals, will risk charges of unwarranted interference in the the internal affairs of a sovereign state.

The scale and fluidity of the problem and the climate of international opinion, therefore, make elaborate plans and provision for large-scale evacuation of nationals (a prominent feature of contingency planning in the 1960s and 1970s, at least in the United Kingdom) unrealistic. It is still possible to turn to account such forces as may be in an area and use them *ad hoc* in acute cases of need; the evacuation of British nationals from Bandar Abbas during the Iranian revolution of 1979, by surveying ships that happened to be at work in the Gulf, was a case in point. And contingency plans at least ensure some of the parameters of a problem, when it arises, are not unfamiliar. But the provision of special forces for this requirement is not something that medium powers need seriously to contemplate.

Counter-terrorist Operations

With this category of low intensity operation we turn to sea denial; all the foregoing have been concerned primarily with sea use. Terrorists are mostly land animals; as a general rule, they look on the sea as a supply route for the arms and explosives that are their stock in trade.

In consequence, states under terrorist threat often endeavour to deny the sea as a route for arms supply. The British have for years conducted such an operation in the waters off Northern Ireland, and in late 1984 it was clear that Irish maritime forces too were working against illegal arms traffic when they arrested and brought to port a trawler that had apparently transhipped a supply of arms from a larger vessel coming from the USA. Similarly, France conducted a very large-scale control operation during the Algerian emergency from 1956 onwards, in the first year of which 4,775 ships were visited and 1,300 searched.[25]

The characteristics of forces required for such operations are essentially those of the constabulary. Intelligence and surveillance are essential components; without them, it is truly a needle-in-haystack matter. Even with these assets, a high level of coverage — much higher than the low-percentage, random-seeming coverage required to deter casual transgressors of ordinary municipal law — is needed, with redundancy enough to ensure that when one unit is off-station searching or detaining there are no gaps where the real gunrunner can slip through. To all the requirements of good communication and data acquisition, agility and stout construction, sea-kindliness and experienced crews, is added a need for further numbers, therefore.

The only consolation to a medium-sized state faced with this problem is that the individual units need not be of great power (though it would be embarrassing in the extreme if they were so feeble as to be unable to subdue a terrorist supply vessel resisting arrest). Even where the jurisdiction claimed extends, exceptionally, beyond the territorial sea — and states have in the past made such claims on grounds of state security — the forces on the spot can be relatively modest in size so long as they are numerous enough and properly backed.

While the interdiction of seaborne supplies is the most usual form of anti-terrorist operation by a medium power, there have been some instances of seaborne terrorist operations in the last two decades. An isolated attack by the IRA on a cargo ship off

Northern Ireland was of little economic but considerable propaganda significance. The guerrilla organisation called *Mukhti Bahini* carried out sporadic attacks on shipping in the approaches to East Pakistan, now Bangladesh, in 1971.[26] But the most systematic and widespread terrorism by sea was that conducted by Indonesian nationals against Malaysian craft, mostly fishing vessels, during the Confrontation of 1963–6. Whether the Indonesians involved were under military control, or were irregulars with the connivance of the Sukarno government, is not certain. Their technique was generally to capture fishing craft, take the crews to a remote spot, rough them up and lecture them in terms that all the sea in that area belonged to Indonesia and they would be killed if they attempted to fish there again, and then release them — sometimes with and sometimes without their craft and gear.[27] There is some evidence from local newspapers of the time that until the situation was brought under control this terrorism was effective in stopping fishing over quite large areas.

In the event, the problem became merged with another form of terrorist attack, the infiltration across the Strait of Malacca of Indonesian guerilla forces. Patrols instituted to control the one threat tended to deter the other, and though the situation remained confused and subject to sporadic acts of violence it never escalated dangerously. Both Malaysian and British vessels were used; this was one of the rare cases where medium-power maritime operations at low intensity have been conducted by two states working closely together. The usual constabulary lessons emerged from Confrontation: the need for numerous, agile, sturdy, quick-reacting craft with good data acquisition, communications and control.[28] Occasionally larger units, with heavier armament, were useful in adding deterrent weight.

The Control of Illegal Immigration

Generally the control of immigration and the checking of irregularities is an administrative matter and a constabulary function in normal conditions. There have been occasions, however, when the scale of unauthorised immigration to a state has taken on some of the characteristics of a mass movement of population, a more or less unarmed invasion. Such incursions can occur across land frontiers, as, for example, from Mexico into the United States; they have also been made by sea, as in the cases of Jewish immigration to Palestine in 1946–7 and Chinese to Hong Kong in 1979.

When they reach this stage, such movements tend to call forth large and highly organised operations to keep them in check. In both the Palestine and Hong Kong cases extra forces had to be moved into the area, extensive patrols set up, and a complex intelligence, information and co-ordinating network established. While constabulary methods were still used, the employment of firearms was not ruled out if immigrant vessels refused to submit to search or detention.

One material problem in such cases is the need for speed and agility. Since the areas being used are often quite extensive, and surveillance particularly at night can be difficult, speed of reaction in the units actually used to investigate possible immigrant craft is most important. So is maximum speed, and agility; the 'snake-boats' used by illegal immigrants off Hong Kong in 1979 were very fast and manoeuvrable, and needed suitable counters.

Nearly always, the perceived need for control is accompanied by sympathy with the plight of the would-be immigrants, who are often in physical distress, usually unarmed, and may be accompanied by women and children. The dilemma was most acute in the case of the Vietnamese 'Boat People' in the late 1970s. In few situations is it more obvious that civil and military policies must go hand in hand. Significantly, the Hong Kong immigrations were checked in 1980 quite as much by administrative and diplomatic measures as by the efficient organisation of the forces employed.

Counter-piracy Operations

The definition of piracy in two succeeding Conventions on the Law of the Sea is unchanged, relatively narrow and precise: 'any illegal acts of violence, detention, or any act of depredation, committed for private ends . . . on the high seas . . . or . . . in a place outside the jurisdiction of any state'.[29] Thus, the Indonesian attacks on fishing vessels referred to above almost certainly were not piracy (because they were not committed for private ends) although, inevitably, they were reported as such in the press. Indeed 'pirate' must be one of the most over-extended words in common use; it was applied to Axis submarines during the Spanish Civil War, to Icelandic and British government vessels in the Cod disputes, and to Mrs Margaret Thatcher in Buenos Aires in 1982. None of these appellations has any basis in modern law, though they can be traced back to some nineteenth-century concepts, since rejected, in which a much broader definition of piracy was put forward.[30]

The pirate is an enemy of all, *hostis humani generis*, and international law allows and enjoins all to use their best efforts to frustrate and take him. However, this applies only on the high seas; within the sovereign jurisdiction of any state, that state must make and enforce municipal law to outlaw and suppress piratical acts. There may, in the new law of the sea containing such provisions as the 200-mile Exclusive Economic Zone, where the coastal state has some functional jurisdiction, and a contiguous zone up to 24 miles from the baselines where it can exercise fiscal, customs and sanitary regulation, be fertile ground for squabbles about anti-piracy jurisdiction. Certainly the interpretation that most maritime powers will give is that coastal states may legislate (and should rigorously enforce) against piracy in their territorial sea but that the pirate should be regarded as the enemy of all in the area beyond that. On the other hand, some coastal states, fearful or suspicious of medium or superpower interference in waters where they have sovereign rights, may claim that they alone have jurisdiction over piratical acts even in their exclusive economic zones.

The question is unfortunately not an academic one. Acts of piracy in certain parts of the world, notably off West Africa and Southeast Asia, are sharply increasing and merchant ship captains and crews are seriously alarmed. A coastal state that on the one hand claims jurisdiction against piracy over wide areas, and on the other does nothing to suppress it, will not be popular with the world shipping community, but it is unlikely to be a rarity.

It is to be hoped, however, that most coastal states will be more responsible and will regard the suppression of piracy as one of their constabulary duties within the territorial sea. The problem is difficult, but at least has this characteristic: that small-scale, sporadic pirate operations can be conducted with minimal resources but are unlikely to do lasting damage; while large-scale piracy depends on bases which inevitably become notorious and can, given determination, be flushed out. All pirates touch the land often, and a vigilant police force is the best first line of defence, but in remote areas this is easier asked for than arranged.

Once pirates are at sea they are more difficult to identify, and reaction rather than arrest before the event is likely to be the sorry tale. But as the dossiers build up, and if proper liaison and communication between land and sea constabularies is maintained (it is astonishing how often this does not happen, even in apparently well-regulated nations), much may be done to neutralise piracy before it reaches epidemic proportions.

Piracy on the high seas is a different problem, for it concerns only vessels (and, rarely, aircraft) and therefore attack on bases, which has historically been the most effective way of ending large-scale piracy, is not an option. The resources necessary for systematic anti-piracy operations on the high seas, even in a fairly limited area of pirate concentration, are enormous, and no medium power, or superpower either, has embarked on such an operation since 1945. It is possible that 'presence' forces may be able to help on occasions when proximity is right, and such fortuitous operations can have a deterrent effect.

The Protection of Offshore Installations

The law of the coastal state extends to fixed offshore installations and in normal conditions constabulary work, though it sometimes involves unusual means of transport for the local copper, follows the same rules as it would on land. Low intensity operations concerning offshore installations are of a different character. They will generally be in response to threats of organised violence, whether from terrorist groups or the specially-trained armed forces of another nation. It will be in their nature, as low intensity operations, that they are sporadic and involve a relatively low level of violence; a full campaign, with the aim of depriving a coastal state of all its offshore energy supplies, would be characterised as higher level operations.[31]

The fact that very few incidents of sabotage, hijacking or deliberate systematic damage to oil and gas installations have been recorded, in the 40-odd years through which these structures have become increasingly common, can give much cause for rational hope to the medium power that the problem is a containable one. The hope is rational because installations are not actually very easy targets for the saboteur or hijacker. He or she has to find a way of getting there, and may also want to consider how to get away. In the geographical and weather situations likely to be encountered, both present some problems. It is also rational because the public impact of any sporadic operation of this sort is unlikely to be as compelling as a similar one on land. Blowing up one power station ashore can, in many countries, spectacularly affect the lives of millions.[32] Severing a gas pipeline at sea generally has no such effect. In short, offshore installations are neither a soft nor an attractive target.

But this is no cause for complacency. There may be particular circumstances where offshore installations are perceived as appropriate targets for attention; and the difficulties of approach and, even more, getaway may be an enticing challenge to organisations such as the 'suicide bombers' of the Islamic Jihad. Thus a medium power with large stakes in offshore exploitation will need to cater for threats of this kind.

The requirement is, as ever, surveillance and intelligence, plus in this case the ability to react quickly, if possible to a developing threat and unfailingly to an actual assault. This demands not only an organisation above the sea-air interface but in many cases beneath it as well, both for intelligence-gathering and for reaction. Special skills and equipment are needed here below; they will also be required in the atmosphere. Enough speedy transport will be needed too.

Rules of Engagement

All low intensity operations, whether for purposes of sea use or sea denial, are subject to rules of engagement which will be imposed on their own forces by the governments of both sides.[33] These will be framed partly to satisfy the requirements of international law, particularly the law of self-defence; partly to ensure that the state's public image is not jeopardised by charges of needless violence or warmongering; and partly to ensure that the conflict remains of manageable proportions with solution by negotiation a possibility. Though O'Connell has called the American-Soviet Treaty on the Prevention of Incidents on and over the High Seas (1972) 'a set of international rules of engagement',[34] the sides in a low intensity conflict very seldom consult overtly about such rules. There is thus ample room for charge and counter-charge, but this is part of the normal commerce of confrontation and is probably unavoidable in any case.

Rules of engagement fall roughly into two categories: those governing intiatives a unit may take, and those governing the reaction it is allowed to make. Initiatives will often be very restricted, limited to manoeuvring, taking up the necessary defensive or covering formations, navigating in certain (perhaps defined) areas of sea and air space, and conducting the necessary surveillance and data-gathering operations. If, however, the operation is one of sea denial or territorial-sea control, initiative-taking rules may well extend to warning, stopping, visiting, searching and if necessary arrest and the use of weapons.

Reactive rules are generally more difficult to frame and more critical in their operation. First, some view has to be taken on whether anticipatory self-defence is permissible and if so in what circumstances; assessment of the opponent's intentions and mood, as well as his equipment and competence, are important. Then, the perennial problems of perception at sea have to be faced. It is not always easy to perceive whether a hostile act has occurred until one is actually hit; neither the Israeli destroyer *Eilat* in 1967, nor the British *Sheffield* in 1982, witnessed the firing of the missiles that destroyed them. Hostile intent is, by an order of magnitude, more difficult to detect. Finally, the problem is once more compounded when the sea-air interface is involved. A submarine is difficult enough to detect and classify in all conscience.[35] But to deduce from its perceived actions whether it is about to fire a torpedo or missile, or whether it is conducting surveillance, or whether it is simply trying to keep clear of trouble, is a task often beyond the most experienced operator and the most advanced equipment.

These problems of perception, and the stringency of international law, led some commentators to formulate what O'Connell elevated into the 'Concept of Initial Casualty'.[36] This is to say that it may be necessary, in the opening rules of engagement, to accept the risk of a casualty before the relaxations necessary to allow prudent self-defence measures can be made. As O'Connell pointed out, it is risk and not certainty that is talked about; for example, in the Gulf of Sidra incident the American aircraft involved risked attack from Libyan fighters which actually fired missiles before the Americans retaliated. And some units are designed to look after themselves even in the event of a first assault of some weight. Nevertheless the command and crew of HMS *Initial Casualty* are not likely to welcome their predicament.

Rules of engagement, then, are an urgent and critical problem that governments and operational headquarters must face at or before the start of low intensity operations at sea, and their development and necessary modification is a continuous task. Medium powers may have to pay them particularly close attention: with more to lose than small powers in their networks of international relations and interests, and with less muscle than superpowers to hack through those networks if need be, they are in a sensitive position. As usual, medium powers have to be as brave as lions and cunning as foxes.

Cover

A general characteristic of low intensity operations is the placing, in forward areas of high tension and possible violence, of units that are not by themselves of overwhelming force. Such units may be at risk if sudden escalation occurs. The problem can be acute for medium powers whose resources are likely to be stretched.

Cover from forces of greater power, able to respond to escalation by an opponent in reasonable time and with a reasonable chance of inflicting damage which he would in the ultimate find unacceptable, is therefore a precondition of well-planned low intensity operations. True to its principle of maintaining sufficient means of power in its own hands, a medium power will want to provide essential elements of this cover from its own resources. In particular, it will wish to have means of extending and multiplying its opponent's problems, to take initiatives and keep the situation open.

But self-reliance to this extent will not preclude some attention to alliances. Some medium powers, indeed, may regard a large part of their cover as coming from this source, either through the operation of a tightly-worded treaty or through the ally's coincidence of interest. Such trust has sometimes been justified in the past, sometimes not. It is unlikely to be put on the line until a substantial escalation from low intensity operations has occurred, and therefore inevitably a medium power cannot rely exclusively on allies for cover; the risks of a *fait accompli* being accepted are too great.

Low Intensity Operations: Summary

Low intensity operations never merit the title of war, are limited in aim, scope and area, and are subject to the international law of self-defence. They require carefully drawn rules of engagement. They may include sporadic shooting incidents with limited weapon systems. Low intensity operations fall into the two general categories of sea use and sea denial. Sea use operations include demonstrations of right and resolve, amphibious landings by invitation and *ad hoc* support of national interests arising out of presence missions in normal conditions. Sea denial operations include counter-terrorist, counter-piracy and counter-smuggling work.

The characteristics of forces organised for low intensity operations include excellent data acquisition and communications, flexible and discriminating weapon systems, and a high level of sea- or air-worthiness and endurance. They need to be backed by a reliable command and control system that is responsive to the direction of government. Particularly if relatively weak forces have been put into the operational area, cover capable of responding in case of potential or actual escalation must be available.

It can all be a tall order for a medium power. Some will choose, or be forced, to limit either the area or the scope even of the low intensity operations they provide for. But it is a dismal fact that in over 130 separate *published* situations since 1946, nations have thought it necessary to embark on operations of this sort, and of these a high proportion were states that have been called medium powers. There is no sign of diminution either of the causes or the practice of such operations. Probably, therefore, low intensity operations at sea by medium powers will continue to be a phenomenon of our time.

Notes

1. Frank Kitson, *Low Intensity Operations: Subversion, Insurgency and Peace-keeping* (Faber and Faber, London, 1971).
2. J. Cable, *Gunboat Diplomacy* (Macmillan, London, 1981), pp. 249, 253, 255; and in G. Till (ed.), *The Future of British Sea Power* (Macmillan, London, 1984), p. 127.
3. In the Corfu Channel incident, 1946, the British destroyers *Saumarez* and *Volage* were mined with the loss of 44 lives while demonstrating the right of innocent passage (subsequently upheld by the International Court of Justice) through an international strait in Albania's territorial sea.
4. F. Seyersted, *United Nations Forces in the Law of Peace and War* (Sijthoff, Amsterdam, 1966), p. 127; G. I. A. D. Draper, 'The Legal Limitations upon the Employment of Weapons by the UN Force in the Congo', *International and Comparative Law Quarterly*, Vol. 12 (1963), p. 401.
5. D. P. O'Connell, *The Influence of Law on Sea Power* (Manchester University Press, Manchester, 1975), p. 64.
6. English text: '. . . if an armed attack occurs against a member of the United Nations'. French text: 'Si un membre des Nations unies est l'objet d'une aggression armée . . .'
7. 'Rules of Engagement', *US Naval War College Review*, January–February 1983, pp. 49–50.
8. Of 136 examples from 1946–79 in Cable, *Gunboat Diplomacy*, pp. 223–58,

56 (or 41 per cent) are classed by this writer as law-based.

9. B. Buzan, *A Sea of Troubles? Sources of Dispute in the New Ocean Régime* (IISS, 1978), pp. 26 and 37.

10. Cable, *Gunboat Diplomacy*, p. 234.

11. Walter Laqueur, *The Road to War 1967* (Weidenfeld and Nicholson, London, 1968), p. 93.

12. J. R. Hill, *The Rule of Law at Sea* (unpublished thesis, University of London, 1973), Annex D.

13. Buzan, *A Sea of Troubles?*, p. 24.

14. Cable, *Gunboat Diplomacy*, p. 82. Although Cable has little time for 'Expressive Force', he concedes that when a Spanish force anchored off Gibraltar after a change in the Spanish government had sparked press speculation of a weaker line, 'a point had been made without the embarrassment of words'.

15. Laqueur, *The Road to War*, p. 140.

16. For example, in the Cod disputes no attempt was made by British warships to aid German trawlers under harassment from Icelandic gunboats although such incidents occurred.

17. Cable, *Gunboat Diplomacy*, pp. 131–3.

18. Hill, *The Rule of Law at Sea*, Case Study D.

19. Cable, *Gunboat Diplomacy*, p. 249; G. S. Bhargava, *India's Security in the 1980s* (IISS, 1976), p. 19.

20. *Navy News*, December 1984, p. 1.

21. *Navy News*, October 1984, p. 1.

22. In *Keesing's Contemporary Archives*, pp. 19963 and 20755, is traced the remarkably swift transition between the Tanzanian government's gratitude for its preservation in January 1964 and its harassment of British nationals and *rapprochement* with China in November of that year.

23. *Keesing's Contemporary Archives*, p. 30643.

24. See below, Chapter 8.

25. O'Connell, *The Influence of Law on Sea Power*, p. 123.

26. *Keesing's Contemporary Archives*, p. 24989.

27. Hill, *The Rule of Law at Sea*, Annex C.

28. 'Gisborne', 'Naval Operations in the Malacca and Singapore Straits', *Naval Review*, July 1967, p. 45.

29. Law of the Sea Convention, 1982, Art. 101.

30. *In Re Piracy Jure Gentium* ((1934) AC 586), the Privy Council favoured the definition, 'Piracy is any armed violence at sea which is not a lawful act of war', but it was never adopted.

31. The three levels in this context are reflected in Vice Admiral Sir Ian McGeoch's 'National Security and Maritime Defence', in *Oceanic Management: Conflicting Uses of the Celtic Sea and Other UK Waters* (Europa, London, 1977), pp. 176–7.

32. On 4 February 1985 Maoist guerrillas in Peru blacked out the capital city in response to the Pope's exhortation to lay down their arms.

33. O'Connell, *The Influence of Law on Sea Power*, pp. 169–80; Hill, 'The Rules of Engagement', *Navy International*, July 1975, p. 8.

34. O'Connell, *The Influence of Law on Sea Power*, p. 179.

35. Hill, *Anti-Submarine Warfare*, pp. 44–8.

36. O'Connell, *The Influence of Law on Sea Power*, p. 82. The concept was first put forward, so far as I know, by me in 'Maritime Forces in Confrontation', *Brassey's Annual 1972*, at pp. 32–3.

8 HIGHER LEVEL OPERATIONS

Higher level operations at sea can be defined as active, organised hostilities involving on both sides fleet units and/or aircraft and the use of major weapons. They are not, however, unrestricted; that is the province of general war. There are still limits to aim, scope and area, therefore, but they differ from the limits of low intensity operations in several important ways.

Aim

Higher level operations tend to have an aim that is expressed in military terms. 'Recapture the Falkland Islands'. 'Occupy the Northern half of Cyprus'. 'Attack and sink Pakistani ships in Karachi harbour'. 'Blockade Biafra'. 'Contain Egyptian missile-armed surface craft and ensure the safe passage of shipping to Israeli ports'. Such could have been the directives, in 1982, 1974, 1971, 1968 and 1973 respectively, to the maritime or maritime-based forces of medium powers involved in higher level operations. The words may not be precise; governments are not very ready to publicise such statements of their objectives. But that was what the forces of Britain, Turkey, India, Nigeria and Israel set about doing, and did.

The existence of a clear-cut military aim does not mean that political objectives can be forgotten. But in higher level operations they may no longer have primacy, either in emphasis or timing. 'Let us get the military job over and sort out the political problems afterwards' is a not uncommon sentiment, at least as usual in politicians as it is in the military men themselves.

But one very important function that political considerations fulfil is in limiting the military aim. Britain did not attack mainland Argentina in 1982, India did not invade West Pakistan in 1971, because however desirable such actions may have been in military terms their repercussions would have been detrimental to the state's political future. Nor do such restrictions apply only to land masses. Objectives at sea can be confined to opposing combatant forces, as they appeared to be (rather unsuccessfully, as it happens, since at least one neutral merchant vessel disappeared without trace) in the 1971 Indo-Pakistan war.

Scope

Such limitations of aim impinge directly on the scope of higher level operations. Restrictions on targets or target sets, whether these be national or by type, will be very irksome to the forces involved, particularly those that depend on speed or stealth for their effectiveness, for they will have neither time nor inclination to make the necessary identifications. Nevertheless, particularly at the outset of higher-level operations, such restrictions often apply.

Other limitations of scope may arise simply through lack, or shortage, of forces in certain media or of certain types. If neither side in a conflict possesses submarines then the conflict will lack a dimension; that is an example so obvious as to be banal. But the same effect is achieved if one side, or both, possesses submarines but is unwilling to risk them; the only difference in such a case is that the armament withheld can be regarded as cover, to deter further escalation or for use if the need becomes dire.

Limitation of the potential scope of a higher-level conflict also occurs in the non-involvement, or partial involvement, of allies. It is striking that in none of the examples with which this section began — all, unarguably, the maritime components of true higher level conflict — was the active participation of an ally ever, in hindsight, on the cards. All the talk of possible Soviet intervention on Argentina's part, China's on Pakistan's, France on Biafra's, was so much claptrap. There may have been more chance of Soviet and American involvement in the Yom Kippur War, but subsequent analysis has suggested that even the celebrated 'alerts' were no more than elaborate signalling between the two superpowers aimed at reassuring their respective champions.

Finally, the scope of higher level operations is limited by Rules of Engagement.[1] Certainly, such rules will be more relaxed than they are in low intensity operations, and less all-pervasive in their effect on the thinking of both operational headquarters and commanders at sea and in the air; nevertheless they will still be there and will be influential. Restrictions governed by an opponent's behaviour may at the outset be almost as severe as in low intensity operations, particularly as regards any new form of combat (for example, an excursion into the submarine medium).[2] But because operations are by definition more widespread and more violent at the higher level, rules of this kind are likely to be relaxed fairly quickly so that the opponent's behaviour — except in such activities as lifesaving — will not be of critical significance in governing the action taken against him. Much more influential will be rules governing the taking of initiatives that would either widen or escalate the conflict: a first use of over-the-horizon missiles, a first use of the submarine arm, even (to complete the gamut) recourse to tactical nuclear weapons.

In its consideration of the rules governing these things the state must take into account both the weight and the discrimination of the weaponry. Some weapons are designed to disable opposing units, some to sink them or shoot them down, many can do either according to where and how they hit, but that is not the end of the story. Who gets hit is also very important in a war of limited scope, and rules of engagement even in higher level operations may make quite stringent stipulations as to positive identification. The weapon that sank the *Lusitania* was, after all, an ordinary torpedo.

Area

The formal limitation of the area of higher level conflict at sea is an appealing idea. It signals desire to keep the conflict limited, it gives fair warning to neutrals to keep clear of the jousting area, it may — if the other side concurs, tacitly or otherwise — afford some possibilities outside the area for the orderly recuperation and turnround of units, and in theory it allows very liberal rules of engagement within the area where military aims may be single-mindedly pursued.

But the idea suffers from numerous defects:

> . . . the principle of self-defence is entirely thrown away; historically such areas have always tended to expand; it gives little scope for further escalation except geographically; and it gives great advantage to the long-range missile-armed unit outside the area, which is in the pleasant situation of being able to float a succession of corner kicks across the goal mouth.

Those words, written in 1972, do not seem to need too much

changing in the light of events since.[3]

The higher level conflict at sea in the Yom Kippur War involved no declared area. The Israeli forces exercised considerable freedom of geographical action and, though the full history of that war at sea has still to be written, it appears that they used it to great effect.[4] Against Egyptian and Syrian forces much more numerous and armed with missiles of longer range, they sank upwards of 15 enemy craft without loss to themselves.

By contrast, in the Falklands conflict of 1982 the British declared a Total Exclusion Zone (TEZ) 200 miles round a geographical point at the approximate centre of the Falkland Islands.[5] In this zone not only Argentine warships and auxiliaries but also any other ship, whether naval or merchant vessel, which was operating in support of the illegal occupation would be 'regarded as hostile' and 'liable to be attacked'. The measure was 'without prejudice to the right of the United Kingdom to take whatever additional measures might be needed in exercise of its right of self-defence under Article 51 of the United Nations Charter'.[6]

The attractions of the TEZ were explained unofficially to the writer as 'political'. Presumably, in addition to the stated advantages at the beginning of this section, there was the added need or wish to strengthen by all possible means the legitimacy of Britain's continued claim to the Falkland Islands. Had a zone of restriction or blockade not been declared it might have been taken as acquiescence in Argentina's occupation.

That legal sophistry might well have been dealt with by an equally legal, as opposed to politico-military, declaration. For, in the event, the TEZ turned out to be a serious politico-military blunder. It was a military blunder, and might have been a military catastrophe, because it allowed the British to be outflanked; if the wind had held on the morning of 2 May, the Task Force would have been attacked by aircraft from the carrier *Vienticinco de Mayo* operating well outside the TEZ to the northwest.[7] At the same time the cruiser *General Belgrano* supported by two surface-to-surface missile armed frigates was ideally placed, outside the TEZ to the southwest, to exploit any success the air strike might have.[8] Whatever the cruiser was doing, and under whatever orders, at 8.00 p.m. on that day when she was torpedoed, at dawn her force was a grave threat operating in what many people had been led to consider sanctuary waters.

Thus, by her sinking, the politically defective nature of the TEZ was exposed. Argentine military commentators afterwards were 'not outraged' by the sinking; they regarded war conditions, and the full risks inherent in them, as having begun with the bombing of Port Stanley runway the previous day.[9] But Argentine authorities generally were entirely aware of the propaganda advantages should the British 'break their own rules', naturally stationed their forces accordingly, and exploited public sympathy to the maximum when it happened.

The fact that the British government had made the caveat about 'whatever additional measures might be needed in exercise of its right of self-defence', including presumably anticipatory self-defence in all relevant areas around the Task Force, has been largely lost in the subsequent hurly-burly. It was the specific TEZ with its defined limits, at first sight comforting in its apparent simplicity, that had caught the public mind and no effort was made by the British authorities to dispel the idea that it was intended in some way to be a sanctuary for the British forces and the area outside it a sanctuary for the Argentines.

When such things go wrong, they are inclined to go wronger afterwards; and at the time of writing, the subsequent inconsistencies of handling, however understandable and however aided by people whose motives must be in severe doubt, rumble on. The real culprit in the *Belgrano* affair was the Total Exclusion Zone itself.

Such strictures do not necessarily destroy the idea that higher level conflict is usually limited in area. The limits, however, are more correctly based in the aims and capabilities of the forces involved. For example, it appears that at no time in the Indo-Pakistan war of 1971 was any restriction claimed. India's decision not to attack West Pakistan by land did not stop Indian missile-boats from attacking Karachi, and in fact this action may well have had effects beyond the inevitable bottling-up of the Pakistan Navy and denial of seaborne reinforcement of the East, which in the time available was probably beyond Pakistan's capacity anyway.[10] Similarly, while undeclared, the USA's operating areas off Vietnam in the higher level conflict there were restricted.[11] It is possible by reference to several other higher level maritime operations since the Second World War — the Spratly and Paracel Island operations, East Timor, the Iran-Iraq war, and earlier Korea — to multiply the cases where a *de facto* limitation of the area was apparent but undefined.

This is of course not an ideal solution for the innocent,

particularly the neutral, bystander; and one of the writer's most abiding memories is the sight of half a dozen merchant ships mixed up with the carrier Task Group in the Eastern Mediterranean in 1956, steaming like mad to get away from what they expected to become a war zone. Such flashes help to illuminate the edges of higher level operations.

Types of Higher Level Operation

Higher level operations still fall into the two general categories of sea use and sea denial, though in operations of large scale the two may be juxtaposed or even merged. The section which follows begins with sea-use operations.

Passage of Shipping Against Opposition

This has been the most important single type of sea-use operation in the two major wars of this century. It has often been said that though it was not a war-winning operation, it was one which if unsuccessful could have lost these wars.[12] Even though the world wars were scarcely to be characterised merely as 'higher level operations', the principle of passage of shipping as a prerequisite for success in cross-sea operations appears entirely valid for such conflicts.

I say 'appears' because in fact there is no record since 1945 of any systematic opposition to the passage of shipping in any higher-level operation. Korea, Suez, India-Pakistan (twice), Vietnam, Yom Kippur, Cyprus, East Timor, the Spratlys, the Paracels, the Falklands: in no case was shipping in the open sea attacked, from under or over the sea, except in the most spasmodic and haphazard way and then, generally, in the course of or in mistake for attacks on warships.

This is a remarkable thing. It is not as though the passage of shipping was an insignificant or peripheral event; in half the conflicts mentioned it was central to the action, for they culminated in seaborne invasions. The failure to oppose is in each of these cases explainable: at Suez the Egyptian forces were at a low state of training; at Cyprus, the Spratlys and Paracels enough surprise was achieved to give a slow-reacting opposition no chance; at East Timor there was no kind of organised opposing force at sea; and at the Falklands the British combatant forces had achieved by 18

May (when the amphibious shipping reached the operational area) an ascendancy at sea that helped to deter the co-ordinated action which alone could have disrupted its advance — and the weather did the rest.[13]

This lack of antecedents has had two effects. First, there is little practical evidence on which to base future concepts of the protection of shipping; exercises and theoretical models are well enough, but operational experience is much more of a clincher. Second, there is a temptation or tendency to say that if it has not happened in eleven operations in 30 years, it is very unlikely to happen again and is not worth planning for.

Both effects are rather dangerous. The first can be mitigated by extrapolation from experience in other forms of sea warfare which actually have happened; for example, the Yom Kippur War and the Falklands both had a lot to say about weapon expenditure, anti-missile measures and the unreliability of theoretical single-shot kill probabilities. The second is much more fundamental; the deduction that a single passage-of-shipping operation can get through without serious opposition may very well hold *if certain conditions are fulfilled*, but there's the rub. A medium power even contemplating, far back in the recesses of its planners' offices, such an operation will need to make a most stringent risk assessment before embarking on any higher-level operation involving an unopposed passage of its own shipping in an operational area. Surprise, deterrence and the incompetence of the opponent may make the risk look acceptable, but it will take a brave planner and a braver commander to accept it.

The techniques of shipping protection, particularly against sub-surface and missile threat, are under endless discussion in the tactical schools of numerous nations. This book is not a tactical manual, and the reader must be referred elsewhere.[14] Here it needs only to be said that for shipping to be passed successfully through an area of opposition two things are essential: the shipping must be *organised* and it must be *protected*. Historically, the idea of 'sanitising' a large area, clearing it of enemy forces so that shipping could operate freely within it, has proved ineffective and costly, and there is no reason to think that it is any more valid today. In particular, any attempt at it is unlikely to be beyond the resources of a medium power. Thus the organisation must be relatively tight, the protection relatively close.

The protection of neutral shipping in the course of someone

else's higher level conflict is a problem which may confront a neutral medium power. Britain and France have clearly prepared for it, to a degree, in the Gulf of Oman patrol. But their non-intervention in the waters of the Arabian (or Persian) Gulf itself, even though numerous attacks on shipping have occurred there, indicates the limits of such protection.

Amphibious Landing

Landings from the sea have been a feature of more than a handful of higher level operations carried out by medium powers since the Second World War. Nearly all have been successful and in fact (as pointed out by Gorshkov) the incidence of unsuccessful amphibious landings, both during and after the Second World War, is astonishingly low.

This is probably because the improvised nature of amphibious operations before that time (when the failure rate was much higher) gave place to well-organised operations conducted by troops trained in the role and using specialised amphibious shipping.[15]

The purpose of amphibious operations, for a medium power, may or may not be connected with sea-based interest. The Turkish invasion of Cyprus was nothing to do with sea communications or exploitation. On the other hand, the occupations by China and Vietnam respectively of the Paracel and Spratly Islands had everything to do with securing rights to resource enjoyment. It is not, in the upshot, something that greatly exercises operational planners. In amphibious operations, particularly, the military aim becomes preponderant. Rules of engagement there will still undoubtedly be, and they will be singularly complex because land as well as sea and air fighting may be involved.

All the requirements for the protection of shipping are present also in the case of amphibious landings, both on passage and in the disembarkation area. The securing of such an area is generally reckoned to be a particularly difficult operational problem, and maximum use has to be made of geographic and hydrographic features, surprise, deception and deterrence, as well as direct protection, to achieve success against a determined enemy. It is clear not only from the Falklands but from Suez and Cyprus that such operations can stretch the resources of a medium power to the uttermost. Indeed, at Suez they were so stretched that the resulting delay leached off all international sympathy, and the cumbersone but effective military landings ended in political failure. It was a lesson that seems not to have been lost on subsequent practitioners.

Bombardment of the Shore

Of all the operations of gunboat diplomacy, bombardment of the shore is probably the most typical in the public mind and usually the most reprehensible too. The fact that it comes apparently impersonally from far away is an important psychological factor.[16] Its effect on civilian populations is also very significant.

Bombardment from ship-based aircraft is, it appears, subject to the same considerations. The American bombardments of Vietnam from the air, while perhaps not so potent a feature of American civil revulsion as some other aspects of the Vietnam war, certainly helped to turn domestic and indeed world opinion against America in that conflict.

In consequence, the bombardment of shore territory from the sea, whether by gun or missile or aircraft, is an aspect of higher level operations to be embarked upon by a medium power only after careful thought and then, almost certainly, in a discriminating fashion as part of an amphibious operation. In the context of the Falklands, where there were well-defined military targets and a small civilian population, it could be used quite extensively. In that of the Lebanon in 1983, where the *New Jersey's* 16-inch guns opened up on reputed militia positions, its efficacy was more debatable; and it would have been little different had the assailant been a medium power in that case. Punitive bombardments, unconnected with landing or operations on shore, seem to have had no part in medium-power conflicts for some years and this is not an unexpected development.

Denial of Passage

Higher level operations are not usually simple in any aspect, but in theory the simplest type of higher level operation is one where one of the antagonists seeks to use the sea for passage and the other seeks to deny such use. Denial of this sort has of course occurred in the last 40 years, but it has not resulted in systematic higher level operations. The Cuba quarantine, the most acute of such affairs, did not involve the firing of a single shot. It does indeed appear that several denial-of-passage operations succeeded at the low intensity level through the acquiescence of the denied party. On the other hand, in one case where there has been a good deal of shooting, in the Iran-Iraq war, the area of concern has been confined within a relatively tiny patch of coastal waters.[17] Interestingly, too, passage has — in spite of minimal arrangements for protection and astronomical insurance rates — gone on.

In spite of all this negative evidence, the option of denying passage to an opponent must form part of the planning of many medium powers. If the use of the sea for such passage confers great advantage, and often it does, then denial — in spite of the drawbacks it may hold of escalation, loss of public support, tit for tat and the necessity of sustained effort — has many attractions. In the present day, where the means of attack are often more cost-effective than the means of protection and attack modes are available both on, under and above the sea's surface, the attractions are proportionately greater.

Denial of Sea Areas

If the denial of passage is a comparative rarity in higher level operations since the Second World War, denial of sea areas is not. Over-defined and constricting though it was, the Falklands Total Exclusion Zone was a clear indication of an attempt at an area sea-denial operation, and it was interesting because the sea denial was taken to be a concomitant of sea use by the denying side.

In the Indo-Pakistan war of 1979, India sought to deny the sea approaches to East Pakistan to all Pakistani shipping, and apparently succeeded.[18] In the Yom Kippur War there were at least two area-denial objectives: Israel sought to deny the area off the Israeli coast to hostile forces, and by offensive action succeeded; and Egyptian forces sought to deny the Strait of Bab-el-Mandeb, calling off their operations apparently on the appearance in the area of USS *Hancock*.[19] It was an Egyptian threat to deny the Gulf of Aqaba to Israel-bound shipping that precipitated the June War of 1967. And, again as a concomitant of sea use, denial by the US of the approaches to its carrier operating areas was a commonplace of the Korean and Vietnam wars.

Some common characteristics seem to emerge. First, area denial operations generally have the very reasonable objective of securing the use of the sea by one's own side; in other words, they approximate to a classical exercise of sea power. Second, they are usually the prerogative of the stronger side. Such has been the disparity of the sides, in most conflicts since 1945, that the weaker has not seriously challenged the stronger and sea denial has been successful in the limited sense and limited areas where it has been tried. In the Bab-el-Mandeb, where a weak power attempted denial, it had to climb down when outfaced — significantly, by the superpower ally of a medium power.

Such refusal of action by the weaker power has, of course, been a characteristic of maritime operations throughout history. But it is not a desirable thing for a medium power to include in its planning. The inability of the Argentine fleet to bring the British task force to action was a crucial failure of the South Atlantic conflict. A determined attempt by a power in higher level conflict to use an area of sea for a strategically critical purpose, and to deny that part of the sea to its antagonist, must call forth from the other party either determined resistance, recourse to allies, or the acceptance of a greater risk of defeat. Resistance may be a precondition of recourse to allies, who are unlikely to rush to help a supine supplicant. Such a situation, where two not wholly disparate powers strive for mastery at sea, is the recipe for that outcome so beloved of the classical theorists of sea power: battle.

Battle

It is a characteristic of battle at sea that it should have a beginning, a middle and an end. The beginning may be long-drawn; as Corbett said, 'the great dramatic moments of naval history have to be worked for'.[20] As has been suggested here, it is likely to grow from a need for and exercise of sea use, backed by an attempt at sea denial. It may be brought on by operations apparently peripheral: harassment or blockade that governments could not stomach. Trafalgar had its genesis in Napoleon's frustration.

However battle comes on, its action does by definition form a tactical whole. By this notion the 'Battle of the Atlantic', so evocative a phrase, is really a misnomer; the passage of Convoy ONS 5 was a battle, the use of the Atlantic from 1939 to 1945 was a campaign. In battle, the commanders on either side will have (or should have) simple and clearly defined objectives in mind, overwhelmingly military in nature: 'the destruction of the enemy's aircraft carriers'; 'the safe and timely arrival of the convoy'; 'the interdiction of the passage of Strait X to enemy forces'. Rules of engagement will be more relaxed than in any other form of higher level operation, confined probably to provisions about the firing of nuclear weapons (which would remain under strict political control) and firing on neutrals.

Battle is likely to involve all the media of the sea environment: surface, air and subsurface. The more diverse these are, the more it will involve intricate arrangements for command and control; under modern conditions the shore headquarters will be much involved in these. Nevertheless, battle at sea inevitably remains primarily the concern of the commander on the spot.

Finally, battles end; always sadly for some, sometimes unsatisfactorily for all. Indecisive results are quite as common as decisive ones, and there is a mass of battles where even the decisiveness or indecisiveness is in doubt. The argument about the effect of Jutland will probably never be resolved. Yet this is not a reason for not fighting, or for keeping operations below the level of battle and confined to a series of incidents. In fact, battle happens because the tensions of sea use and sea denial have come to a head. If the end of battle is decisive victory, that will no doubt affect all other aspects of the conflict. If it is, as Pepys once said, 'only we keep the sea . . . but no great matter to brag of', that may be all that is needed. But if medium powers plan never to have a battle, they may get one on very unfavourable terms.

Notes

1. D. P. O'Connell, in *The Influence of Law on Sea Power* (Manchester University Press, Manchester, 1975), pp. 169–80, shows how rules of engagement based on self-defence become modified and relaxed as the higher level of operations is reached.
2. See above, p. 128.
3. J. R. Hill, 'Maritime Forces in Confrontation', *Brassey's Annual 1972* (William Clowes, London, 1972), p. 33.
4. N. Safran, *Israel — The Embattled Ally* (Belknap Press, Harvard, 1978), p. 311.
5. The orientation round a point ought to have precluded any claim that the British were in some way proclaiming a security zone coincident with an Economic Zone, which (if declared) would have been 200 miles from the baselines of the Falkland Islands. However, the figure of 200 miles was an unfortunate choice in this context.
6. *Keesing's Contemporary Archives*, p. 31709.
7. J. Ethell and A. Price, *Air War South Atlantic* (Sidgwick and Jackson, London, 1983), p. 75.
8. Rear Admiral Sir John Woodward, 'The Falklands Experience', RUSI, *Journal*, March 1983, p. 28.
9. R. L. Scheina, 'The Malvinas Campaign', US Naval Institute, *Proceedings*, May 1983, p. 107.
10. Vice Admiral S. N. Kohli, Lecture to the Indian Staff College, 1979.

11. O'Connell, *The Influence of Law on Sea Power*, p. 177.

12. P. M. Kennedy, *The Rise and Fall of British Naval Mastery* (Allen Lane, London, 1976), p. 259.

13. Ethell and Price, *Air War South Atlantic*, p. 98.

14. P. Nitze *et al.*, *Securing the Seas: The Soviet Naval Challenge and Western Alliance Options* (Westview Press, Boulder, Col., 1979); J. Winton, *Convoy: the Defence of Sea Trade 1890–1990* (Michael Joseph, London, 1983); J. R. Hill, *Anti-submarine Warfare* (Ian Allan, Shepperton, 1985).

15. In *The Military Balance, 1983–84* can be counted ten NATO, four Asian and five South American countries possessing Marine Corps. The inception of some of these forces may have less to do with strategic perception than the glamour generated by the US Marine Corps.

16. Argentine diaries in the Falklands had many references to the unsettling effect of bombardment, particularly the morale-lowering effect on infantry who could not hit back.

17. While information is incomplete it appears that most but not all of the attacks have occurred within the territorial sea of one or the other antagonist. See O'Connell, *The Influence of Law on Sea Power*, pp. 130–1.

18. Kohli, lecture.

19. J. Cable, *Gunboat Diplomacy* (Macmillan, London, 1981), p. 20.

20. Quoted in G. Till, *Maritime Strategy and the Nuclear Age* (Macmillan, London, 1984), p. 105.

9 GENERAL WAR

By definition, general war is an armed struggle between both superpowers and their allies. By general consensus it carries a great risk of eventual escalation to the widespread use of nuclear weapons and is therefore a conflict to be discouraged by all possible means.

Medium powers are likely to share that sentiment. Some of the physically larger and more remote, such as Australia and Brazil, may fancy their chances of keeping clear of mortal involvement in such a conflict, and some aspects of their force structure might be designed to maximise that possibility. But for most medium powers, populous, industrialised and strategically placed, there would be no such option and they must concentrate on seeking the maximum security of deterrence.

In both deterrence of general war, and in general war if deterrence fails, the role of a medium power is bound to be contributory. However independent their postures at lower levels of conflict, and however much independence may be built into some of their general-war provisions, they command military resources an order of magnitude below those of the superpowers which are bound to dominate the main conflict both by land and sea.

This is not to say a medium power is necessarily a *mouche du coche a l'envers*, a fly trying to stop the turning wheel; some contributions will certainly be individual and a few highly influential. Situations can be envisaged, for example, where the French and British strategic nuclear deterrents might be very important in deterring the superpowers from certain courses of action, and in land warfare in Central Europe the form and timing of French participation could be critical.

At sea, too, medium powers can be expected to bear a part. History suggests that the forces of subsidiary powers operating closely with dominant allies are not always effective or welcome. Spanish and French combined fleets usually fared particularly badly; Italian submarines did little to help the German effort in the Atlantic in the Second World War; the British Pacific Fleet was a poor relation of the Americans for a long time in 1945–6. Where a medium power had a sphere of operations in support of a dominant ally, things often worked better. The 1939–45 anti-submarine campaign in the Atlantic was, for example, very largely left to the British (scarcely perhaps in that context a medium power), and was successful.

While much has been done, particularly in the highly-structured alliance of NATO, to allow for integrated operations by allied maritime forces, there is room for doubt whether in time of war the core naval groups will admit of much allied dilution. This could not happen with the Warsaw Pact anyway, since no East European navy is capable of ocean operations; but there are a good many indications that US Carrier battle groups operate and in particular communicate in a way that would make it hard for any allied vessels or aircraft to work with them in an integrated way. Support, yes; total participation, no. And, of course, many European navies are deliberately regional in their scope.

These considerations suggest that even for general war tasks a certain degree of autonomy is desirable in a medium-power maritime force. Reliance may be placed on allies for certain capabilities both operational and logistic, but it needs to be well established by precedent and procedure, and in the multi-threat environment that general war is bound to bring with it national forces must be able locally at least to look after themselves to a large extent. The US Cavalry is not always within reach of the smoke signals.

The characteristics of general war maritime operations are potentially as varied as can be conceived; but, in general terms, they follow the lines that have already been suggested for higher level operations — the passage of shipping, amphibious landing, bombardment of the shore, denial of passage, denial of areas and battle — with overwhelmingly military aims, and little limitation of area and scope. They will impinge on each other to a very great extent, not least in the preoccupations of the main forces of the dominant superpowers.

One aspect, however, must be considered in some detail since it can affect quite radically the qualities of medium-power maritime forces. This is the likelihood of the widespread use of nuclear weapons at sea. While they would certainly be subject initially to political control, tactical nuclear weapons do confer considerable advantages to their users in anti-submarine and anti-surface ship warfare. Lethal ranges are considerably enhanced, and tactical constraints are imposed on the other side by way of forcing the adoption of formations that minimise the effect of blast and fallout on a force as a whole but are not in other ways tactically desirable. Moreover, the superpowers do have very large armouries of nuclear weapons at sea. It is said that 65 frigates, 78 destroyers and 27 cruisers of the USN carry nuclear weapons.[1] Presumably all their carriers do so.

How much provision a medium maritime power should make for the incidence of such warfare is an important question. It is not simply a matter of deciding whether to make, and carry, tactical nuclear weapons oneself; this is within the compass of a few medium powers, and may be within that of more soon, but given the vast size of superpower tactical armouries it may be thought a relatively small and low-priority contribution for an ally to make. More critical in many ways is the expensive provision for nuclear, biological and chemical defence which if taken seriously has to be an important feature of ship design.

Finally, in general war those medium powers that have chosen to deploy a strategic nuclear deterrent by sea will be doubly pre-occupied with its safe operation. There may have to be increased emphasis on the approaches to the bases from which ballistic missile submarines operate, and if the war becomes protracted the sailings and arrivals of the submarines would become matters of vital concern.

But when all is said and done, provision for general war is a matter for the most fundamental political discussion in the councils of a medium power. On the one hand will be the need to deter such war above all others, the price to be paid for superpower alliance, the weight to be carried among the like-minded. On the other will be the inherent unlikelihood of general war, the dominance of the superpowers if it happens, and the distortion of the force structures needed for other tasks if over-provision for this kind of warfare is made. It is a discussion that all too often is taken as read.

One short cut, however, is not permissible for the medium powers of the West. Planning for general war of short duration only, on the grounds that a long war is unsustainable, is for a sea-dependent alliance planning merely for defeat. No amount of stockpiling or prepositioning can sustain a conventional war in Europe without reinforcement and ultimately resupply from the United States; and early recourse to nuclear weapons is a good way of ensuring that everyone loses. Consequently, no successful outcome of any major NATO campaign can be contemplated without the continued use of the Atlantic Ocean.

Notes

1. Joel J. Sokolsky, 'The US Navy and Nuclear ASW Weapons', US Naval Institute, *Proceedings*, December 1984, p. 153.

10 REACH

Reach can broadly be defined as the distance from home bases at which operations can be carried out.[1] Reach was one of the focal points of discussion at the Gosport Seminars of 1981 and 1982; before then it had held a similar place in the work of Professor Kelleher and her team at the University of Maryland.[2]

Many of the statements that need to be made about reach look obvious the moment they are made. But on this subject, as on many others concerning maritime power, what is not exposed as obvious is too often ignored. Considerations about reach, in conceptual terms, fall into four categories: interest, type of operation, level of operation and sustainability.

Interest

If a medium power has no extended vital interest beyond its economic zone then it may judge that its reach need extend no further than the limit of that zone. Such powers, as has been suggested, are rare; certain South American states, medium powers by the criteria adopted in this book, confine their maritime activities very largely within these limits, but that is more due to budgetary constraints than to perceived needs.[3] The Economic Zone, vast as it is in the cases of Brazil, Argentina and Chile, by no means exhausts the area of maritime interest that these states aspire to cover.

This exemplifies the tension between interests and resources which is implicit in most planning for maritime power and is particularly acute in the matter of reach. As always, one returns to the fundamental question; which interests are to be regarded as vital? Does it really matter to India that one Indian tanker is bombed at Kharg Island? Would it matter if all Indian tankers going to Kharg Island were singled out for bombing? The examples and hypotheses can be multiplied; scenarios are a bad basis for planning but are useful tests for plans in the formative stage. In this case, they can be useful in establishing the limits of the tolerable, and thence the element of risk in allowing long-reach interests to take care of themselves.

Clearly it is not only the operation of trade and access that can be the preoccupation of medium powers when reach is being considered. Overseas possessions and responsibilities, albatrosses round the neck though they may be, are a fact for some medium powers; and those same medium powers may feel moral obligations to fully independent states at great distances from their shores. A general atmosphere of stability and goodwill in a particular area of interest may be regarded as something that can be fostered by maritime reach into that area; conversely, such reach could be considered in some cases as a disability or goodwill-reducing factor.[4]

All this suggests that the interaction of interest and reach is a subtle, cumulative and many-sided affair demanding a careful analysis in which statistics will be only part of the arguments.

Type of Operation

The type or types of operation for which reach is required, if they can be defined, will clearly help to govern and limit the forces to be provided. A prime example was the decision by the United Kingdom government in 1966 that amphibious landings against opposition would not be undertaken without allies.[5] That this turned out to be misconceived (at least by the lights of the Government of 1982) is neither here nor there in the context of this chapter; it was a strategic assessment closely concerning reach, and it did have an effect on force structures since it was the critical conceptual decision in the scrapping of plans for a new generation of fixed-wing aircraft carriers. The characteristics of amphibious forces were less clearly affected, overlaid as they were by the NATO role in northern Norway that the Royal Marines swiftly embraced at that time; but it is clear that this is another critical type of operation where force structure *vis-à-vis* reach is being considered.

Similarly, some states may consider that the whole range of sea-use operations is not for them beyond certain limits of reach, but will think it worthwhile to be able to conduct sea-denial operations considerably further from their shores. This can be held to safeguard the territorial integrity of the state against all but ballistic-missile bombardment; to deter interference in local conflicts; and to discourage too large a build-up of outside powers in a region of interest.[6]

Presence, particularly non-permanent deployment with a programme of port visits, is a fairly common and a fairly easily attainable long-reach function. The days when such deployments were a great adventure, requiring tremendous diplomatic preparation and logistic forethought, are largely behind us, though emerging medium powers may still need to take very seriously the planning for their first few ventures in this field.

Even the regulatory functions of seapower may be affected by reach considerations. As has been suggested, some economic zones are of immense size and where coastal bases are few, the reach of the forces involved may need to be considerable. Distant-water fishing fleets too may require support far beyond the economic zone; such support is often para-military or non-military in character but is still of concern to the state.

Level of Operation

The level of operation at which any particular degree of reach may be needed is also a critical planning assessment for a medium power. 'How far?' when combined with 'How much?' leads to a large set of subsidiary questions. How much, to protect a given interest, need be done there and how much can be done closer to home? What contribution can be made by other elements of power? When, and to what extent, are allies expected to stir?

These questions are for deep pondering. They bring in many of the basic elements of maritime power, as practised by medium powers. For example, the reluctance of British governments to plan for higher level operations at extended reach led to several gaps in Britain's maritime armoury which were exposed in the Falklands campaign; the most critical, the lack of airborne early warning, was costly in lives and ships, in the event.[7] On the other hand, the French deployment in the Franco-Brazilian Spiny Lobster War (1963) was kept by the French at a deliberately low level although they probably had the reach to escalate the conflict to a higher level.[8] It may be, however, that the sort of operational considerations attendant on matters of reach — the logistic effort required, the sustainability on station of higher level forces particularly carriers and submarines — did influence the French in keeping the confrontation at low intensity.

More than most maritime planning, the combination of Level of Conflict and Reach requires careful assessment (and, for medium powers, probably acceptance) of Risk. There will be, always have been, medium powers who possess covering maritime forces that can in theory escalate to the higher level, or re-enter a conflict that has escalated to that level, with reach sufficient to back up the low intensity forces that are on station. But more than most situations, that of Long Reach sorts out the men from the boys, and as planned by some medium powers the covering forces will be more effective in theory than in practice. In the event they may not sail because they will fail if they do. It does not mean they have no utility; the opponent may be unable to ignore them; allies may be unable to ignore them. But the more obvious the bluff (and sometimes it may not be obvious even to the planners themselves) the more likely it is to fail.

In such risk assessments, scenarios can be useful for testing plans. Indeed, it is probably in the field of level/reach combinations that one most often hears the anguished planner's cry: 'Give us a scenario'. But the cart must absolutely not go before the horse. Plans must be based on interests, threats, resources and allies, usually in that order, and scenarios come afterwards as a test. Cable has pointed out the dangers of the single scenario as a basis for planning.[9] But even multiple scenarios, though more robust, are no substitute for orthodox planning processes that are at once more general and more precise.

Sustainability

It is once more a statement of the obvious that reach must be complemented by sustainability. It is not much use being able to deploy forces to an area at a long distance from the home base if an hour later they have to return home for want of fuel. Logistic support, therefore, is an important element of reach and in modern times, with few formal bases available to medium powers outside the home country, it is either necessary to cultivate friends or to provide autonomous means if reach is to be sustained.

But another element of sustainability is the ability to keep forces on station. A maximum effort from a medium-size fleet may be mounted quickly enough from a non-bluffing power; but if it is not quickly effective, then to achieve the necessary remissions for men and machinery some phasing of the effort will be necessary. If further forces to fill the gaps are not available, the effort up front will diminish. It is often calculated that three ships on the order of battle are required to keep one on station; for all but the most protracted emergencies this may be a rather pessimistic figure but it indicates the scale of the problem.

Sustainability takes in both human and material factors. On the human side, the level of training of ships' companies is an important factor, and just as important will be their habituation to long periods away from home ports and in unfamiliar waters. This includes the acceptance by their families of relatively long periods of separation; the security of each individual's home base means a great deal to morale.[10] Separation will be disliked but is more bearable if familiar. This is a set of factors that gives the British method of group deployments a distinct advantage over the French system of small maritime garrisons covered by a home-based fleet. Exercises of medium scale, as practised by the British deployments far away from any kind of shore support, were immensely important in maintaining the operational autonomy so necessary in the South Atlantic campaign and gave the command an opportunity to consider the tactical problems that might confront such a force.[11]

On the material side, sustainability means a combination of qualities in warships and auxiliaries themselves. They must be able to keep not only the sea but the ocean; weatherliness and watertightness are only part of the story, for ships and aircraft must work as well as float and the design of machinery and equipments to minimise so far as economically possible the incidence of operational defects is highly desirable. Moreover, equipments must be designed to work not only in all expected sea states but in all expected climatic conditions. Many medium powers will not need to take an extreme view here; Indian and Australian planners are unlikely to insist that their ships and aircraft be fully 'arcticised'. The converse, tropicalisation, is likely to be a much more general requirement since even in subtropical latitudes temperatures and humidities can rise to severe levels. Finally, units must carry or have access to adequate stores of fuel, food, gear and ammunition to sustain deployment of adequate length, and must offer sufficient standards of crew comfort to ensure low fatigue and stress.

Reach and Alliances

In her valuable work on the modelling of medium-power European navies, Professor Kelleher distinguishes three main categories.

Model I. Blue water reach with capacity for some major independent maritime action — United Kingdom, France.

Model II. Some reach beyond coastal defence; designed within coalition warfare assumptions — Holland, Italy ('blue water reach'); Germany, Spain, Turkey, Greece ('regional navies plus'); Belgium, Portugal.

Model III. National and local defence; assumptions of coalition framework and support — Norway, Denmark, Sweden, Iceland.[12]

The reach of these navies has, it need hardly be said, been arrived at not only by a national assessment of national and alliance needs but the operation of a whole host of factors including what the navy was like (and what it was thought to be for) 30 years ago, how much money was deemed to be available in the interim, how the perceived requirements have changed in the same period, what the pressures were from indigenous and foreign armaments firms and how powerful were the voices of individuals advancing more or less logical arguments about force structure. But one influence, certainly, has been the collective voice of the Alliance suggesting on the one hand burden-sharing — with the connotation that, say, the denial of the Danish Straits to the enemy in time of higher level conflict and above is a primary task for both Denmark and Germany and should form the basis for a large part of their maritime planning — and on the other demonstrations of solidarity, with the additional connotation therefore that frequent participation by Germany and occasional participation by Denmark in the medium-reach Standing Naval Force Atlantic is desirable.

The point is that the superpower partner in the alliance tends to see the essential function of medium-power partners as a relatively short-reach one, and that any ability to operate at oceanic reach is a bonus. This sentiment is even more clear in the case of the Soviet Union, which confines the non-Soviet Warsaw Pact to local waters. It may be that the United States values United Kingdom and French participation in oceanic operations, particularly at low intensity outside the NATO area and in higher level operations within it, but it is unlikely to regard those contributions as absolutely essential.[13]

At the other side of the world, Japan has been much preoccupied with reach for about the last decade.[14] The clear dependence of the Japanese economy on ocean-going trade, most notably but not exclusively the oil supply from the Gulf, and the insistence of the Constitution on a narrow interpretation of the principle of self-defence, set up tensions within the administration that were singularly hard to resolve. The formula that anti-submarine defence may be applied to 'sealanes' out to 1,000 miles from Japan, however arbitrary a strategic concept it may be and however shaky it is in tactical terms, at least forms a basis for force planning and has helped to define the relative maritime roles of Japan and the United States under the Treaty.

Home or Away

Reach is a kind of cross-hatching to the other concepts that have been discussed in this book. All the operations that have been described in various chapters, at whatever level, can take place at long or short distances from the shore of the state conducting them. Their objectives will be the same in abstract terms, their character similar, their rules will not be greatly different. Yet the characteristics of the forces that will be necessary respectively for home or away matches, if one can so trivialise them, will be vastly different.

When operating close to home frequent recourse may be had to shore bases and ports, logistic and repair problems are likely to be more tolerable, shore-based air resources are likely to be available and communication easier and more precise. Away Teams need much more specialised support and, in these days when foreign bases are seldom within the compass of medium powers to maintain permanently and likely to be accorded grudgingly if at all on an *ad hoc* basis, that support will have to be largely at sea.

Lucky is the medium power that regards its vital interests as ceasing at the boundary of its metropolitan Economic Zone, or that assesses its superpower ally to be sufficient to protect such interests in the oceans beyond. For the rest, the problem of Reach must be tackled if only as an unsatisfactory and partial fulfilment of a perceived need. Away matches are always the most difficult to plan for and play.

Notes

1. J. R. Hill, 'Maritime Forces for Medium Powers', *Naval Forces*, Vol. 5, No. 2 (1984), p. 29.
2. Catherine M. Kelleher, 'Alternative Models for Medium Power Navies', in G. Till (ed.), *The Future of British Sea Power*, pp. 240 and 242.
3. D. P. C. Ferreira, *The Navy of Brazil* (National Defense University, Washington, 1983), p. 37.
4. Indian writers and politicians have argued forcefully that the United States' presence in the Indian Ocean, and particularly the Diego Garcia facility, are just such a destabilising influence: P. K. S. Namboodiri, J. P. Anand and Sreedhar, *Intervention in the Indian Ocean* (ABC Publishing House, Bombay, 1982), pp. 129–30.
5. Cmnd 2901 (1966), Section II, para 19.
6. Capt. K. R. Menon, 'The Sea Denial Option for Smaller Navies', US Naval Institute, *Proceedings*, March 1983, pp. 119–20.
7. Cmnd 8758, para 228.
8. J. Cable, *Gunboat Diplomacy* (Macmillan, London, 1981), p. 239.
9. J. Cable, *Britain's Naval Future* (Naval Institute Press, Annapolis, 1983), pp. 93 and 167; and 'Surprise and the Single Scenario', RUSI, *Journal*, March 1983, p. 38.
10. For the importance of family support to submarines on patrol see Jonathan Crane, *Submarine* (BBC, 1984), p. 187.
11. Rear Admiral Sir John Woodward, in conversation with the author, July 1982.
12. Kelleher, 'Alternative Models for Medium Power Navies', p. 242.
13. In *The Future of British Sea Power* (ed. G. Till), p. 238, Vice Admiral M. S. Holcomb USN makes it clear that the United States is engaged in a 'bid to regain maritime superiority' over the Soviet Union — on its own.
14. For the background information to this paragraph, as for many of the other entries on Japan in this book, I am much indebted to Ivan Cosby and to Dr Seiichiro Onishi of the Research Institute for Peace and Security, Tokyo.

11 MATERIEL

The engines of power at sea are of enormous complexity and fascination. Detailed discussion of their characteristics, let alone their technical workings, could fill more than one book. The distillation here is intended to point out those characteristics of maritime materiel which are of most interest to a medium power in planning for what it thinks it needs to do.

Although the discussion will concern mainly military power, it will begin with a brief reminder on interests since their nature is itself a strong influencing factor in the choice of military measures. The remainder of the discussion will concern military systems, with frequent reference to the question of cost. Platforms and weapon systems will be treated in separate sections. Although some naval planners hold the view that a ship, submarine or aircraft ought to be considered as a single, fully integrated weapons system, the practice and evolution of warship and aircraft development suggests otherwise; unless they are very small and simple, a surface ship and a submarine carry multiple systems for different purposes, and aircraft too have always potentially been and increasingly now are multi-system, multi-role vehicles. Strap-on systems for use in emergency have recovered some lost prestige lately. Moreover, during its life a platform may prove adaptable to a whole new series of systems. Thus there are good reasons for the differentiation of platforms and systems, and that method will be adopted here.

Interests

By way of reminder, the maritime interests of a medium power include the maintenance of territorial integrity and political independence, trade and access, economic exploitation, overseas commitments and stability. A very high proportion of these interests is manifested at the sea's surface even though some of the means of defending them — for example, strategic deterrent missiles — may be placed beneath or above the surface, and the chief threats to them may also come from either side of it.

Changes in the technology of maritime trade and exploitation may have a considerable influence on the provision for safeguarding these interests. For example, according to Couper it can be taken that one 300,000-tonne Ultra Large Crude Carrier (ULCC) replaces eight or so 28,000-tonners in the crude oil trades and nine container ships replace 60 conventional liners in parts of the Australian trade.[1] And given the economics of ship operating, it is the large and intensively used vessels, the ULCC and the container ship, that will increasingly predominate. Both their numbers and their characteristics may predicate novel methods for their protection and therefore generate new requirements for maritime forces. Similarly, in fishing the increasing use of factory ships is an important factor in the pattern of exploitation and therefore regulation; while new types of mineral-resource exploration and exploitation platform, constantly emerging, may bring not only new constabulary problems but demand new methods of protection against sabotage.

Nor should it be forgotten that the maritime interest starts before the sea begins. At home, ports (ever more specialised as marine technology increases) are an essential ingredient of the maritime system of trade, as are shore terminals of the exploitation of maritime resources. Indigenous shipbuilding, aircraft, weapon and electronics industries may be regarded as important elements of maritime power; and whether so regarded, or considered as an economic embarrassment, they will have an important influence on materiel. Overseas, the atmosphere of diplomatic and business relations is the breath of trade and access.

Finally, the fostering of alliances, particularly a superpower alliance, is such an important means of supporting the interests of a medium power that it is sometimes considered as an objective, even the primary objective, of medium-power materiel policy. It will be clear by now that that extreme view is not taken by the present writer. However, materiel provision must take alliance considerations into account, even though it is the vital interests of the medium power itself that are the ultimate objects of strategy.

Platforms

Surface Ships

Like man, the surface ship is a creature of the interface, following the natural laws of gravity, buoyancy and stability without trying too hard by the aid of machinery to circumvent them. In consequence it can carry very large payloads; this is its principal virtue as a trading vehicle and one of its easily-forgotten advantages as a warship.

The advantage is easily forgotten because it is desirable to pack so much into the available space. Machinery both propulsive and auxiliary, fuel, weapons, ammunition, sensors, accommodation and stores: all make their demands and the judgements involved in making the right allocation, taking full account of the interactions involved and always bearing in mind the tasks the ship is to be called upon to do, are critical matters in ship design. Pervasive to these provisions will be the view taken about how far the ship is to be able to withstand action damage: great stoutness did in the days of armour demand great weight allocation, nowadays it is likely to require allocations more of power and space.[2]

Nevertheless, the fact remains that a surface ship can provide multiple weapon systems and sensors, and the bigger it is the more varied these can be. Moreover they can with some ease be deployed on both sides of the interface. Air-riding weapons, whether ballistic (which actually includes shells) or aerodynamic missiles, are natural weapon systems for a surface ship, and considerable though by no means inexhaustible stocks of ammunition can be carried. Underwater weapons (torpedoes, depth-charges and mines) can equally be carried and launched in considerable numbers. Where sensors are concerned, surface ships are again capable of great variety. Communications of both world-wide and local range, more and more rapid, comprehensive and secure as technology advances, are commonplace. Radar can cover a large area of sky, a smaller area of the sea's surface, with a high probability of detection of air and surface units. Search equipments can give warning of hostile radars operating in the area, and electronic countermeasures can be used to deny information and disrupt weapon systems. Beneath the surface (and half of a surface ship is beneath the surface), sonars (whether hull-mounted or towed) can be operated in the active or passive mode, and communication with friendly submarines can be attempted over relatively short distances by underwater telephone.

Payload also allows the surface ship, if over a certain size, to offer the ability to carry aircraft. Helicopters can land on very small flight decks but for keeping on board need hangars, too. Fixed-wing aircraft, even those of the very short take-off and

Table 11.1: Surface Ships — Typical Characteristics

Type	Tonnage	Propulsion	Crew	Armament	Range n.m.	Cost
Attack Carrier	35,000–100,000	Steam Turbine or Nuclear	2,000+	50–100 Aircraft SAM	8,000 Unlimited if Nuclear	$2bn+
Support Carrier	18,000–30,000	Steam or Gas Turbine	1,000+	20–40 Aircraft SAM	5,000	$400m.+
Cruiser	10,000–25,000	Steam or Gas Turbine	800	SSM, Guns ADMS 2–4 Helos	6,000	$400m.+
Destroyer	3,000–8,000	Gas Turbine	300	SSM, Gun ADMS 1–2 Helos	4,500	$250m.+
Frigate	2,500–6,000	Gas Turbine/ Diesel	150+	SSM, Gun PDMS 1–2 Helos	4,500	$150m.+
Corvette	600–2,500	Diesel	60+	SSM Light Gun Close Range A/S Weapons Helo Deck	3,000[a]	$50m.+
Fast Attack Craft	150–500	Gas Turbine or Fast Diesel	30	SSM or Torpedoes Light Gun	500[a]	$20m.+

Note: a. Weather-limited.

All figures are illustrative and do not represent any particular class in any navy. They are based on 1985 in-service date and price.

Abbreviations:

SAM Surface-to-air missiles
ADMS Area defence missile system (surface to air)
PDMS Point defence missile system (surface to air)
SSM Surface-to-surface missiles.

landing type, need larger and more complex facilities including, for regular operation, flight decks running the length of the ship.

Finally, payload can include large numbers of troops and equipment for amphibious landings. Deployment at the landing end can be by helicopter (the large number of helicopters required to land troops in a combat posture demands a specialised ship), or by landing craft, or through bow doors in a specially-constructed beachworthy ship, or a combination of these.

The surface ship also has the advantage of high sustainability. Soviet vessels appear to have little difficulty in maintaining deployments of many months, though their work rate is not high, and at the start of the Beira patrol HMS *Eagle* clocked up 72 days continuously under way without noticeable ill effect.[3] For fossil-fuelled warships this naturally means topping-up at intervals of a few days and a fleet train, at least of oilers and probably store ships as well, is needed. The two functions can be and increasingly are combined in a 'one-stop' comprehensive stores ship.[4] The virtue of sustainability extends quite a long way down the surface ship scale. The Soviet Union maintained *Petya*-class corvettes for many months on out-of-area station and these are ships of 1,000 tonnes standard displacement. However, fast attack craft generally have lower levels of sustainability and their ability to fuel in the open sea is very limited.

Finally, among the surface ship's virtues must be counted visibility and public impact. When a surface warship is about, there is not much doubt that it is there. It may assuage or alarm, be emollient or abrasive, but it will be noticed. In general, also — and this may be simply a function of its visibility or it may have deeper psychological roots — the surface ship is a more conciliatory symbol than any other manifestation of maritime military power. Aircraft are sudden, potentially lethal, frightening; submarines are stealthy, sinister killers. That may be a slightly colourful way of expressing a widely-held public vision, but the overstatement is not great.

The surface ship's virtues, then, as both a purveyor and a demonstrator of maritime military power, are considerable. But it has also a number of drawbacks of which medium-power planners must be acutely aware.

First, it does, as Moineville in Compton-Hall's excellent translation says, ride 'horseback on the air-sea interface'.[5] The horse can buck, and however many stabilisers are fitted a surface ship of moderate size will often find weather and sea conditions where its fighting and movement abilities are severely degraded. This effect is particularly marked in the underwater sphere where hull-mounted sonars can be of little use in very high sea states.[6] But weather and ship movement can have a severe effect too on radar and above-water weapon performance, helicopter operations and crew efficiency.[7] Seakeeping and weatherliness are of course constantly sought in surface ship design and are an item of current controversy in the United Kingdom.[8] But the general fact of surface ships being subject to sea effects cannot be gainsaid.

Second, although a surface ship can carry almost any form of sensor it can carry very few in the optimum manner. Above the interface, the best sensors are either optical or in the electromagnetic spectrum, and the most critical fact about these is that in the overwhelming number of cases their ray paths are straight. Visual, radar and electro-optical systems such as lasers are all therefore, for practical purposes at sea, limited in range by the horizon, if a limit has not been applied closer in by such factors as weather and attenuation. The classical solution is to raise the sensor; the lookout in the crow's nest. But ships' masts are limited in height by stability and structural considerations, so surface ships will never be able to hoist their above-water sensors as high as they would wish.

Beneath the surface, ship-carried sensors are subject to a different set of circumstances. Here the principal sensing medium is sound; radar cannot penetrate at all, and light not far. The temperature, pressure and salinity structure of sea water is complex and causes aberrations in sound paths. Typically, these result in what is colloquially described as a layer or layers, horizontally at a depth of some hundreds of feet, across which sound passes with difficulty.[9] Sensors near the surface are considerably degraded in such conditions against targets below the layer. Surface ships can seek to get round this problem by towing sensors at the optimum depth but the manoeuvring limitations imposed detract from their mobility and hence effectiveness in other tasks.

Third, most surface ships are still dependent on liquid fuel and require replenishment at relatively frequent intervals — typically every four or five days. They also tend to carry sizeable ships' companies in order to operate their machines, sensor and weapon systems at sustained rates and readiness, and their stores requirements are considerable; and in hostilities they are likely to need frequent replenishment of ammunition.[10] Thus access to logistic support, whether this be ashore or afloat, is a requirement for sustained surface ship operations; and while replenishing, surface units are not only unable to do their full operational task, they are — particularly when replenishing at sea — more than usually vulnerable.

Fourth, the surface ship's visibility is an operational drawback as well as a diplomatic virtue. When the only sensor was the human eye and its greatest limit of vertical travel was a masthead, or a high cliff on shore, this was not such a serious matter. Now that sensors of many kinds can be put aloft not only into aircraft but, at least by the superpowers, into space, the disadvantage is much sharper. Strategic surprise, which up to this century was not an uncommon aspiration for naval forces, is now a virtual impossibility. Tactical surprise may still be achievable but against a sophisticated opponent, particularly one with access to space-based surveillance systems, it will require much ingenuity as well as luck. Moreover, the visibility of the surface ship to electronic as well as visual sensors makes it relatively easy to acquire as a target for weapons and hence more vulnerable.

Vulnerability is the fifth and greatest advertised drawback of the surface ship in modern conditions. There is nothing new about the controversy over the scale of the problem which has most recently been revived since the Falklands campaign.[11] Advocates of the submarine before the First World War, and of the aircraft immediately after it, were quick to pronounce surface ships dead; the advent of the nuclear-propelled submarine and the aerodynamic homing missile, both deadly menaces to the surface ship, have sharpened a dilemma that was already apparent and was demonstrated often in both World Wars, most dramatically perhaps in the sinking of the cruisers *Aboukir*, *Hogue* and *Cressy* by a single submarine in 1914 and the Royal Navy's very heavy losses to air attack off Crete in 1941.

Those incidents were not only dramatic but significant in that they involved unbalanced and unsupported forces of surface ships, and they point up the classical answer to the vulnerability problem: to concentrate a force with an array of defensive talents which is extremely difficult and expensive to assail. This is the American solution, using large carriers and cruisers equipped with extremely sophisticated sensors and making full use of air and submarine assets. Scaled down, and against relatively unsophisticated opposition, it was the preferred British method of operation in the Falklands campaign. But because of the lack of one or two important components, as well as operational imperatives that dictated departure from the general scheme in, for example, the isolated position of HMS *Ardent* on 21 May, the vulnerability of surface ships to air attack at least was exposed.[12] Four destroyers or frigates, a sixth of the number employed, were sunk.

The conclusions that the medium power can draw from the foregoing discussion on the surface ship's virtues and drawbacks seem to be these.

The surface warship is visible, versatile, controllable and

un-sinister. It operates in the most common medium of sea use. Therefore, it is is clearly of value in those operations that require careful politico-military handling. Many of the functions of normal conditions — demonstrated effectiveness, presence, overt surveillance and constabulary duties — are entirely suited to it. Equally, it is admirably capable of carrying out the majority of low-intensity operations, where its versatility and responsiveness to changes of policy (including rules of engagement) are singular virtues; demonstrations of right and resolve, amphibious work, the sea denial functions of counter-terrorism and the protection of offshore installations are all meat and drink to the surface unit.

It is at the higher level of operations that the surface warship's defects become apparent. Its sphere of action begins to look limited, its visibility ceases to be an asset and becomes a liability and its vulnerability to more lethal weapon systems becomes apparent. This may be nowhere more acute than at the point of transition to the higher level, where the onset of hostilities can, unless their governments and superior commanders are alert and wary, catch surface units unprepared. The measures that have been suggested in this and previous chapters — cover, integration with subsurface and air assets — need at once be brought into play in higher level operations, but medium power resources on their own are bound to be limited.

The dilemma, and of all medium-power dilemmas it is one of the most critical for planners, is that for many operations at the higher level surface ships, however vulnerable and limited, are still essential. In amphibious operations, in those concerned with the passage of shipping, in the fire support of forces ashore, it is not possible to do the job without them. So, even if the proportion that are not going to survive their first battle is expected to be high, surface ships must form part of the structure at all levels of operation.

Aircraft

The distinguishing characteristic of an aircraft is that it defies gravity. To do this it needs either to have much of its space taken up with lighter-than-air gas, a currently unfashionable mode, or to ride on wings gaining their lift by motion through the air, a process very demanding of power and fuel.

The consequence is that the payload of an aircraft is relatively low, and that a high proportion of that must be given over to fuel.

Table 11.2: Maritime Aircraft — Typical Characteristics

Type	Weight (tons)	Speed (knots)	Endurance	Armament	Sensors	Base	Cost
Long-range Maritime Patrol	80	500	10 hr	Torpedoes Depth Charges	Radar Sonobuoys	Shore	$50m. +
Carried-based Patrol	20	500	4 hr	Torpedo Depth Charges	Radar Sonobuoys	Attack Carrier	$40m. +
Strike/Attack	25	supersonic	3 hr	Bomb Rocket ASM	Radar	Attack Carrier or Shore	$30m. +
Fighter	20	supersonic	2 hr	AAM Guns	Radar	Attack Carrier or Shore	$30m. +
STOVL Fixed Wing	10	high subsonic	1½ hr	Bomb Rocket AAM Gun	Radar	Support Carrier	$20m. +
AEW Fixed Wing	25+	400	12 hr (4 hr carrier based)	—	AEW Radar	Shore or Attack Carrier	$60m. +
AEW Helo	10	130	4 hr	—	AEW Radar	Support Carrier	$25m. +
Heavy ASW Helo	10	130	4 hr	Torpedoes Depth Charges	Radar Sonar Sonobuoys	Carriers Cruisers Some Frigates	$25m. +
Medium Helo	5	150	2 hr	Torpedoes Light ASM	Radar Lightweight Sonar	Destroyers Frigates	$15m. +
Troop-carrying Helo	10	130	4 hr	—	Radar	Support Carrier	$20m. +

Note: All figures are illustrative and based on 1985 in-service date.

Abbreviations:

ASM Air-to-surface missile
STOVL Short take off and vertical landing
AAM Air-to-air missile
AEW Airborne early warning
ASW Anti-submarine warfare.

The equations between range and payloads are a constant feature of the planning of air operations and are further complicated by the profiles — high or low flight, attack mode or speed — dictated by any particular mission. Finally, the aircraft is particularly sensitive when getting into, or returning from, the air; it habitually needs specially constructed facilities, and may require certain conditions of wind or weather or light, to enable it do do so safely. It was because all these equations did not work out that the Skyhawks from the *Vienticinco de Mayo* did not carry out their attack on the British Task Force on 2 May 1982.[13]

If the aircraft has these generic limitations as a vehicle of war it also has great generic virtues. First, it is capable of tremendous mobility; it can go a long way in a very short span of time, and its speed may also give it the military advantage of surprise. Even the relatively slow aircraft of the Second World War often achieved attacks on unalerted ships; modern aircraft operating near, or beyond, the speed of sound pose much sharper problems to the surveillance of defending forces.

Second, the aircraft can carry sensors aloft. This is an enormous advantage in surveillance and warning. The horizon is expanded by orders of magnitude as the sensor is raised, so much indeed that maximum range tends to be governed by the sensor's power or sensitivity rather than the physical horizon itself. But this lofting of sensors has another most important application. It can also be used to indicate (though not usually to identify) targets, particularly targets on the surface, to weapon systems carried in the aircraft itself or in other units. In this way the potential of self-homing missiles can be maximised.

Third, in spite of their limited payload aircraft are generally capable of carrying weapons of great lethality. The bomb, the self-guided missile and the unguided rocket are all capable of scoring successes against medium-sized ships, and anti-submarine aircraft are capable of carrying both depth-charges and torpedoes. Allied to tactical mobility and lofted sensors, the weapon loads that can be carried by modern aircraft make them formidable machines of war.

Apart from their general characteristics, particularly the range/payload equations, aircraft have certain other limitations. First, they are complex equipments with no maintenance facilities on board the aircraft. Consequently they require extensive bases either ashore or afloat. When such bases are efficient, high serviceability can be achieved, like the 95 per cent overall in Harriers in the

Falklands campaign.[14] But such facilities are expensive to provide and to maintain; and if on land they may not be in the right place. Whether on land or at sea they may be liable to attack; the vulnerability of an aircraft is to a large extent the vulnerability of its base.

But not only: for the second disadvantage of aircraft, particularly those that have to loiter or patrol in order to survey sea or air with their airborne sensors, is their vulnerability in the air. The provision of self-defence weapons, even if feasible (and it will only be so against other aircraft), reduces the payload available for other purposes.

Third, the limited endurance of aircraft means that for a sustained effort large numbers are required. As an example, to keep one Nimrod airborne some six *operational* airframes are likely to be needed, and this probably entails two more in deep maintenance. The number of trained crews to keep one in the air may be somewhat lower, around four. But it costs a great deal to train aircrew.

Fourth, aircraft no less than ships require communication facilities, but in addition need highly-trained and well-equipped air traffic control organisations to see them safely from and to their bases, and, for many missions, tactical controllers and equipment 'on the ground' or in another aircraft. This applies whether the aircraft are land based or shipborne.

Finally, the relatively small size and payload of aircraft tends to make them platforms with a limited range of roles. A Nimrod long range maritime patrol aircraft is not suited to air-to-air combat; a Harrier cannot fly airborne early warning missions. Even multi-role aircraft may have to carry armaments specific to their mission; medium-sized helicopters can carry torpedoes or air-to-surface missiles but not both at the same time.[15]

Aircraft are an important component of most maritime operations. Surveillance and information gathering is, as has been shown, a pervasive activity in normal conditions, low intensity operations and operations at the higher level; aircraft must be prime vehicles here. As cover, too, means of putting on the frighteners to deter escalation from normal conditions or low intensity, combat aircraft are important; while at the higher level, in operations of sea use (particularly amphibious operations), of sea denial, or in battle, they are indispensable.

But there must be a caveat against too early a use of combat aircraft, particularly fast fixed-wing aircraft, in any scale of conflict. Their very speed and suddenness does, and is bound to, make it difficult for them to be discriminatory in low intensity operations. Put another way, no properly-trained combat aircraft is going to stooge around making positive identification of targets because he is much more likely to be shot down if he does. Thus rules of engagement are very difficult to draw tightly enough to satisfy political requirements in such operations. The world public knows this very well, which is one reason why 'bombing' is such an emotive word.

There is, then, a definite link between the levels of conflict and the characteristics of certain sorts of aircraft; fixed-wing patrol types are pervasive to all the levels; helicopters also in their surveillance, rescue and logistic modes, while at low intensity they may carry out isolated operations and at the higher level the combat tasks for which they are mostly designed; fast combat aircraft are suitable for cover and for the higher levels of operation.

There is also a link between aircraft and the concept of Reach. Here it is necessary to remember the difference between Range (the distance from its point of origin at which a system can be militarily effective) and Reach (the distance from the home base at which operations can be carried out). The range of aircraft can be increased by air-to-air refuelling, which demands large numbers of tanker aircraft and bases from which to operate them. Their reach can be increased by operating them from land bases abroad, if these are available, or by basing them in ships, which need special facilities in order to operate and maintain them and impose limitations on aircraft size and characteristics. The balance between these considerations and solutions, given the required reach, is a critical decision for any medium power. It is interesting, but in view of the distances involved not surprising, that Britain's Falklands operations in 1982 employed all three of the methods: air-to-air refuelling, advanced bases and shipborne aircraft. Though for the current garrison task they do so still, the balance has changed; during the conflict nearly all the combat aircraft were shipborne, now they are forward based on land.

Submarines

If the aircraft defies gravity, the submarine defies buoyancy. More precisely, it controls buoyancy in order to submerge and stay at its desired depth. In order to achieve the strength, stability and buoyancy control necessary for this unnatural characteristic, submarine design has to surmount many technical and physical problems.[16] In general, although there have been some design and operating disasters in the last four decades, these problems have been satisfactorily coped with and well over 30 nations now operate submarine forces, though by no means all build their own boats.[17]

The submarine is, of all the platforms being considered here, the one that has experienced the most important step-change since the end of the Second World War. Submarines then were propelled by diesel engines on the surface and battery-powered motors when submerged; running on diesels was needed to recharge the batteries, and although this could be done at periscope depth using a snort mast for air, it even then exposed the boat to detection from the atmosphere. The endurance of a boat on batteries alone was a matter of a few days at most. The introduction of nuclear propulsion changed all these parameters. The closed cycle system is independent of the atmosphere and provides enough power for life-support services — air purifying and so on — as well as for powerful propulsion, weapon and sensor systems. Thus a nuclear powered submarine can remain at depth for weeks at a time.[18] However, nuclear propulsion is not an easy goal to reach; so far it has demanded a large home-grown atomic research and development base for its achievement as well as an indigenous nuclear industry, and apart from the superpowers only Britain, France and China operate nuclear powered submarines. While conventional submarines of the diesel/electric type mentioned above have been subject to immense improvement, they continue to have the basic characteristics and limitations of their Second World War predecessors.

The prime virtue of the submarine as a platform of war is concealment. Sound is the principal method of sensing beneath the sea, and is, as has been shown, subject to vagaries caused by temperature, pressure and salinity variations, extraneous noises, surface effects and shallow water. A submarine using these variations to optimum effect can much increase its already inherent chances of hiding in the wide spaces of the ocean. Its designers will, in these days, have done their best to ensure that it is as silent as can be managed. In conventional submarines that still have to use diesels from time to time, that period can again be minimised by design that makes snorting and battery-charging as efficient as possible.

A second virtue of the submarine is endurance. The diesel is an economical engine and fuel for a voyage of many weeks can be carried; 60-day patrols were not uncommon even in the Second World War. Nuclear-powered submarines can do even better, but in general patrol lengths seem to remain at about the two-month mark, probably for reasons of crew morale.[19] This endurance is, it must be stressed, independent of any outside source of replenishment. The hotel services may be rudimentary, the food lacking in freshness and the routine wearing, but submariners are trained to that environment and value their independence.

The submarine's third great virtue is its striking power. Partly this is a function of concealment — virtues are nearly always interactive — but mainly it is because, as an underwater vehicle, it can strike at the vulnerable underwater portions of ships and other submarines. And it has no difficulty in carrying weapons of considerable weight; the heavy torpedo really is heavy, and carries a corresponding charge.[20]

Finally, among the submarine's virtues is its ability to gather underwater information. This depends on the proficiency with which it uses the sea conditions as well as the innate efficiency of its sensors, and it is not a quality that lends itself to precise analysis. But certainly, because the submarine can adjust its depth and orientation in a way that is open to no other system, it does have an inherent advantage in this field.

All these virtues of the submarine as an engine of war have led many to characterise it as 'the capital ship of the future' and to pronounce that 'navies must go under water'. It is not only a distrust of slogans that makes the present writer bridle at such extremities; for the submarine has identifiable disadvantages too.

First, it is not an easy craft with which to communicate when it is submerged. Only very low frequency radio waves penetrate more than a few feet below the surface, and even then only a couple of hundred feet or so; moreover the data rates of such transmissions are not high. Neither are submarines good transmitters of information, though this is primarily for another reason: by transmitting they doubly expose themselves, by coming to a less-than-optimum depth for concealment and by making tell-tale emissions that can be detected and localised.

Second, its ability from deep to assess what is going on in the surface area around it, and even in the depths of the sea within its sensors' span, is limited in that imperfectly understood medium by the sensitivity of those sensors and the skill of their operators.

Generating the necessary localisation and tracking, particularly in a complex situation, is a process requiring patience, accuracy, flair and a good deal of time.[21] Short cuts can be taken, involving the use of speed and of the periscope (which in any case is required for positive identification of surface targets); they invariably involve a greater risk of exposure to detection.

Third, the submarine has no armoury of discriminating weapons. It cannot fire a shot across anyone's bows, either with missile or torpedo, in any way that can be identified as such; any shot from a submarine is bound to be taken as fired with intent to kill. Similarly, self-defence as exercised by a submarine can only be evasion, concealment or lethal counter-attack; proportionality is not its forte.

All these characteristics point the submarine clearly in one direction: to be a lone predator, at its best when operating in an area clear of friendly or neutral forces and given great freedom of offensive action against both surface units and opposing submarines; in other words, suited admirably to operations at the higher level and particularly to those of sea denial, but trammelled and confined when the rules of engagement are strict or too much co-operation with surface or air units is required. In normal conditions the submarine is a most useful vehicle of clandestine surveillance; in low-intensity operations it is a valuable component of cover, a fine stick to shake; but it is not until the transition to higher level operations that it comes into its own. At that point it is a formidable protagonist.

Sensors and Weapon Systems

Air Defence

In hostilities, ships (and installations and port facilities) need to be defended not only against aircraft but against aerodynamic homing missiles which can be fired from a variety of platforms. They may also be under threat from ballistic-trajectory missiles, and since no way is in prospect for stopping these once in flight they pose a particularly severe air defence problem; fortunately, however, their inability to conduct precise homing on a moving target has so far imposed severe limitations on their tactical use.

The first line of air defence is generally held to be at source: in other words, to destroy or incapacitate the missile-carrying platform. This requires systems, usually airborne themselves, of considerable range. As an example, the shooting down of a Soviet Backfire equipped with a 250-mile range AS-4 missile has to take place at least at that distance from the threatened unit, which requires sensors and probably airborne fighter aircraft stationed in the direction of the threat to give any chance of a timely interception taking place.[22] The neutralisation of missile-armed submarines is an even more intractable problem although such submarines have difficulties of their own and may have to close a force to gain fire control information.[23]

Air defence at source, then, is likely to be only a partial solution, and the direct defence of units against both aircraft and missiles is required. A system requires several distinct components to give a reasonable chance of success.

First, there must be warning of incoming threats. The atmosphere is a less capricious-seeming medium than the sea, and the ranges of electronic sensing devices designed for warning can be measured in hundreds of miles. They are of two kinds: active, which to all intents and purposes means radar, mounted either ashore in ships or in airborne early warning (AEW) aircraft; and passive, which means electronic intercept devices that detect and find the direction of hostile radar emissions. Such emissions may themselves give evidence of hostile intent.[24] The advantage of taking sensors aloft has already been mentioned, and this can be particularly beneficial if low-flying aircraft or missiles are the principal threat. But, necessarily, such sensors are of less weight and power than can be carried in ships, and communication links between the sensor-carrying aircraft and the ships and fighter aircraft are also necessary.

In general, maritime fighter aircraft are not yet in the business of shooting down missiles, though the development of 'look-down shoot-down' against cruise missiles is bound sooner or later to have an application at sea. Even now, however, they are (if available) an important line of defence against low-flying attacking aircraft detected by AEW or by their own radars. However, a significant part of the air defence of ships still falls to the ships themselves.

They need, first, precisely to localise the incoming threat. Warning is not enough; generally speaking, two further sensing processes are needed, the first by a target indication sensor (usually radar) and the second by a tracking sensor (sometimes radar, sometimes the eye). The tracking sensor, once it acquires the target, needs to be kept on it long enough for a successful engagement to be carried out.

There are several ways of arranging this, and the details are not appropriate here; they are covered in the technical literature.[25] But one or two general points can be made. First, it is much easier technically to defend oneself than one's neighbour. A crossing target is notoriously difficult to hit; and even when one's neighbour is close, problems of co-ordination may arise.[26] Second, the closer an incoming missile (or aircraft) is the easier it is to hit, but conversely its momentum even when hit may be enough to allow it to hit you. Third, missiles at very low or very high elevations are unusually difficult targets for radar sensing; the former because of sea and weather returns, the latter because of the characteristics of most radar envelopes. Fourth, the times involved from first detection to impact may be very short — a matter of seconds. Fifth, ship motions must be fully compensated by stabilising equipment in sensors and mountings. Finally, channels of fire should be sufficient to cope with multiple attacks.

The consequence has in general been a perceived need for very sophisticated, agile systems depending on a great deal of automation. In all navies the emphasis has been on what are called 'hard-kill weapons', which aim actually to destroy the incoming missile before it comes within the lethal range of its own warhead. The American Standard and Sea Sparrow missiles, the British Sea Dart and Sea Wolf, the French Masurca and Crotale, the Soviet SA-N series, are all missiles of this type; nor are gun systems neglected, the Dutch-American Goalkeeper being a typical close-in air defence gun system.[27] Many such systems are available off the shelf to medium powers; the trade journals are full of advertisements for them.

There are also passive air defence systems. Electronic countermeasures (ECM) seek to disrupt or jam the target acquisition, control or homing systems of incoming threats. Potentially they are of great value in thickening the fog of war and imposing confusion and eventual attrition. However, they require intimate knowledge of the opposition's systems in order to be fully effective, and if operated with ignorance can even be counter-productive; no doubt some missile homing heads positively enjoy riding down the beam conveniently provided by a jammer.

Decoys are another matter. They aim, by being positioned far from the true target and making a large radar reflector or infra-red emitter, to seduce stupid missiles away from the target towards themselves. Such are the chaff-dispensing rockets and shells that are, again, frequently seen in the advertisement pages. There is no doubt that these can, given sufficient warning and released at the appropriate moment, be an effective attrition device; not only the Falklands operation, but the Yom Kippur War, showed several occasions when they were a significant factor in keeping hits to manageable levels.

Perhaps that is a suitable note on which to end this section. Even to the Americans, the idea of a 'leak-proof' air defence is scarcely credible. To a medium power it must be much more dubious. There will be casualties if a surface force comes under determined air attack, whether from aircraft or standoff missiles or both. Planners and operators (which includes politicians) between them must contrive to keep them to mangeable proportions.

Anti-submarine[28]

Anti-submarine warfare is dominated by the environment in which it takes place. The complexity of that environment and its broad effects have already been noted; in summary, the principal sensing medium, sound, is subject to vagaries and distortions that make position and manoeuvre (particularly in depth) essential elements of tactics, and measures to minimise the effects of physical laws essential elements of equipment.

Sensors in the antisubmarine field are overwhelmingly sonic. Before discussing these, however, it is worth remembering that submarines are sometimes forced, by either tactical or design constraints, to expose part of themselves above the surface, and if they do, airborne radars have a chance of spotting them. This is particularly germane to medium powers because the submarines most often having to expose themselves in this way are the conventional types — and of the submarine operating nations only five have any nuclear-powered ones at all. Moreover, the mere threat of detection by airborne radar has a unsettling effect on the hardiest submariner; there is probably a folk-memory of the effect the very long range Liberators had on the U-boat campaign in the spring of 1943, reinforced by many an exercise since.

But it is necessary to return to sonics, the principal sensing medium. Sonar is divided into two categories, active and passive. Active sonar is the emission of short pulses of sound in the hope that they will bounce back off a submarine and indicate range (by measurement of time difference between transmitted and received pulse) and bearing to the receiver. Passive sonar listens through arrays of hydrophones for sounds in the sea that are emitted by submarines, and can at any moment give only the direction of the sound, not its range. While some sonars have both active and passive modes, modern equipments are mostly single-mode though both active and passive may be available in the same platform. The power required by active sonar is considerable because of the attenuation of sound energy on its two-way journey; passive sonar does not emit power, but may need large and heavy arrays and processing equipment.

The anti-submarine process leading up to a successful attack on a submarine can be divided into the phases of detection, classification, localisation and tracking. All these can be carried out by a single sonar working from a single platform, but modern practice suggests that even against a single submarine a number of systems and platforms are likely to be involved. Thus initial detection might be made by a fixed bottom array (passive sonar), a general probability area passed to a patrolling aircraft, sonobuoys dropped, the contact classified and localised and then passed to a helicopter which would further localise and track by active sonar before attacking. This is only one possible sequence; numerous others can be envisaged involving submarines generally using passive sonar, and surface ships using either towed passive arrays or hull-mounted active sonars. And the initial detection may be made under much more tight and urgent operational conditions than the example given; for example, a detection following on from a submarine attack on ships in an escorted force or convoy.

It is not simply that anti-submarine warfare *offers* a wide variety of sensors and platforms from which to operate them; it *requires* such a mix for its successful prosecution against a widespread and diverse submarine threat. Even in the rigidly defined single scenario of transatlantic reinforcement devised as a determinant case for the Royal Navy in the NATO context, it was hotly (and rightly) argued that reliance could not be placed on barriers operated by submarines and long-range aircraft in the Greenland-Iceland-UK gaps, but that defence in depth was needed. In the more realistic circumstances of a threat handled with initiative and a conscious exploitation of any weakness, that need for comprehensive defence is even more apparent.

In the face of these huge demands, what may a medium power

do? First, perhaps, it ought to remind itself that only the superpowers operate very numerous, very sophisticated and predominantly nuclear-powered submarine forces, and that it cannot hope to tackle one of these for very long without either triggering help from a superpower ally or giving in. Against the more modest submarine forces of other medium or small powers, the problems may be more manageable so long as the areas of interest are firmly defined in the minds of the command and wild-goose chases avoided. It is not of very much comfort, in the field of sensors, that active anti-submarine operations are a function of higher level operations; for at low intensity, if opposing submarines are in the area, there will be powerful pressures from authority to keep tabs on them and this may demand considerable expenditure of resources. Sonobuoys in particular are non-recoverable items and can be spent rapidly in such circumstances; the towed array, a relative innovation, could turn out to be a most useful passive monitor in low intensity conflict.

Compared with the proliferation of sensing devices and platforms, anti-submarine weapons are not of great diversity. They are of two kinds; torpedoes and bombs.

Nearly all anti-submarine torpedoes now have self-homing acoustic terminal guidance. This may rely on noise emitted by the target submarine, or use echoes from the torpedo's own active transmissions, or a combination of both. In any case the effective range is only a few hundred yards. Therefore, the torpedo has to be placed within this distance of the target submarine.

This is done in the case of heavy submarine-carried torpedoes by wire guidance from the attacking submarine; in fact this guidance can be used up to the moment of impact but it seems generally agreed that for final precision the better mode is for the homing head to take over the final attack. In the case of light airborne torpedoes, either they must be parachute-dropped by aircraft within the circle in which they can hope to detect the target (the low, slow aircraft is preferable to the high fast one for this job) or transported to that circle by pilotless aircraft such as the British Ikara, the French Malafon, the American ASROC and the Soviet SS-N-14. Ships increasingly carry such torpedoes as anti-submarine weapons for urgent counter-attack.

Modern torpedoes are meant to be clever, and need to be if they are to be effective. There has always been some doubt about torpedo reliability and the writer will not labour it here, except to say that claims of very high single shot kill capability have usually proved to be false in the past.

Bombs are crude. They can be dropped or fired by most vehicles by air or sea, and (by means of air-flight weapons that swim out of torpedo tubes) by submarines too. The use of patterns of bombs to plaster the area of a submarine target may seem a very hit-or-miss operation and certainly disrupts subsequent tracking for a time if unsuccessful; but it has sunk many a submarine in the past, including the only one (the Pakistani submarine *Ghazi*) sunk while submerged since the Second World War. So far, no homing torpedo has sunk a submarine in action.

The point which it is necessary to make above all others is that anti-submarine warfare is a chancy, complex and imperfect business in a very difficult medium. In so far as anti-submarine capability can be made comprehensive, it demands massive resources. In this field, more than any other, it is desirable, as Cable says, to 'choose the threat'.[29] Medium powers cannot always do that; but they can do their best to assess the likely scale, level and reach of anti-submarine operations they need to be able to carry out on their own, and tailor their forces accordingly.

Anti-ship

'I would not put anything on the surface of the ocean', said Edward Teller, 'it's too good a target'.[30] Those words, written though they were in the nuclear context by a proponent of superpower, encapsulate the opinions of many people, lay and professional, who think about modern maritime warfare in general.

It is necessary first to say, therefore, that surface ships are not necessarily sitting ducks. They are without doubt increasingly difficult to conceal and indeed, from ocean reconnaissance satellites as operated by the USSR and USA, virtually cannot be concealed within those satellites' area of coverage. But, as has been shown, medium powers are not necessarily going to be preoccupied with superpower threats, nor are they necessarily going to be operating in areas of primary superpower interest, nor are their quarrels necessarily going to be in the ocean areas where the satellites do their job best. Finally, they may encounter deliberate superpower standoff; non-involvement up to a certain point is a logical stance for a superpower to take, and refusal to pass on satellite information a logical part of that stance.

Surface ships can also of course be detected, tracked and

sometimes identified by patrolling aircraft, submarines and ships. But the coverage and the accuracy of the information will be very much a function of the opponent's resources and the efficiency with which they are managed. The large British landing force did, with the aid of thick visibility, achieve tactical surprise in landing at San Carlos on 21 May 1982. One of the reasons for this was the age and poor material state of the Argentine reconnaissance aircraft.[31]

When all these caveats have been entered . . . the surface ship is a good target. Its radar echoing area is immense, and it tends to lie in an area of little radar clutter (particularly from airborne radars). It is visible to the naked eye from long distances. It tends to make a lot of noise that can be heard by submarines. It is a powerful infrared emitter. None of these characteristics can be eliminated, and measures to minimise them can be very expensive.

The means of attacking a surface ship are as diverse in detail as the means of detecting it, but basically they are three: missiles of ballistic trajectory, aerodynamic missiles and underwater weapons.

Ballistic missiles can range from shore-based, very long range systems to shells. The longer end of the scale need not perhaps concern a medium power too much. While there are indications in the writings of some Soviet authors that the Strategic Rocket Forces could be used in such a way against concentrations of surface ships, this is very much a general war function in the superpower versus superpower domain, and it is most unlikely that a medium power would wish or need to operate such systems itself. The short end of the scale poses a problem familiar to warship planners for at least a century: the provision of effective gun systems that can outrange an opponent. Because targets move during the shell's unguided flight, the question has always depended on accurate range, bearing, course and speed assessments at ranges that may reach out nearly to the horizon, and now that aerodynamic systems are available the 'outranging' problem may be insuperable. Nevertheless the ballistic trajectory, because it cannot be intercepted by the target, is an attractive one and has been completely forgone in very few medium-sized surface designs.[32] It is theoretically possible to design a maritime missile of composite type, powered and guided in its initial trajectory with a final ballistic phase; this would give over-the-horizon range and the advantages of terminal ballistic attack, but it would require a clever missile as well as good target acquisition.

Missiles which are aerodynamic throughout their trajectory

depend for hitting on terminal guidance, usually from an active radar homing head in the missile itself, sometimes on infra-red or other emissions from the target. The Soviet-designed Styx which sank the Israeli destroyer *Eilat* in 1967 is typical of such missiles of the first generation, the Exocet which came into such prominence during the Falklands conflict of the second. The difference between the generations lies in higher speed, sea-skimming flight and smaller size and radar echoing area. Further improvements are likely to be in the direction of longer range (a characteristic that is of limited value for ship-to-ship use unless intermediate target indication, probably from an aircraft, is available), more agility and preprogrammed evasive manoeuvres, and resistance to countermeasures. The size of many second-generation missiles allows them to be launched by aircraft as well as ships, and they can even swim out of submarine torpedo tubes, rise to the surface, ignite and go on their preset way. The American Harpoon and Tomahawk missiles (the latter of many hundreds of miles range) are designed for air, surface and submarine launch.

Given their effectiveness, relative ease of fitting and far from crippling cost, it is no wonder that anti-ship missiles are now fitted by 70 navies around the world.[33] Many such navies have nothing larger than fast attack craft on which to mount these, their reach can be considered as limited to local waters, and they may be short of both training and reserve ammunition; nevertheless the amount of high explosive that can be flying about in a dedicated way, in most of the seas of the world, is a moving consideration for a medium power.

Finally, underwater weapons have for over 100 years been a very serious menace to iron and steel hulled ships, which tend to sink when punctured underwater. 'Damn the torpedoes', said Farragut at Mobile in 1864; he meant mines, actually; but in fact both the mine and the torpedo have taken a heavier toll in ships sunk, since then, than any other maritime weapon.

This is in spite of the fact that powered torpedoes, particularly at the onset of conflict, have generally been of low reliability. At the start of the Second World War the German, British and American torpedoes all suffered very high failure rates; the frustration of the German U-boat captain who claimed to have heard three torpedoes clang against the side of the battleship *Nelson* with no subsequent explosion was typical. This does not mean, however, that medium powers can ignore the torpedo either as weapons for themselves, for use at the higher level, or as threats to their own forces. There is so far no hard-kill defence against torpedoes themselves; they are too difficult to detect and counter in the time available. The acoustic-headed sorts can be decoyed though many now have anti-decoy measures. In the torpedo more than most weapons the trade-offs between reliability and sophistication can be critical, and are worth very careful consideration by a medium power. The torpedoes that sank the *General Belgrano* were designed in the early 1920s; the torpedoes that the Argentine submarine *San Luis* claimed to have fired at a British frigate, without result, were of modern German design.[34]

Mines are also subject to increasing sophistication. Even in the Second World War they were of four sorts — contact, magnetic, acoustic and pressure; they now include a genus of listening mines which, when triggered by certain sorts of ship or submarine noise, release a torpedo or other device intended to blow up the intruder.[35] While the later weapons are untried in war, the earlier ones certainly are not. Nor are they expensive or particularly difficult to lay. A medium power concerned mainly with intrusions in its local waters, and not scrupulous about discrimination or identification, may well consider the declared minefield to be a cost-effective way of dealing with a short-reach problem. But the option is more likely to commend itself to medium powers with less than affluent populations; defensive mining of the coasts of Brittany or Cornwall is not, at first sight, likely to commend itself to local fishermen or yachtsmen.

However, though the mine may sometimes be a useful option for a medium power it is just as often to be thought of as a threat to be defended against. Such a threat may occur at any level of conflict, and any reach though, as a general rule, the lower the level of conflict, the less likely are an opponent's mines to be found in one's own home waters.

The business of neutralising mines is governed by the nature of mine mechanisms and by the nature of the sea environment. The variety of mechanisms demands effective means of detecting mines lying on the bottom and exploding them by remotely triggering their acoustic or magnetic mechanisms (this usually involves some automated vehicle operated by a parent unit outside lethal range); and of sweeping moored mines by cutting their wires. The sea environment imposes on the parent units the requirement to navigate precisely in often marginal weather and water conditions and strong tidal streams. Mine countermeasures craft, whether water, air or air-cushion borne, must have small acoustic and magnetic signatures as a safeguard against undue risk of themselves triggering the mines they seek to sweep.

To this clear problem of variety and sophistication (and consequently expense) there can be added the problem of numbers. A medium power with large and scattered maritime interests, taking counsel of its fears, may view a large-scale mine threat as insurmountable. And so, carried to the ultimate, it is; Britain would probably need upwards of 500 mine countermeasures craft to guarantee keeping all its ports open against such a threat. The only solution for a medium power is to play the percentages, and concentrate in its mine countermeasures on the more likely contingencies and conflict levels as well as its most vital points of vulnerability.

Anti-ship weaponry, then, can be presented in a variety of options, many of them potentially lethal and able to be launched from platforms above, on and beneath the sea. A criticism of some medium power maritime forces is that they are over-provided with such systems. This may sometimes be so; it is always tempting to buy gear that is impressive and relatively easy to operate rather than grapple with the more difficult air defence and anti-submarine problems. But there is a case for diversity in anti-ship weaponry. As has been demonstrated, the surface ship is the preferred unit for low-intensity operations; and it is in the interest of all in controlling such operations that the weaponry available against it should not consist just of killing weapons. Guns are useful in this context; as any gunner will tell you, you can miss all right with a gun. Equally, you can shift quickly to firing for effect if warning is unavailing. That sort of flexibility is not so readily available in missiles and it is not present at all in torpedoes or mines.

Command, Control and Communications

The co-ordination of operations towards a common aim is a principle of war taught in all Staff Colleges. In conflict it is the principal function of command, ranging from the high command at governmental level through Commanders-in-Chief to Commanders in the field or at sea.

The means of gathering information have been discussed already in this chapter; this section is concerned with the collation and exchange of such information and with the passing of orders and instructions.

First, the collation within a unit of information that has been gathered by its own sensors is now available to a high degree of speed and sophistication. Modern electronics enable even small units to process tactical information to the extent that is required for their mission. It is now feasible for any craft of, or larger than, the size of a heavy helicopter, fast attack craft or conventional submarine to be fitted with processing and display equipment that provides more than enough collated information, so that selection of what is necessary becomes important.

Similarly, when it comes to exchanging information the speed and capacity of modern communications, particularly if they are routed through satellites, make it imperative to be selective at some point in the process. This at present is an important staff function, and one on which commanders need to give well-judged directions; in the future it may employ intelligent machines with an ability, given expert programming, to sift the wheat from the chaff.[36]

Finally, the ability to pass orders and instructions rapidly from a commander to above-water subordinates is also available, given modern equipment and normal propagation conditions. Again, selection is likely to be a bigger problem than feasibility. There is still a problem when attempting to communicate with submarines at depth; measures to minimise it tend to result in loss of tactical flexibility for the submarine, and no major improvement is in prospect.[37]

The material problems confronting a medium power in the Command, Control and Communications field are therefore numerous and have to do really with how far they should strive to keep up with a fast-moving, highly complex technology that offers them more than they probably need at a price they may not be able to afford. Yet the fact that the technology is so fast-moving means that out-of-date equipments may be pitifully slow and inadequate when faced with modern ones. Selection at all levels — planning and operational — is the watchword, and given the enthusiasm with which such dazzling advances are often greeted may be difficult to control.

If the problem was simply a national one, it would be easier to handle. In alliance matters, however, communications make very great demands for commonality and comprehensiveness, and here too a medium power has to make a number of fine, and not always popular, judgements.[38]

Platforms and Systems

The dictum that 'in an age of precision-guided munitions of increasing range, the dominance of the platform on land, air and sea is sharply declining', is one of the most nonsensical and dangerous pseudo-scientific generalisations inflicted on the public for many a day.[39] It might have been thought that the 'unguided', aged torpedoes that — fired from a highly modern, sophisticated and expensive platform, HMS *Conqueror* — sank the *General Belgrano* might have sunk this silly slogan with it; yet, having been peddled before the Falklands conflict in an effort to justify naval reductions, it appears somehow to have survived.[40] Perhaps, indeed, the shards of it are worth preserving, not only as an example of the dangers of oversimplification but in order to provide, with the word 'dominance', a point of departure for discussion of the interaction of platforms and systems.

In one sense, a platform cannot dominate, and never could as such. It can move; and as Moineville has well shown, the ability to move and manoeuvre, by air and sea, increases.[41] It can provide common services — data acquisition and processing, power, ammunition, management — for the weapons it carries; and here too the facilities available can be constantly improved by the application of modern technology. It can, with its weapons, form a military entity, perceived as a piece of coercive power; what people see is the warship, the military aircraft. In this sense, perhaps, a platform can dominate: but by virtue of the weapons it carries and the facility it has in managing them.

Whether the weapons are primarily offensive or defensive in nature is not of such critical importance as might be thought. First, very few weapons are solely one or the other; the torpedo, a weapon of the offensive *par excellence*, may be fired by a submarine in mortal danger from surface-ship attack and be regarded as defensive on that occasion; the Sea Cat missile provided for close-in air defence can be used offensively against surface craft. Moreover, ability to withstand or repel an attack vastly improves a unit's ability to counter-attack successfully; in the Battle of the Philippine Sea, the American carriers had conducted the greater part of their 'turkey-shoot' against the Japanese attacking aircraft before turning to the offensive themselves.[42] Dominance in this tactical sense must be an outcome of the platform-weapon combination and its balance of offensive and defensive functions.

There is another sort of dominance, though, and this is in design. There is a rather simple view, and like most simplicities that are not the outcome of long and complex thinking it is a dangerous one, that warship design between the wars was a matter of building a good hull and machinery, and throwing armament, stores and men into it so that they lay where they fell. As analysis of destroyer design of those days shows, that was not a fair statement of the case, although accommodation certainly took rather lower priority than modern standards would tolerate.[43] In any event the myth persisted, and — certainly in the Royal Navy — resulted in the 1960s in rather too large a swing the other way, towards highly integrated units like the Type 42, where systems were interdependent to an extent that seems to have been unhealthy particularly in the case of HMS *Sheffield*.[44] The less tightly-designed ships of later decades may well strike the right balance in this respect at least; and, it is said, will also have a higher weapon density than previous ships.[45] Without doubt some foreign designs such as the *Madina* class frigates built in France for Saudi Arabia provide a variety of powerful conventional weapon systems on a hull of under 3,000 tonnes.[46]

Weapons do, then, exercise some dominance in the design of platforms, but it should not be so complete as to shut out other factors such as mobility, stoutness and sustainability. These factors are of course particularly important in forces of long reach, and it cannot be overstressed that however good a weapon may be, if it cannot be taken to where it is needed for a particular task, then for that task at any rate it is useless. Fast attack craft with missiles are very well in coastal waters, but have great difficulty crossing oceans and are unsustainable and unmaintainable, without elaborate shore facilities, when they get to the other side.

The relatively large and sea-kindly ship platform, then, cannot readily be forgone any more than the relatively large and air-kindly maritime aircraft platform. But modern technology does give opportunities for some flexibility and adaptation. The United States, oddly for a power with so many integral military resources, led investigations in the late 1960s and early 1970s in the ARAPAHO concept, an idea which takes a fast container ship and, using specially designed and prepared bolt-on equipment, converts it into a vessel carrying aircraft, troops or both. The same can be done for self-defence systems, possibly even for surface-to-surface missiles. Clearly such things are more comfortably done if they have been prepared in tranquillity, but they can be done at the rush and be effective as was shown in the South Atlantic campaign.[47] Medium powers may take some comfort from the experience but should not be deceived; the common services provided by a platform even for strapped-on systems must be sufficient to work the weapons so strapped on. There are all sorts of problems, technical and administrative, that have to be tackled with immense determination if the systems are to be effective.

Costs

All medium powers are likely to suffer severe cost constraint in their provision for maritime power. In a comprehensive description of a new programme for the Saudi Arabian navy, Bonsignore points out that it is likely to be unique because only that nation has the wealth to handle such an ambitious expansion.[48] Established medium powers of course have a more long-standing materiel and training base, but this brings financial commitments of its own, for the running costs of such an infrastructure have to be added to the capital costs of new development in order to arrive at the, no doubt daunting, bill.

Budgeting for national security is an immensely complex business not only in its details but in its fundamentals. The nation's wealth, as represented by its gross domestic product (GDP), is only one factor. The remaining factors can very broadly be represented as perception of the immediacy of threat; perception of the utility of various means of countering the threat; influence of allies; and national custom. All interact to result in unusually high, or unusually low, proportions of GDP spent on defence at any time. In 1982 Israel, for example, regarding herself as embattled, spent over 30 per cent; France and Germany, regarding themselves secured to some extent by alliance, 4 per cent; Brazil, with many development commitments and a low perceived threat, 0.8 per cent.[49] There is, without doubt, a very great degree of inertia and even tradition in defence budgets, but they can swing markedly over the years in response to variable factors.[50] Portugal's defence provision when she was attempting to hold on to her African colonies was over 10 per cent; now it is just over 3 per cent.

The complex working-out within a defence budget of allocations to the various elements of a force structure is not a matter for detailed discussion in this chapter. It is appropriate, though, to make one general point and to indicate some of the big spenders in the maritime field that may, by their very cost, negate or check certain strategic concepts.

The Ruthless Exponential

The phenomenon of the 6 Per Cent Multiplier is now almost ingrained in defence financial planning, in Britain at least. This is an empirical law which states that real cost growth from one generation of equipment to another is about 6 per cent per annum.[51] Thus, an air defence aircraft (let us say) which cost £10m. in 1975 will cost, before any allowance is made for inflation, £19m. in 1985. The assumption is that in each case the piece of equipment is typical of its generation.

The implications are obvious; if the real GDP does not rise at least at the same rate as the multiplier and the proportion of it allocated to defence does not rise, numbers are driven down in each generation of systems. In the older medium powers, this is exactly what has happened.

It must be stressed that this exponential law is an empirical one. It deals with equipments as they have emerged from the mill of staff requirements, development and manufacture. They are therefore the outcome not only of technologies but of threat perceptions, strategic and tactical concepts, and national economic and institutional practices. At this point, and in order not to succumb to such an apparently damaging law, it is permissible to look in quite another way at the ruthless exponential.

For any equipment, figures of merit can be established. For a ship, for example, there are measurable quantitities such as range, speed, range and weight of weapons, data acquisition, communications; to these can even be added, if one has the courage, strength, sustainability, impressiveness, the more imponderable and unquantifiable characteristics. They add up to an overall assessment of performance. When looked at against cost, performance increases but not in a linear way; it follows an exponential curve (see Figure 11.1).

This is because, in broad terms, extra performance in any field demands beyond a certain point greatly increased effort, and this is just as much so in design and development (the extra 10 per cent of designed range in an active sonar demanding an extra 50 per cent power) as in operation (the extra fuel consumed in travelling flat out).

Figure 11.1: Weapon Systems: Relation of Performance to Costs

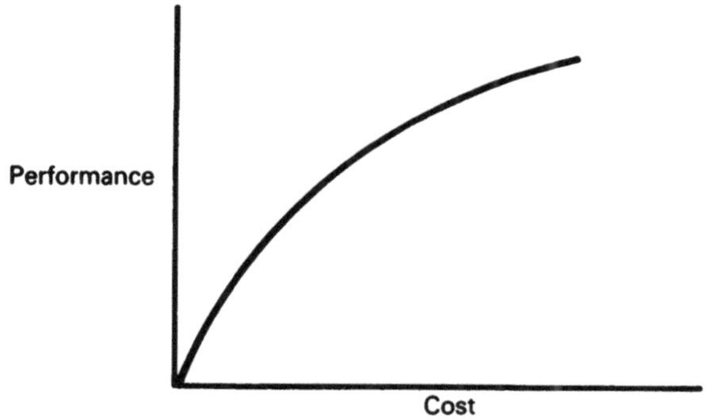

But when expressed in terms of effectiveness against threat or opposition, the curve looks different. At the lower levels of effectiveness, however pleasantly cheap it appears, a unit may be fatally outranged, unsustainable, or even uncomfortable in a seaway to the extent of incapacitating its equipment or crew. When such parameters are taken into account the curve tends to look like this:

Figure 11.2: Weapon Systems: Relation of Cost to Effectiveness

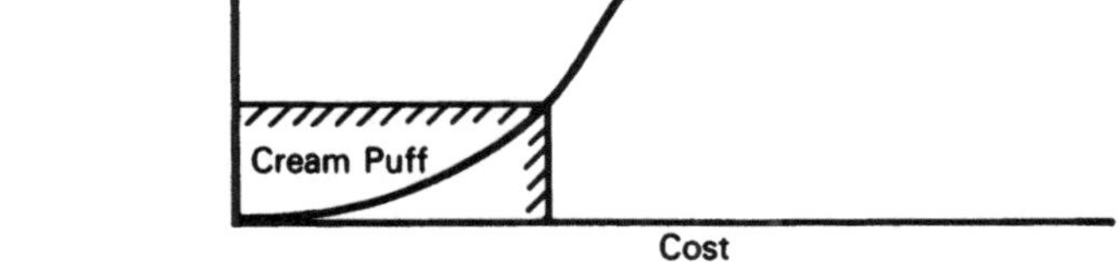

The area at the bottom end may be called cream-puff; the units look all right but a serious threat can brush them aside. At the top end, however, remains an area called gold-plate; up here there is very little extra chance of success against opposition, for a high extra cost outlay.

It is at least arguable that medium powers, particularly if for alliance or other reasons they ape superpowers, are likely to end up at the gold-plated end of the exponential. Only the coolest appraisal of what maritime forces are really there to do, and tailoring their cost and effectiveness to that job, will keep them out of that dangerous area — and perhaps at the same time break the tyranny of the 6 per cent multiplier.

The Big Spenders

But however rigorous is the planning and the cost-control process, some maritime activities are bound to be big spenders and will require constant scrutiny by a medium power, first as to their necessity and then as to their scale.

First, nuclear development, both as to weaponry and as to power plants, demands tremendous initial outlay in both materiel and intellectual resources. Once a programme is on stream it may be tolerable, but this does not cushion the early shock. Moreover, nuclear technology is not readily transferable and the political as well as the financial cost is likely to be high.

Second, the development of any radically new vehicle shape, particularly that part of development that covers the transition from supertoy to operational vessel or aircraft, is an extremely expensive process. Had money been thrown at the hovercraft in sufficient quantity, a useful war role might have been found for it; but so far even for mine countermeasures, to which it seems well suited, no country has adopted it. The much more potentially versatile and ocean-going Small Water Plane Area Twin Hull (SWATH) ship requires innovation of mind-boggling scope; if it is the maritime unit of the twenty-first century, it will be a superpower that first produces it.[52] Granted that there have been some notable major innovations since the Second World War that originated in medium powers — the most notable, probably, the VSTOL aircraft that became the Sea Harrier — there is less and less money about to make similar developments, and any that are sanctioned must have a clearly-perceived part in a future force structure. The Harrier had no such status for years; only its private enterprise backers preserved it.

This was ironic, for the third big spender in maritime force structures is the large fast platform for operating conventional fixed-wing combat aircraft; and it was the cancellation on cost grounds of the British version of such ships that brought the Harrier into its own as a maritime aircraft. The 'big carrier' is indeed an extremely costly ship, having to provide very extensive and sophisticated services for its aircraft; while small carriers, which most medium powers manage still to operate, can accommodate few and generally old-fashioned aircraft.

Fourth among the big-spenders is a comprehensive, autonomous ocean anti-submarine capability. It demands such a diversity of assets, plus high levels of knowledge and training, that high cost is inevitable. There are no short cuts in this field; attrition is the pattern, and defence in depth the only method that can give it successful meaning.[53]

Fifth is the capacity to defend against large scale and near-simultaneous missile attack on surface ships. Granted that casualties in higher-level operations have to be accepted, and that leak-proof defences are not sought because they are not feasible, enough ships must remain operational to achieve the aim, and survival against a large scale threat cannot be bought on the cheap.

Finally, any excursion into space, except with the crudest kind of ballistic missile, is an extremely expensive venture.[54] Medium powers have not for decades embarked on such projects singly; Britain uses US rockets to put her communication satellites in orbit, France collaborates with other European states in the ESRO as in almost no other project, Japan and Australia buy their various ways into American facilities.

Even for a medium power seeking stringently to set limits to its maritime autonomy by all the conceptual tests that have been suggested — by assessments of the rival claims of deterrence, economic and diplomatic measures, sea use and sea denial, levels of conflict and reach — the list of big spenders may be a daunting one. How to keep it within manageable bounds is one of the themes of the next chapter.

Notes

1. A. D. Couper, 'The Shipping Industry' in G. Till (ed.), *The Future of British Sea Power* (Macmillan, London, 1984), p. 58.
2. R. J. Daniel, 'The British Shipbuilding Industry' in ibid., p. 190; and Admiral Sir Anthony Griffin, 'Weapons and Platforms', ibid., p. 223.
3. J. Cable, *Gunboat Diplomacy* (Macmillan, London, 1981), p. 125.
4. Director of Public Relations (Navy) *Broadsheets* (HMSO), 1983, p. 22 and 1984, p. 14.
5. H. Moineville, *Naval Warfare Today and Tomorrow* (Blackwell, Oxford, 1983), p. 63.

6. J. R. Hill, *Anti-Submarine Warfare* (Ian Allan, Shepperton, 1985), p. 41.
7. D. K. Brown RCNC, giving to the author information based on Institute of Naval Medicine and the US Navy, suggests that severe degradation occurs at sea state 6, corresponding to wind force 7 on the Beaufort scale. This is disputed by some sea officers who consider the threshold to be higher. That there is a threshold, however, is not doubted.
8. For the case for the 'Short Fat Frigate' see D. Giles, 'Want of Frigates', *Naval Forces*, No. 2 (1984), p. 58.
9. R. J. Urick, *Sound Propagation in the Sea* (DARPA, Washington, 1979), Chapters 3 and 5; Kosta Tsipis in *The Future of the Sea-Based Deterrent* (MIT Press, Cambridge, Mass., 1973), p. 174.
10. Ships of the British Task Force fired 8,000 rounds of ammunition in Naval Gunfire Support (shore bombardment) alone in the Falklands campaign: Cmnd. 8758, para 235b.
11. For an unusually gloomy view see *Strategic Survey, 1982–83* (IISS, London), pp. 128–33; for a more sanguine one, G. Till, *Maritime Strategy and the Nuclear Age* (Macmillan, London, 1984), p. 258.
12. J. Ethell and A. Price, *Air War South Atlantic* (Sidgwick and Jackson, London, 1983), p. 103.
13. Ibid., p. 75.
14. Cmnd. 8758, para 222.
15. *Jane's All the World's Aircraft 1984–85* (Jane's, London, 1984), p. 296.
16. Norman Friedman, *Submarine Design and Development* (Conway Maritime Press, London, 1984), Chapter 2.
17. Hill, *Anti-Submarine Warfare*, pp. 34–6.
18. Friedman, *Submarine Design and Development*, pp. 134–40.
19. P. Lacoste, *Stratégie Navale* (Nathan, Paris, 1981), p. 46.
20. Hill, *Anti-Submarine Warfare*, p. 91, Table 11.
21. Jonathan Crane, *Submarine* (BBC, 1984), pp. 31–2, describes a nuclear-powered fleet submarine's uncertainty of the position of surface forces under exercise conditions.
22. Data from *The Military Balance, 1984–85* (IISS, London), p. 135.
23. Hill, *Anti-Submarine Warfare*, p. 29.
24. D. P. O'Connell, *The Influence of Law on Sea Power* (Manchester University Press, Manchester, 1975), p. 82.
25. *Jane's Weapon Systems 1984–85* (Jane's, London, 1984), pp. 131–57; *Combat Fleets of the World, 1984/85, passim*.
26. Ethell and Price in *Air War South Atlantic*, p. 145, describe how HMS *Broadsword*, equipped with Sea Wolf and stationed as a 'minder' to HMS *Coventry*, was frustrated from defensively firing her missiles by a manoeuvre from *Coventry* which caused the missile control radar to break lock.
27. *The Military Balance 1984–85*, pp. 7–8, 20, 33, 38.
28. For a more comprehensive treatment of this subject see Hill, *Anti-Submarine Warfare*, Chapters 3 and 4.
29. J. Cable, *Britain's Naval Future* (Naval Institute Press, Annapolis, 1983), p. 105.
30. Edward Teller, 'The Nature of Nuclear Warfare', in *US Air Force Magazine*, January 1957.
31. Ethell and Price, *Air War South Atlantic*, p. 94.
32. The British Type 22 frigate was designed with no medium-range gun, but the third batch — Nos. 11 and 12 — will carry a 4.5-inch gun mounting. All other European designs — The Dutch *Kortenaer*, the German MEKO and the Italian *Maestrale* — have medium-calibre guns.
33. *The Military Balance, 1984–85*.

34. Ethell and Price, *Air War South Atlantic*, p. 74.
35. Ted Hooton, 'Naval Mines', *Military Technology*, No. 9/84, pp. 27–33.
36. M. Gerencser and R. Smetek, 'Artificial Intelligence on the Battlefield', *Military Technology*, No. 6/84, p. 86.
37. This is the generally-held view and in the author's opinion the correct one. However, some commentators predict a great improvement through unconventional systems: see Roland J. Starkey Jr, 'The Renaissance in Submarine Communications', *Military Electronics*, April 1981, p. 44.
38. J. M. Sochaczewski, 'The Role of Communications in NATO', *Military Technology*, No. 6/84, pp. 150–6.
39. British Atlantic Committee, *Diminishing the Nuclear Threat* (London, 1984), p. 33.
40. Cmnd. 8288, para 5.
41. Moineville, *Naval Warfare Today and Tomorrow*, pp. 80–1.
42. S. W. Roskill, *The War at Sea*, Vol. III, Part II (HMSO, London, 1961), pp. 196–7.
43. Edgar J. March, *British Destroyers* (Seeley Service, London, 1966), pp. 267, 398, 467, outlines the progression to more precise design particularly of accommodation spaces.
44. M. Hastings and S. Jenkins, *The Battle for the Falklands* (Michael Joseph, London, 1983), pp. 154–5.
45. Sir Ronald Mason, 'Problems of Fleet Balance' in *The Future of British Sea Power* (ed. Till), p. 216.
46. Ezio Bonsignore, 'The *Madina*-Class Frigates', *Military Technology*, No. 1/85, p. 30.
47. Cmnd. 8758, para 308.
48. Bonsignore, 'The *Madina*-Class Frigates', p. 30.
49. *The Military Balance, 1984–85*, pp. 140–2.
50. Sir Frank Cooper, 'Economic Constraints in Britain's Defence Planning' in *The Future of British Sea Power* (ed. Till), p. 172.
51. See, for example, Cooper, 'Economic Constraints', p. 178; J. R. Hill, 'Apocalypse When?' RUSI, *Journal*, June 1981, p. 63.
52. Captain S. E. Veazey, 'New Shape in Ships', US Naval Institute, *Proceedings*, February 1985, p. 40.
53. Hill, *Anti-Submarine Warfare*, pp. 108 and 110.
54. Norman Friedman, 'Real-Time Ocean Surveillance', *Military Technology*, No. 9/84, pp. 76–81.

PART THREE

AVAILABLE STRATEGIES

12 PLANNING, ORGANISATION AND DEPLOYMENT

Planning for maritime power, in the writer's experience — which spanned some 15 years — is a complex, iterative, often frustrating and always absorbing process. As Moineville has well observed, the problems seem greatest for countries 'in an intermediate situation, where they certainly cannot be prepared for all events but where they have, all the same, enough resources to have options to choose from' — in other words, the medium powers.[1] Superpowers and small powers might not agree; they have problems of their own; medium powers, in this book at least, must be allowed their moment of self-pity.

The planning process is not tidy, and attempts to tidy it up by analysis can be dangerously misleading. Some sort of description of the normal process must be attempted, however; it may look like and indeed is an idealised scheme, but it is something against which the all too frequent aberrations can be set.

A medium maritime power will already, at any given moment, have a maritime power structure. There will be ships, ports, fisheries, naval and air forces. Therefore, the process of planning will not be end-stopped but cyclic. Where one enters the cycle will depend on one's particular interest and preoccupation; but since this book began with national characteristics and interests, that is no bad place for it to be entered here.

The idealised process then goes through the stages shown in Figure 12.1. At a point near the start, the notion of 'expected developments' is included; it must be stressed that planning ought to take account of a period for many years ahead. The mismatch between (for example) the scientists' futuristic visions, the intelligence officers' cautious predictions and the foreign office officials' day-to-day preoccupations must be minimised as far as is possible.

After that point, every element of the diagram into which an arrow points represents an area for deep assessment *and decision* by government. It is safe to say that in most medium powers the right-hand side of the diagram is generally neglected; the reluctance of the British establishment to deal with these matters has been

Figure 12.1: The Planning Process

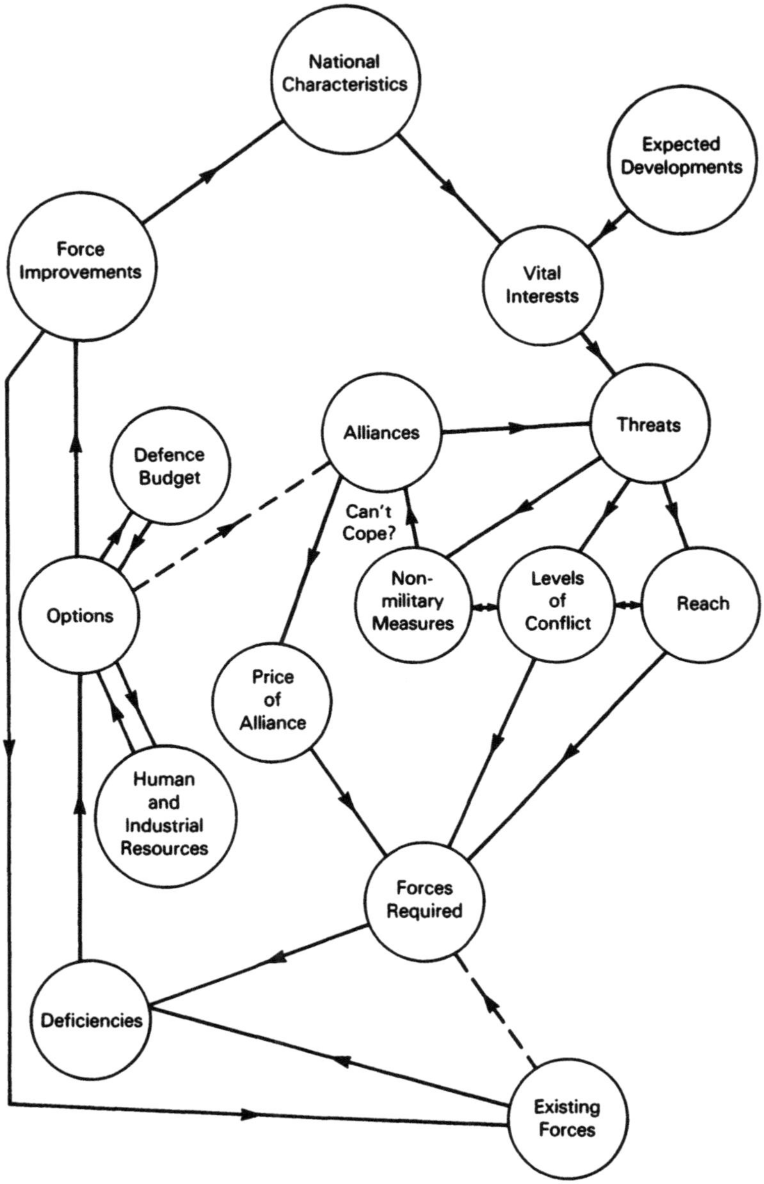

mentioned all too often above, and all the indications from India, Brazil and even Japan are similar. Israel, having for more than two decades had a strategy that well matched its appallingly difficult security problems, appeared in the early 1980s to have made, for short-term reasons, seriously mistaken changes in both the structure and employment of its forces. France has a better record, as is suggested not only by the writing of individuals but by the institution of a Ministry for the Sea. Australia, too, seems to agonise quite deeply over the fundamentals of maritime defence, and indeed could be criticised for neglecting the left-hand side of the diagram rather than the right.[2]

In fact, the right-hand side of the diagram follows very largely the pattern of this book, with the observation that the threats here shown are strategic threats to vital interests and not the specific technical threats beloved of materiel planners. Because of the long lead times involved in the development of most equipments, performance against a specific, known, existing threat is not the best of criteria. Development on those lines is likely to result in at best inflexible, at worst obsolete, new equipments. Like scenarios, specific threats are useful tests but are not a basis for planning.

To return to strategic threats, these when considered against vital interests generate one of the most critical decision-areas in maritime force planning: level of conflict and reach. Since no one wants to fight unnecessarily, alternative non-military methods of coping with threats stand to be considered here, and interact constantly with the military measures. A powerful trading position, strong linguistic and cultural links, overseas aid and political bargaining may all serve either to keep threat to manageable proportions by themselves, or greatly to reduce requirements for level of operation. For example, France does not appear to plan for anything but low-intensity operations in the Indian Ocean on the grounds that the interaction there of interests, threats and non-military measures makes higher-level operations an unlikely contingency. It goes without saying that there is an element of risk in such an assessment, and the fact that French forces of sufficient reach and higher-level capacity could probably be put together in emergency is significant.

There will in any case for most medium powers be areas beyond their economic zones where non-military measures cannot be relied upon and where provision for operations up to the higher level is necessary. Here the question of reach becomes a critical element of force planning. India, for example, has to judge how far her desired influence should extend. The Indian Ocean is much larger than charts drawn on Mercator's projection suggest, and the ability to operate at its peripheries, even from India's central position, demands a reach of some 2,000 miles. Yet, as is clear from much Indian writing by no means all of which is from naval officers, India regards her vital security interests as extending all over that Ocean.[3] Japan's agonising over 'defending the shipping lanes' up to 1,000 miles from her shores is another typical example of the consideration of reach in the planning process.

Discussion at this stage of planning is a complex polyphony and decisive thinking is needed to achieve satisfactory resolutions. Where the consideration of only medium-power threats is concerned, indeed, resolutions of the problems may look possible and it is permissible to clench one's teeth and go on to the next stage. But a discordant note is almost always introduced by a superpower threat.

Here a medium power may quickly conclude that it cannot cope at all; or it may assess that it can make a stand at low intensity if the stakes are high enough; or it may be bold enough to decide that, *in extremis*, it must be prepared for independent action at the higher level. It is, however, constantly confronted by the superpower's capacity for escalation beyond any which it could itself manage, and at some stage therefore of the vast majority of confrontations with superpower it will be in a position where it cannot cope.

Alliance and Its Price

Therefore, alliances; and specifically superpower alliances. Once these are entered into they will change the threat-pattern and an iterative process begins, because levels-of-conflict and reach requirements have to be looked at again. It is quite easy to turn this into a closed cycle, so that threats are perceived to have been entirely negated by the alliance and strategic planning is replaced by jog-along complacency. That ought not to happen, for it is more than likely that the ally will not be interested in all the threats that concern the medium power.

There is one other effect of alliances, and that is their price. No ally commits himself out of pure altruism. Even the coincidence of interests and culture, if it exists, may not be regarded as enough to justify a disproportionate commitment by the more powerful to the less. The medium power therefore must be able to offer some kind of price.

This may be strategic position. Britain's place on the Eastern side of the Atlantic, distanced alike from the USA and possible front lines in Scandinavia and Germany, is of great strategic value to the USA and the alliance it leads. The same goes for France, particularly in its possession of the Brittany ports (which are further from the Soviet Union than are Britain's) and land communications with Europe. Linked with strategic position may be base, communication or intelligence facilities; one of Australia's major contributions to the ANZUS alliance is a Very Low Frequency radio transmitting station that can communicate with American submarines, a facility opposed by some Australians on the ground that it might make Australia a nuclear target.[4] A third kind of price may consist of resources, whether in skills or raw materials, that can be provided by the medium power. Even if the market price still obtains, security of supply of such resources may make a superpower seek or preserve alliance where otherwise it would not. Britain's relationships with the Baltic States in the eighteenth century were based on mast-and-spar supply; the USA's cultivation of Saudi Arabia in the twentieth on oil. The record suggests that understandings rather than formal alliances are more usual in such circumstances.

Finally, the price of alliance may be the contribution by a medium-power ally of forces: either dedicated to the alliance where they would normally be under national control, or specially provided for alliance purposes where they would not be needed for national tasks. The German destroyer force since the Second World War is an example of both; even when German maritime defence policy was based entirely on the battle for the Baltic exits, there were some ocean-going ships because NATO was an oceanic alliance and it was thought appropriate that a major member like Germany should make some blue-water contribution. Their dedication to NATO tasks made for regular participation in the Standing Naval Force Atlantic. However, the provision of such forces, as a price for alliance, can be overdone; as O'Neill rightly said, 'it is Australia rather than ANZUS which is important in American eyes'.[5]

Force Requirements

Maritime force requirements for the medium power, then, proceed along two lines: national needs, the forces required by levels-of-conflict and reach considerations for tasks which — even taking alliances into account — must be nationally tackled; and the price of alliance, which must take into account all other tradeworthy assets as well as the forces the alliance may demand.

The interweaving of these two strands becomes a statement of the forces required. Clearly, even at this stage some account must be taken of the forces that already exist. They were spacious days indeed when Fisher was able to roar 'Scrap the Lot' and embark on his dedicated Dreadnought fleet; and not only was more money then available, lead times were much shorter. At this end of the twentieth century, replacement of one kind of maritime force by another that is radically different is bound to be a matter of half a decade at least and usually much more.

This is no excuse for inertia, however; there is a vast difference between deliberate and purposeful movement on the one hand, and planning drift on the other. Size-and-shape studies are a frequent phenomenon in defence ministries and institutions of learning; what is important is that they should stem from the roots of strategy and not cling to its branches.

The first consideration of medium-power maritime force planning is likely to be that closest to home: the protection of the territorial integrity of the state and good order in the waters round its shores. Much of this can be provided by constabulary forces optimised at most to low intensity operations: shore-based aircraft of relatively low speed and cost but well-equipped with surveillance and communications gear, weatherly but not necessarily ocean-spanning surface craft with mostly light, discriminating armaments of the surface-to-surface type, and the necessary base support and command facilities to make them effective. The other maritime services of the state — survey, navigational warning, traffic routeing, buoyage, port approach control, all comprehended in the now-modish phrase Vessel Traffic Services (VTS) — form part of what ought to be a well-ordered whole, and it goes without saying that the better-ordered it is, the less chance there will be for the state's ill-wishers, whether on a small or massive scale, to violate its territorial integrity without its full knowledge and the opportunity for reaction.

Whether such order is to be achieved by a centrally controlled service such as, in many ways, the US Coast Guard and the Japanese Maritime Safety Agency are, or whether it is to be done by a diffuse and empirical organisation such as Britain's, is partly a matter of national history and character. The seams between the various functions are going to exist anyhow, and how they are sewn does not in practice seem to matter all that much.

In either case one thing is sure. There must be cover in case serious threats do arise. In some cases, for example danger to offshore installations from terrorists, quick-reaction forces of specially-trained and probably helicopter-borne troops are needed. In others, such as invasion by surface means, shore-based fixed-wing aircraft may be an important form of cover, as may surface warships with missile armament. Mines can be an extremely useful and inexpensive means of defending coastal areas and are a useful deterrent in periods of tension. Coastal submarines of small size and conventional power plant are in theory a highly effective form of cover against major invasion forces, and the survival of the *San Luis* in the Falklands operation — in spite of her lack of positive success against the British Task Force — will have encouraged proponents of the submarine in this role.

For any medium power with a substantial coastline and economic zone, then, there is an irreducible requirement for constabulary air and surface forces, linked with a well co-ordinated VTS organisation and backed by cover including more powerful air and surface forces and probably quick-reacting troop cadres, coastal submarines and mines. The majority of such forces should have a reach at least to the limits of the economic zone — not such an easy matter in the case of vast countries such as Australia and Brazil, with relatively few bases on a very long coastline.

If this was the whole requirement, probably most medium maritime powers could cope. But as has been shown, their interests generally extend far beyond the 200-mile limit of the economic zone and here the really big spenders begin to be part of the force requirements.

The first consideration, clearly, is to what level of conflict the medium power is to be prepared to go and against what kind of opposition. The forces needed to conduct no more than low intensity operations against small powers or unsophisticated medium powers — with the clear implication that if outfaced they either withdraw or rely on an ally to continue the struggle — need be no more than frigate-sized, with organic helicopters and simple anti-submarine equipment. Cover, by definition, comes from the ally and not from national forces.

This is not a common general proposition for a medium power to accept, though there may be some regions or commitments — for example, Britain in Hong Kong — where it is the only sensible policy. It is usually unacceptable as a general rule simply because alliances cannot be relied upon to operate at such a low level of conflict. The outcome has to be forces that are capable of operating on their own at the higher level. Here at once the questions of sea use, sea denial and reach that have become so familiar in this book are applied to the options for force structure. Sea use is likely to be at the heart of what a medium power wants to do at considerable distances from its shores, and as has been shown it demands, at the higher level of operations, the ability to defend against attack from above and beneath the surface.

Above-water defences may include only shipboard weapons and countermeasures, but aircraft add a tremendous increment for surveillance, warning and attrition of attackers and a medium power contemplating operations at the higher level, even against another medium power, is likely to view them as a requirement. To a reach of several hundred miles from home bases this requirement can be met by shore-based aircraft so long as they are appropriately equipped and trained and their command and tasking organisations are responsive to maritime needs. Beyond that reach — which may for surveillance aircraft be extended to a thousand miles or more — the air component must operate either organically from ships or from advanced shore bases. The latter are few and far between now, and expensive both politically and financially to maintain; moreover, they cannot be moved, so their reach is fixed and inflexible. The ship basing of these assets is, therefore, more and more the preferred mode, and is helped by the development of both the VSTOL and ARAPAHO concepts. These, described above, give opportunities for keeping within bounds the very considerable expense of providing ship platforms for sea-based combat aircraft.

It must not be forgotten however that even if a force is aircraft-equipped very considerable resources will also be needed to provide further lines of defence against above-water threat. Here, almost certainly, a medium power will regard the most sophisticated systems, such as the United States designed AEGIS, as beyond its means. The emphasis will be on self-defensive measures, both hard-kill and decoy particularly against missiles; and there will be great applause for the first inventor of an easily strapped-on, cheap close-in weapon system capable of defending its host unit against missile attack. The possibilities include anti-missile missiles, electronic means, chaff decoys and in the future even high energy lasers.[6] All, however, to have a chance of defeating low-flying missiles, must be able to detect and usually to acquire their targets quickly and accurately, and it is often in this area rather than in the business end of the systems that the expense is greatest.

Above-water defence can also be taken to comprehend attack at source against surface-to-surface missile carriers, and here the situation may be a trifle rosier for the medium power — particularly if it has made a decision in favour of organic combat aircraft. These are a longish-range counter-surface force; closer in, shipborne surface-to-surface missiles, even if they do not outrange the opposition, can if allied to good surveillance and tactical control be a useful counter. Finally, the possession by a medium power of submarines probably gives it the most powerful anti-surface asset of all, though the difficulties of information and control across the interface must never be minimised and submarines as a sole means of countering surface threats are unlikely to be sufficient.

If the above-water means of preserving sea use are complex, the underwater means are unfortunately no less so. It has already been suggested that there is no way of destroying torpedoes once fired, although decoys may be effective; and a submarine-launched airflight missile is essentially an air defence problem. For the rest, defence against underwater threats is a matter of neutralising submarines themselves.

Again, out to a thousand miles or so from its shores a medium power may deploy shore-based air assets and, in the form of large, long-endurance and well-equipped aircraft, these are highly important. They may operate in close co-operation with surface forces, or independently, or, if satisfactory communication arrangements are feasible, with submarines. They are not only formidable search and attack units but also exercise a powerful deterrent to free use of the surface by opposing submarines. However, a glance at even a 1,000-mile circle with a few typical long-range maritime patrol areas superimposed indicates the scale of cover that a limited number of such aircraft can provide.[7]

Inevitably other assets are needed, and if they are to be effective, they must be disposed in order to focus the activities of opposing submarines, to complicate their tactical problems to the maximum extent and to impose on them the need to expose themselves to detection. This is the classic method of convoy or the defended force, and still has validity even in the day of the towed array, the anti-submarine helicopter and the nuclear-powered submarine.[8]

It may be in this field of anti-submarine warfare that a medium power has most difficulty in working out its force structure. First, will it need to make provision for fighting against nuclear-powered submarines at all? While modern conventional boats, with their weapons, make potent systems and are difficult to detect because of their quietness, they are less of a recurrent menace than nuclear boats, and probably need a lower scale of counter. It is also a rather different kind of counter, with more emphasis on radar and less on passive sonar and ASW submarines. If it is possible for a medium power to choose its threat, then savings in this field may be possible. But the risk is considerable; nuclear power plants for submarines may be coming within the reach of more states in the next couple of decades. It is also at this point that there can be a mismatch between national and alliance requirements; it is most acute at present in the case of Britain, which has accepted a responsibility for a very high level of ASW sophistication, on alliance grounds, which is probably an over-provision for national purposes.[9]

The difficulty is of course compounded by the fact that long-range maritime patrol may not be available over the full required reach. This is a difficulty that confronts even the world's greatest maritime alliance in the recesses of the ocean; American carrier battle groups may provide enough organic air assets to look after themselves but this cannot extend to the full protection of shipping. *A fortiori* this applies to a medium power, and inevitably may set very severe limits to what it can try to do in the way of shipping protection against submarines at distances far from its shores. The case is not hopeless, particularly against less than first-rate opposition; but its solution is likely to be partial, limited and by no means risk-free.

A special element of higher-level forces, and one which becomes more special and more demanding as reach increases, is the ability to land amphibious troops. While this use of sea power is as old as the sea itself — Alkibiades' campaign against Syracuse was nothing if not an amphibious operation — it retained a remarkably extempore character until the Second World War. It then became correspondingly stylised, to the extent that after the war its chief exponents, the United States Marine Corps, invented a new name for it ('the projection of power ashore', which promptly became somewhat muddied by its upward extension into strategic deterrence from the sea) and founded a permanent amphibious establishment of great size and cost.

The questions before a medium power are: first, whether it needs such forces; second, their reach if needed; and third, the degree to which they can rely on improvisation.

In a recent study, taking particular account of Angola, Ethiopia, Chad and Afghanistan, Neil Macfarlane questions the long-term advantages of military intervention.[10] He accepts, however, that pinching-out operations like that of the United States in Grenada are more likely to achieve success.[11] Cable makes the same point; in his commentary on 'island-grabbing' in the 1970s he observes that all the amphibious operations concerned were 'definitive' in nature.[12] It is noticeable that operations of this kind seem to occur either across land frontiers (as for instance in the Indian annexation of Goa) or by sea. Intervention-by-invitation, however, may take place in a more administrative way and on a small scale can often be managed by air-lifted troops alone.

When all these considerations are set against a medium power's interests, it may well be found that hard and fast commitments and justifications are few and far between. Yet — certainly in the case of post-imperial powers — they can be potentially humiliating if not honoured.

A medium power's need for long-reach, assault-capable amphibious forces, then, is likely to be a matter for considerable internal argument. The cost of standing forces of this type, the possibility of using alternative deterrent or garrison measures, the real value of the assets under threat or the potential gains to be made, are all important factors. Many states compromise; some like Greece have landing craft but no specially-trained marines.[13] In general the pattern is a limited force of trained amphibious troops and some specialised vessels of limited reach. These may be adequate for set-piece operations against light opposition. The ability to conduct successful operations at long distances from home demands higher levels of training, more expensive equipment and probably improvisation too. If the choice for resource allocation has to fall between the provision of trained, seasoned and resourceful troops on the one hand and excellent specialised equipment on the other, the wise medium power will go for the former. Some risk must be taken somewhere.

Risk is a good word with which to end this brief discussion of operational force structures for the medium power at the higher level. The risk of the wrong choices having been made in planning when the balloon does go up; the risk of systems not working as well, in the event, as advertised; the risk of casualties, without which no operation of war ought to be contemplated; the risk of alliances not being triggered when their help is needed; all these need constant thought.

One way in which some risk-limitation can be sought, and at costs that are not excessive, is in the provision of logistic reach. This is not particularly difficult to provide on a permanent basis — twelve navies have at least two ocean-going replenishment tankers[14] — nor is augmentation of it too difficult to improvise, as the Russians showed in the early 1960s when they started the Mediterranean deployments and as did Argentina in 1982.[15] The systematic provision of ammunition and solid stores is more difficult but, again, *ad hoc* arrangements have been made to work. The corollary of such arrangements is of course that there must be enough ships of the national flag to be taken up from trade in emergency. But, in general, the provision of seaborne logistics may well be an area where the top level of sophistication begins to hit the gold-plated end of the effectiveness exponential.

Finally, the medium power must, however reluctantly, consider the question of general war. First, it must decide how far its general purpose forces should be equipped and fitted to cope with such a struggle, involving as it does the full engagement of the superpower and likely escalation to the general use of nuclear weapons. The ability to survive in such a war demands a number of expensive qualities that are not necessarily required at lower levels: the ability to steam through fallout clouds, to decontaminate, to withstand electromagnetic pulse effects, to be proof against underwater shock much greater than high explosive demands. The ability even to put up a fight demands air defence and anti-submarine assets of great scope, range and weight. Naturally, the fact that a superpower is bound to be engaged on one's own side will ensure that not all the enemy fire comes down upon the medium power; nevertheless, it is likely to be of disproportionate scale.

The principles put forward in this book imply that only certain medium power maritime forces should pay this particular price of alliance. Units optimised to low-intensity operations, and even to the general run of higher level operations, should not necessarily be of the quality required to fight and survive in general war. There will in fact be many useful jobs they can do even in such a conflict, but in the face of the ultimate menace they must — like so many other elements of the national infrastructure — take their chance.

Certain units, however, are intrinsically suitable for general war operations and can and do form a most important part of allied forces in them — notably nuclear-powered submarines and long-range maritime patrol aircraft so long as their bases last.

The second question to be answered by a medium power in the general war context is whether it should provide its own strategic nuclear deterrence. This is not a question that admits a one-page answer valid for all medium powers, and it does in any case spread far beyond the sea affair, even if the choice falls on sea-based systems. It is clear, however, that, first, its possession puts a medium power in a quite different category as regards the defence of its territorial integrity and, second, it imposes a considerable load — between 5 per cent and 20 per cent — on the national security budget; third, it demands, if sea based, substantial ancillary forces as well as the submarine ballistic missile force itself. The extra strain imposed will make a medium power consider very carefully what advantages it can gain from such measures; how beleaguered it is; how threatening are those powers that have similar systems; how separable its own case may be, *in extremis*, from those of its allies. And it must do this not only for today, but for at least two decades' worth of tomorrows. It is no wonder that some of the powers made a subject of particular study here — India, Brazil, Israel — have hedged their bets by investing in nuclear power to the extent of near take-off but have not gone into the business of producing a thoroughgoing, operational strategic deterrent force. Neither is it any wonder that powers already in possession of such weapons, and with the capacity to make more, hold on to this strategic asset and work for its preservation in national hands.

Forces for the Requirement

All these considerations, then, go into the planning pot. When the stirring is complete, out should come the stew called a Force Requirement. Like any good stew, it will be a balance of flavours.

For, however well-defined the medium power's vital interests, the threats to them, the alliances that help to safeguard them, and the non-military measures that look after them may be, the fact remains that they are diverse, variously assailable and often of unpredictable nature. Forces tailored narrowly to a set of perceived needs today may fit very uncomfortably after tomorrow's blow-out.

Balanced and versatile maritime forces, then, are a general requirement for a medium power. But this does not mean having a lot of the best of everything. That kind of *folie de grandeur* is a way to arbitrary and damaging reductions when the economic heat comes on; and it may have even more dangerous long-term effects on strategy, since it tends to discount national strategic thought, lead to the adoption of arbitrary defence policies and confine all defence discussion to ways and means rather than ends.

Rational and limited force structures that avoid such excesses, however, can be arrived at, and the method should be clear enough in the light of what has been said earlier in this book and particularly this chapter of it. The combination of vital interests, threats, alliances, levels of conflict and reach is the core of maritime strategic planning and the basis for designing forces within reasonable limits. A good general rule is that every unit ought to be optimised for the level of conflict and reach at which it is generally expected to operate.

A prime example is in the field of medium-sized surface ships — corvettes, frigates and destroyers — which even in the case of the highly submarine-orientated British Navy form the most expensive single procurement item.[16] It is very easy, in the name of 'quality', to seek to pack into every unit of this kind as much equipment, habitability and indeed crew as can physically be managed; what comes out is a generally versatile but very expensive ship, as the cost escalation from Leander to Type 22 frigate, for example, shows.[17] This may be needed if the requirement is for a ship to operate in a heavy submarine environment at the higher level. But it is not needed when the ship is conducting low-intensity operations even at long reach. And, indeed, because it is optimised so much towards the higher level the Type 22, with no medium-calibre guns, may not even be very suitable for some low-intensity operations.

The same considerations may be applied to submarines: how many medium powers need nuclear-powered submarines, or, put another way, is there a set of vital interests that are most cost-effectively safeguarded, at plausible levels of threat and conflict, by such submarines? Would conventionally-powered submarines be almost as effective at lower cost? Equally, the test applies to aircraft both shore-based and shipborne. If a state does not seriously contemplate higher-level warfare against any opponent with submarine assets, then it may be able to make do with coastal surveillance aircraft that cost only a fraction of the price of long-range maritime patrol machines.

This book is not in the business of providing blueprints for individual medium-power maritime forces. But what is shaped by the conceptual tools of the trade seems likely to be as follows:

(a) constabulary forces for good order and regulation in the economic zone, optimised to normal conditions and short-reach low-intensity operations;
(b) long-reach surface forces optimised to low intensity operations;
(c) a strictly limited number of surface, air and submarine units of long reach optimised to higher level operations.

It should be noted that all the requirements stated here are national requirements. The price of alliance may have to be paid, of course, in some force capabilities that would not be nationally required. But, it needs to be said again, the price can be paid in other kind than in forces, and all such other measures — facilities, diplomatic support, even denial of support to a rival superpower[18] — must be brought into the equation.

Deficiencies and Options

When the desired force structure has been worked out and compared with the existing one, the result is likely to be a statement of deficiencies. (It would be nice to think it could be a statement of surpluses; I suppose it has happened.) Options for correcting them, as well as for sustaining the existing force structure, must then be studied.

The interactions here are with the defence budget, not only for the year but for the next decade or so, and with the human and industrial resources available. This process of defence procurement is, particularly in a democracy, a highly complex and stressed affair subject to all kinds of factors not all of which are logical or even ethical.[19] For the medium power, some particular points stand out.

First, defence procurement is by its nature a long-term business. Fisher may have built the *Dreadnought* in a year and a day, but nowadays even in the Soviet Union lead times are ten years and more for major equipments[20] and in the West can be even longer. In consequence, short-term perturbations in the defence budget can be very damaging to projects and ought to be avoided.[21] Stability in defence budgets year on year requires in its turn, however, that defence planners — who are after all the *demandeurs* in the case — formulate their plans soundly, cost them honestly and amend them seldom.

Second, the existence of indigenous defence industries is generally considered to be an element of strategic power but it is not an unmixed blessing. An extreme example may be found in the ailing shipbuilding industries of Western Europe, which have imposed on many national procurement organisations distortions in naval programmes in order to stabilise activity levels in the shipyards.[22] Economically attractive offshore procurement can easily be jammed by national lobbying; in Britain the shore-based Nimrod 3 airborne early warning system, which as a British solution was almost universally applauded in Parliament when it was selected in the late 1970s, ran into costly development problems that certainly would not have been experienced had the American AWACS been chosen. The same effect may yet be encountered with the new British heavy torpedo, chosen in preference to an American design.[23]

Medium powers are increasingly unlikely to be able to sustain efficient armament industries offering a comprehensive range of products. But collaboration and specialisation measures have been pursued, particularly in Western Europe, with only limited success.[24] In general, it seems that nationalist procurement policies are still more prevalent than strict logic or economics would demand. This sorts oddly with what are, at least by the tenets of this book, over-collective defence strategies: a fundamental mismatch indeed.

That mismatch does not apply to medium powers outside Europe — nor to France, which is firmly nationalist in both strategy and procurement. India, Japan and Australia all make what they can and buy what they cannot. Brazil is a most interesting case; she now has a major arms-exporting industry aimed very much at the low-intensity end of the market and produces such weapons for herself also.[25]

Third, the medium power has a decision to make in the extent of its research and development base. Most such states seem to spend between 3 and 6 per cent of their defence budgets on research and development; Britain, as a result perhaps of historical factors going back to the performance of her scientists in the Second World War, spends over 10 per cent, although in the early 1980s efforts were in hand to retrench.[26] How much needs to be done nationally is as ever a critical question; views vary from the comprehensive British approach, which sometimes extends to areas of research where national development would be out of the question, to the highly selective Dutch, who use mainly for evaluation of equipments on offer — both homegrown and foreign — their sophisticated facilities at Oegstgeest.[27] It seems to this writer that the comprehensive approach, particularly if publicly funded and bureaucratically controlled, is not only gold-plated in itself but encourages gold-plating right down the line as far as production.

Finally, the medium power has to consider how its human resources match the options available. The attempted sudden expansion of Iran to medium-power status, assiduously sponsored by the United States throughout the 1970s, encountered very serious difficulties because although the population base was large enough to sustain such growth the educational base was not. The quick reversion, in the Iran-Iraq war, to tactics reminiscent of the Western Front in 1917 was unsurprising. In the reverse sense, Israel for decades matched population resources to armed services to strategy with uncanny accuracy; the use of mobility, excellent organisation, tactical aggression and high technology to sustain a strategic position that was essentially defensive succeeded with brilliance, no less at sea than on land. It was only when the services became bogged down in the largely static activities of an army of occupation in the Lebanon that there was a serious mismatch between national character and population resources on the one hand, and force structure and deployment on the other. The full effects have not yet worked through.

These considerations tend to apply more forcefully to developing medium powers than they do to established ones, and they can of course be amended with time if the population base is large. Where it is small, as in Saudi Arabia and Oman, training and education of indigenous personnel can be added to expatriate skills to go a long way towards significant fighting capacity at relatively short reach.[28]

Even in the discussion of options to improve maritime forces and bring them into line with the strategically-dictated requirements of a medium power, the question of alliances looms. How much can an ally be relied upon to supply, in case of need, those assets that a medium power would much rather not have the expense of providing for itself? Particularly this goes back to the question of the big spenders: nuclear assets of all kinds, surveillance from space, comprehensive anti-submarine cover at the higher level. Reliance on an ally always entails risk; however tightly alliance treaties are drawn, they tend to be pragmatically interpreted in the event. Moreover, some of the assets described — particularly the nuclear ones — are precisely those that superpowers are reluctant to deploy. This is not to say that a medium power will necessarily want to produce its own; it is to say that it must seek to make its own forces robust enough to ensure that the engagement of allies' high-grade resources, in case of need, is a clear possibility.

Alliance considerations do, of course, work also in some of the details of the options for force improvement, although it is a clear corollary of the arguments advanced in this book that they should not dominate force requirements. Compatibility of communications and logistic arrangements with those of allies is a sensible policy for a medium power; dependence in such major aspects of maritime power is not.

Eventually, then, the outcome of the planning process is or ought to be an improvement in maritime forces in line with national strategy and resources. The process is a continuing one, looping back on itself as new evidence emerges and arguments unfold. This is healthy so long as there are real and timely outcomes. But the iterations must always include all parts of the diagram, the strategic as well as the material and organisational; the shortest questions are often the most telling, and 'why?' is just as important as 'how?'

Organisation and Deployment

It is tempting to declare that of course a medium maritime power ought to have an integrated maritime policy directed by a single department of state. This would comprehend offshore exploitation, the fisheries, overseas trade, the merchant marine, shipbuilding, and the military and diplomatic means of furthering and protecting all these aspects of maritime power. In this way, it can be argued, all such activities can be channelled in accordance with government policy and can be made consistent with each other; aid and subsidy can be applied where it will do most good and financial resources economically managed. Moreover the constituency thus established will have a powerful voice that will ensure the maritime aspects of national life are not neglected.

The logic of this is not, however, clear cut. In fact the various constituencies that would make up such an organisation are very diverse. Offshore exploitation, for example, connects much more strongly with the patterns and economics of world fuel extraction and use than it does with any maritime activity. Fisheries depend quite as much on national eating habits as they do on quotas and fishing methods. Shipbuilding and the merchant marine, unless operated in a totally centralised way by a state economy, are responsive to every kind of international economic pressure. Thus there is a strong case for all these activities, maritime though they may be, to be handled by departments of state which are not specifically directed to maritime matters.

What in the writer's view is absolutely necessary — and more so for medium maritime powers than others because their maritime activities are generally of wide scope but not so gigantic that they fragment of their own accord — is that a powerful inter-departmental body, ideally under the chairmanship of an impartial minister, should be charged with co-ordinating maritime affairs. In this way the various constituencies can carry proper weight, and resources may be bid for where they are most needed.

Such co-ordination can and should be carried down into the working levels of the departments of state. At those lower levels, indeed, Britain — which seems to have come in for a good deal of stick in this book, probably because the writer has seen so much of its workings at first hand and no organisation comes well out of detailed scrutiny — has probably a more effective machinery than any other medium power. The improvisations of the Falklands campaign did not all spring fully-armed from the heads of British industry. They were in many cases the result of planning and liaison between official and commercial organisations, patiently built up over the years at middle management level.[29]

Operationally, too, particularly in relation to the exclusive economic zone and close inshore, the minimum requirement is for tight co-ordination. It may not be necessary for a medium power to put all the good-order requirements of its sea estate under a single agency, though Japan and Canada, for example, get very close to this on the model of the United States Coast Guard. But it is necessary for activities to be co-ordinated so that they are responsive to all the needs of international and municipal law and to the requirement for the efficient conduct of maritime activity, and so that they do not duplicate or run counter to each other.

Finally, the organisation and deployment of maritime military forces is for medium powers a critical concern. Since the days are largely gone when overseas Commanders-in-Chief wielded power that ranged from the merely magisterial to the near-divine,[30] the operational command of maritime forces tends to be exercised from a single headquarters in the home country. The higher direction of that command, including the political direction which ought at all times to be its mainspring, is handed down from the seat of government. As has been suggested, in normal conditions and for low intensity operations such direction is responsive mainly to political considerations; at the higher level both objectives and direction are more military in nature.

How command is organised at the operational level and delegated to the field raises more contentious issues. The first question concerns the command of shore-based maritime aircraft, which exercise such a pervasive influence on operations for surveillance, anti-submarine warfare, attack on surface ships and air defence, all within their effective operating range. The problem of command is intrinsically difficult, because the operational factors point clearly in the direction of the maritime commander being in charge of all available forces so that their combined effort may be organised to the best effect, while procurement, training, basing and logistic factors all point to their being part of the nation's main air force. A study of recent medium-power practice does not help much because nations mainly influenced by the United States subordinate maritime air to the navy, while those most influenced by Britain subordinate it to the air force. France and India, probably the most free of outside influences, both make their maritime patrol aircraft part of the navy.[32] The question will remain a difficult one, but it is at least clear that all aircraft which may be called upon for maritime tasks must be suitably equipped and trained for such tasks, and exercised in them often enough to be effective; moreover there must be a reasonable expectation of their availability at need. This points to at least a strong operational input from the maritime commander.

Second, to what extent command and control is exercised from the shore and how far it should be done at sea is a matter whose contentiousness has increased with what a colleague (a communication specialist) called 'the disaster of modern communications'. Given the comprehensiveness of such systems, including satellite communications, it is tempting not only for shore headquarters but actually for governments to attempt to exercise minute-to-minute direction of operations.[33] Such temptations may be particularly dangerous in sea use operations at the higher level, when response to rapidly-developing threats, redisposition of forces and control of air assets are all very much the business of the commander on the spot. Sea denial operations are more traditionally conducted from shore, though whether that tradition is a correct one is an open question. As for low intensity operations, the political considerations surrounding them will always invite government and higher-command intervention, but this must be tempered with common sense. The fragmented and often reactive nature of low intensity operations requires quick and politically sensitive responses from commanders — who may well be the commanders of quite small single units — on the spot, and direction must be equally sensitive. Clear and well-considered rules of engagement are often the key to success.

The very nature of maritime forces makes their *ad hoc* regrouping a relatively simple task, much easier than that of either land- or shore-based air forces. This does not mean that a newly-formed task force will be able at once to operate *op rolletjes*, as the delightful Dutch expression for well-oiled precision has it; but it does mean that in a matter of a few hours for specialised forces, and a few days for large, all-arms groupings, good operational teamwork can be achieved. This inherent flexibility can be fostered by frequent exercises and training beginning with relatively formalised events and going on to more complex and exacting work. Sea training organisations such as the British set-up at Portland provide the basis on which later, more complex fleet exercises can be built.[34]

It is here that in normal conditions a medium power may find to the maximum the advantage of having balanced forces capable of operating in all media. The lack of any arm of maritime forces — submarines, reconnaissance and combat aircraft, even a shortage of frigates — can take away a whole dimension of experience from the other arms as well as being a strategic lack in itself. Allies can fill a gap here as they do in the strategic sense; but dependence for any facet of training is irksome, and the more basic the lack the more irksome it may be.

Thus, the main organisations in medium-power maritime forces are likely to be administrative and training in their nature. Operational organisations and deployments can be much more flexible and indeed need to be in order that economical use can be made of the forces available.

Similarly, deployment need not necessarily follow rigid rules. If the Quai d'Orsay requires a small frigate to be stationed at Djibouti, well and good; if the small French Indian Ocean force can use its mobility to look after Mayotte and La Réunion as well and do some useful work visiting East African ports on the way, so much the better; if the job can be done by less permanent stationing of ships and allow the deployment of balanced forces that can exercise *en route* and reach a high pitch of operational efficiency, perhaps best of all.

But those observations bring us back to the heart of the matter. What one's forces are meant to be doing; what they may be called upon to do; the extent of the cover they need; the extent to which allies can help; and how the situation may change in the future: all these considerations govern not only deployment but reach back into organisation, planning and procurement. In however evolutionary a way, the medium power must constantly re-evaluate these basic factors in order that its forces serve its strategy, and its strategy serves its interests.

Notes

1. H. Moineville, *Naval Warfare Today and Tomorrow* (Blackwell, Oxford, 1983), p. 91.
2. Australia has not abandoned the 'self-sufficiency' policy adumbrated by most contributors to *Australian Defence Policy for the 1980s* (Australian National University Press, Canberra, London, 1978), ed. R. O'Neill, and reflected in Sir Arthur Tange's address 'Australian Regional Defence Commitments' at the *Seapower '81 Seminar* of the Australian Naval Institute. But, as shown, for example, by Lieut. Cort D. Wagner in 'Australia', US Naval Institute, *Proceedings*, March 1983, pp. 84–90, her forces do not measure up.
3. G. S. Bhargava, *India's Security in the 1980s* (IISS, London), p. 23; Brig. Y. A. Mande,'India's Security Environment', *USI Journal* (New Delhi), October-December 1983, p. 307.
4. Noel Butlin in *Australian Defence Policy for the 1980s*, ed. O'Neill (University of Queensland Press, Queensland, 1982), p. 97.
5. O'Neill, *Australian Defence Policy for the 1980s*, p. 292.
6. Capt. A. Skolnick, 'Too Light on Lasers?', US Naval Institute, *Proceedings*, December 1984, p. 30.
7. Air Vice Marshal G. Chesworth, 'Maritime Alliance: Practice and Future', *Maritime Strategy Seminar*, 15 October 1981 (RUSI), pp. 26–30.
8. J. R. Hill, *Anti-Submarine Warfare* (Ian Allan, Shepperton, 1984), pp. 102–3.
9. Sir Ronald Mason, 'Problems of Fleet Balance' in *The Future of British Sea Power* (ed. Till), p. 213. Sir Ronald discusses British ASW assets entirely in the 'contribution to NATO' context.
10. Neil Macfarlane, *Intervention and Regional Security* (IISS, Adelphi Paper

No. 196, 1985), p. 55.

11. Ibid., p. 61.

12. J. Cable, *Gunboat Diplomacy* (Macmillan, London, 1981), p. 22.

13. *The Military Balance, 1984–85*, p. 42.

14. Labayle-Couhat (ed.), *Combat Fleets of the World 1984/85, passim* (Canada, Chile, China, France, Germany (Federal Republic), India, Italy, The Netherlands, United Kingdom, USA, USSR). Another six navies have one such tanker each.

15. R. L. Scheina, 'The Malvinas Campaign', US Naval Institute, *Proceedings*, May 1983, p. 105.

16. Cmnd. 9227-II, p. 9, Table 2.3.

17. Cmnd. 8212-I, p. 45.

18. G. Liska, *Alliances and the Third World* (Johns Hopkins University Press, Baltimore, 1967), p. 31.

19. For the financial aspects as they affect the United Kingdom, see Sir Frank Cooper, 'Economic Constraints on Britain's Defence Planning' in *The Future of British Sea Power* (ed. Till), pp. 171–84. A more general survey, including other resource aspects, is in Roger Facer's *Weapons Procurement in Europe — Capabilities and Choices* (IISS, Adelphi Paper No. 108, 1975).

20. Hervé Coutau-Bégarie, *La Puissance Maritime Sovietique* (Economica, Paris, 1983), p. 79.

21. Sir F. Cooper, in *The Future of British Sea Power* (ed. Till), p. 79.

22. Daniel Todd, *The World Shipbuilding Industry* (Croom Helm, Beckenham, 1985), p. 318.

23. Cmnd. 8529-I, para 214.

24. Trevor Taylor, *European Defence Co-Operation* (Chatham House Papers No. 24, 1984), pp. 55–8.

25. *The Military Balance, 1984–85*, p. 114.

26. Cmnd. 8529-I, paras 413 and 425.

27. A name even the Dutch have difficulty in pronouncing.

28. Bonsignore, in 'The *Madina*-Class Frigates', p. 31, describes the comprehensive training programme in connection with these ships.

29. Official views of the efficacy of improvisation remain cautious nevertheless: see Cmnd 8758, paras 237–40.

30. A story is told of W. W. Fisher (and probably several other Commanders-in-Chief of the 1930s): a small girl was taken to church in Valletta in the heyday of the Mediterranean Fleet and looked on in awe at the proceedings and particularly the arrival of the bemedalled, full-white-uniform-clad C-in-C. When asked about it afterwards she said she had liked the service and thought God had looked wonderful. They told W.W. 'H'm' he said, 'an intelligent child, and a natural mistake'.

31. This book does not address the question, sometimes raised, of the command and control of shipborne air forces. It is not possible to find an example of such command in any but naval hands in any medium power navy, and the deduction may be drawn that such specialised forces are in fact a naval concern although their operations can affect land campaigns and overland air operations.

32. *The Military Balance, 1984–85*, pp. 38–9 and 99.

33. In Cmnd. 8758, paras 205, 206, it is clear that HM Government were acutely conscious of the need to keep the balance during the Falklands campaign and in general this had a successful result, though the Total Exclusion Zone was an exception — see p. 136 above.

34. See J. R. Hill, *British Sea Power in the 1980s* (Ian Allan, Shepperton, 1985), pp. 108–11, for a description of the 'work-up' process.

13 TOWARDS A GENERAL THEORY

Theories that rest on no assumptions at all are rare indeed. It has been the intention of this study to keep the downstream arguments as assumption-free as possible; but the basis of the theory is an assumption sure enough. It is that the states under discussion seek to preserve their identity and to create and maintain conditions in which their interests can flourish.

This may look like a statement of the obvious but it needs to be made. Most states make declarations of loyalty to supranational organisations and aspirations; they are part of the common currency of modern diplomacy and are a helpful basis for its conduct. There is a tongue-in-cheek flavour to most of them that is, again, entirely accepted in international exchanges. It is when the tongue is removed from the cheek, and the interests of the nation-state are lost, even in its internal counsels, in favour of the policies and machinery of inter-state groupings or international movements, that strategies can become muddled. So the primacy of the nation-state is the bedrock of the theory advanced here.

What is not an assumption is the existence of medium powers. This is based upon evidence. Like all manifestations of power it is not easy to define, but when a number of parameters — economic, cultural, intellectual, military, geographical — all point in the same direction, towards a significant autonomy and capacity for self-help in the preservation of national identity and vital interests, then medium-power status can be accorded until it is shown to have been abdicated. You know one when you see one.

Maritime-ness too is evidential. It is only partly a matter of present dependence on the sea. It rests also on geography, on the popular consciousness, on economic potential, on the extent of overseas territorial interests, on the use that is or can be made of the sea for strategic deterrence (and at the other end of the scale for diplomacy), and, even, on the expectation of other states that one's own will act in a maritime way. But at the back of maritime-ness, in the strategic context, must be the extent to which vital interests are maritime or can be secured by maritime means.

For strategy must be a whole, and the maritime side of it must serve the whole and not unduly distort it. Overreaching abroad and weakness at home is a danger. Britain, because she is an island and her large maritime establishment could in the eighteenth and nineteenth centuries fairly easily cope with invasion threats as well as foreign campaigns, managed for some time to attain a reach and scope quite out of proportion to her size; the Netherlands in the seventeenth century lasted a much shorter time as a prime maritime power, and one of the reasons was its vulnerability by land.

That said, the medium power cannot neglect the preservation of its interests *at* sea nor the chance of safeguarding and promoting its more general interests *by* sea. Both these lines of strategy can be complex, subject to national choices; lucky the medium power for whom those choices are not already constrained by the current situation, the legacies of the past and plans for the future. But even if the choices are relatively free of such trammels, there will always be one restraining factor, particularly in the military aspect of strategy: the medium power's limited resources.

The mismatch between what one would like to be able to do as a nation-state, a strategic entity, and what one's resources will allow one to do is the central dilemma for the medium power. The dilemma is not at all confined to the maritime scene. Germany, with the hugely powerful Group of Soviet Forces Germany facing her, confronts it in stark form. India, for all her alarm about the United States' presence in the Indian Ocean, no doubt regards China on her northern border as the greater threat. Moreover, maritime interests are often at a considerable remove from home and it is easy enough for governments to regard them as ultimately disposable, while the option of safeguarding wider national interests by sea may look financially unattractive compared with home-based solutions. Nevertheless, when all is said and done many medium powers will find much they need to safeguard, much they would like to do, at sea in strategic terms — and all too few resources with which to do it.

Therefore, allies. However medium powers may wish to remain non-aligned in this split world, and India in particular has made strenuous effort to do so, they are bound to seek superpower backing even if it is only in the contingency of imminent superpower threat. Alliances that do not involve superpowers are, possibly because of their clear incapacity to influence events in the pre-1939 era, quite rare in the post-war world. Zones of peace and neutrality, whether in a nuclear or general context, are on the evidence regarded as useful declaratory aspirations and when in force, like the Treaty of Tlatelolco, as worthwhile dampers or lids to put on the level of conflict; but they are not — again on the evidence — regarded by medium powers as reliable guardians of state interests.

But if alliance, and particularly superpower alliance, forms the exterior vertebra of a medium power strategy, that structure can take many forms. The tight formation of NATO and the even tighter one of the Warsaw Pact (which allows no medium power status, on the terms put forward in this book, to any of its members, even to Poland which has extensive maritime interests) are not followed outside Europe. Even the ANZUS agreement uses much less demanding formulae and institutions, while India, Brazil and Japan rely on generalised treaty language and informal and non-permanent international staff arrangements.

As the example of France in the 1960s showed, the options for the medium power are not closed by history. In leaving the permanent military structure of NATO she achieved, *de facto*, a special relationship with the Atlantic alliance that gave her minimum (though by no means nugatory) formal commitment and maximum national freedom of action while she continued to enjoy the ultimate protection of American engagement in the defence of Western Europe. This had been regarded by many as a cynical piece of freeloading, but it is argued by many Frenchmen that it could and should be taken as a pattern for other Western European nations to follow, and that an Atlantic alliance of much looser structure would be more, not less, effective than NATO in politico-military and deterrent terms.

It is worth following such an argument some way down its track in the light of the ideas expressed in this book. The model is a multinational alliance containing a superpower, covered by a treaty of general rather than specific commitment in case of emergency and served on a permanent basis by a very small co-ordinating staff whose planning comprehends the command and communications machinery for use in emergency, broad concepts for joint operations at need and fostering, through its diplomatic elements, mutual trust between the political power centres of the alliance.

The operation of a loose alliance of this sort in emergency is, to use a dangerous metaphor, less mechanical than chemical. A highly-structured alliance has machinery in place that, when levers are pulled, moves in a planned and pre-organised way; as an example, at Simple Alert the Flag Officer Plymouth becomes COMCENTLANT and COMPLYMCHAN and his staff, with augmentation, becomes a NATO staff. A looser-model alliance operates more by catalysis; events themselves, often initiated by individual national actors, dictate the particular forms of mutual help and organisation that emerge, although because the constituents of the alliance are the same in each case the resulting compound will always have identifiable characteristics.

From the maritime point of view the looser form of alliance has many attractive features. It is emphatically not tied to a single scenario or area; the treaty wording and the small flexible staff structure will see to that. Thus it is likely to be more, not less, responsive to the unexpected contingencies that can occur at sea. Moreover its method of response, the catalytic action as a result of events, lends itself to initiatives of a maritime nature in support of vital interests: initiatives that may be independently taken by a medium power. Finally, it allows no less grass roots co-operation; exercises and joint training, even to some extent joint doctrine, can be made largely independent of centralised alliance machinery.

The dangers of a loose alliance, however, should not be blinked. There is after all great reassurance in ringing treaty phrases like 'An attack on one is an attack on all', however subject this may in practice be to *de minimis* interpretation; a loose alliance gives less certainty of support. And the large staff, planning and command machinery that goes with a tight alliance, though it may be cumbersome in operation, does make for co-operative and friendly relations between allies at staff level and provides a strong communications infrastructure that is perhaps its most important single contribution in military terms. Finally, what is good for the maritime gander may be less good for the land/air goose; the idea of a loosely-structured alliance on land can suggest a vision of various national armies roaming at will round the Continent. However there is much evidence now of disjunctions not only of logistics but of doctrine and even of command in the land theatre, and looser structure properly handled might not much exacerbate these.

In choosing the right form of alliance for itself or in interpreting its existing alliances — and it is implicit in the assumption of this book that for the medium power those choices are extant and remain open — a state has finally to ask what the price of alliance is. As has been shown, this may be in terms of bases, other logistic facilities, political support, the contribution of specially-configured forces, the special stationing of forces, or a combination of these. In the outcome the single strategic question for the medium power is: how does this affect my autonomy and given the need to safeguard my national interests can I afford it? If the answer to this question is no, then two courses are open to the medium power. Either it moves towards a looser form of alliance with less structured commitment, and consequently less strain on its force plans for independent operation, or it moves to a position of greater dependence on its superpower ally. In NATO over the past two decades France took the former course, Canada — in spite of its agonising over defence policy — the latter. Britain has steadily tended towards the path of greater dependence.

After so many pages of argument, that path looks no more attractive than it did at the outset. Dependence represents a diminution of power not an accretion of it. The state's interests become less identifiable as they become less independently defensible. Freedom of action, restricted in the military sphere, becomes more and more constrained in diplomacy, and finally in economic matters. The end may not be satrapy in the extreme form suggested by Mr Barnett in his more comminatory passages, but it is distasteful and it is not necessary.

It is not necessary because, in fact, the price being paid is a good deal more than could be reasonably asked and than would, given fair negotiation, be exacted. A regrouping of British forces to give them more operational autonomy would do no more than bring them into line with those of most other NATO nations, which are structured primarily for national needs and then assigned to the alliance, and with those of all the medium powers — even Japan — which have been used as exemplars in previous chapters. With this change would logically come a greater flexibility in the Western alliance reflecting far less dependence on a single scenario and a much greater potential response to diverse, not necessarily Soviet, threats in a wider world scene. But that response would not depend on rigid contingency plans so much as *ad hoc* arrangements that could stem as easily from medium-power as from superpower initiative.

If the writer emerges from this discussion as a half-baked Gaullist, that is probably not an unfair description. There is a distinct logic in French defence policy during and since the time of that tall figure, and it is singularly appropriate to medium powers as described in this book. Where Gaullist policy seems somewhat to falter is in its insistence on the primacy of nuclear deterrence as a safeguard against *conventional* attack on metropolitan France; this may have worked well enough in the days of the great General himself (if he did not say *'La dissuasion, c'est moi'* he certainly should have done) but it lacks credibility in a less monolithic political scene.

Whether a medium power, even one in the first rank, needs strategic nuclear deterrence even for the ultimate case of *nuclear* threat to the homeland is a subject that this book has uneasily fudged, on the grounds that it is not essentially a maritime matter; it must rest so here, with the perhaps lame observation that the decision, momentous as it is, must rest on the medium power's particular situation and perceived deterrent needs for several decades to come. Whether the alliance to which it belongs is loosely or tightly drawn is, no doubt, an important factor in that perception; but the continuing debate about the depth of American nuclear commitment to NATO, for example, suggests that that single question cannot be regarded as critical.

Given, then, that a medium power chooses or interprets its alliance arrangements to ensure that they offer considerable freedom of initiative in support of its vital interests, and that allies are engaged in emergency by catalysis more than by formal procedures or machinery, a rational way of planning the necessary forces for use at sea is available. It rests on assessment of vital interests, of threats to them, of the reach and level of conflict that may be required for their preservation, of the help that allies may give; it goes through the mill of force requirements, comparisons with existing forces, options for improvements and the far-from-merry-go-round of matching these to resources. What emerges will be, inevitably, forces that do the best they can. There are two words that exemplify the planning process for the medium power: Limits and Risk.

Limits ought to be apparent not only in resources, where they are all too obvious, but much further back in the planning process. Even in the assessment of vital interests distinction must be made and a wary eye kept on the difference between desirable and essential, though the cumulative effect of small aggressions and erosions of trade and access must not be forgotten. Further into planning, the limits of level of conflict and reach are immensely important, as are the subsets — particularly of higher level operations: if, for example, a medium power foresees no requirement for amphibious operations, having good land communications at home and no commitment abroad, then it ought not to strain after them; and if its interest, perhaps local only, can be secured mainly by sea denial then it can with relief eschew most of the expensive demands of higher-level sea use. The second case will be rare but Israel, for example, models effective forces on this pattern. Finally, limits can be imposed by an assessment of when an ally is likely to find it necessary to intervene — of, in fact, the point of catalysis. It has been suggested above that this is unlikely to occur in low intensity operations, and that at the higher level in conflict with another medium power it may not occur either. In the event of superpower intervention on the other side, or in the highly dangerous situation where a medium power finds itself opposed to a superpower from the outset, the ally's engagement is much more reliable.

This is all risky stuff, one can hear experienced planners saying. Indeed Risk is part and parcel of the medium power's planning process. A prime plea of this book is that risk should be recognised as such and coolly assessed. Of course on the day the escalation may be sharper, the foe may be more powerful, catalysis may operate later than the limits of planning foresaw; what is the risk of this, and what extra resources will cut it significantly? Scenarios can be used to test this; that is what they are for. That sort of method is much less risky than founding maritime forces on a single scenario which makes them unsuitable for other contingencies that may arise. The single scenario that postulates an alliance conflict escalating quickly to general war is the most risky of all in planning terms for the medium power, since it forces it to concentrate on force characteristics that are exacting, expensive and quite often unusable at the levels at which, from recent history, conflict and confrontation may be expected to occur.

It is on these questions of limits and risk that the advice of planners and the judgement of statesmen will be most severely tested. Probably they are not enough discussed in the administrations of any medium power, being too often replaced by comfortable formulae and assumptions that begin half-way through the proper thought-process. But it seems that in emerging medium powers — India, Brazil, Australia — there is considerable realism and some hard assessment is going on, while France has come to terms with the logic of her strategy and makes as good a fist of it as her resources allow. Japan, still agonising over the philosophical implications of military preparedness, is nevertheless occupied in assessments of level of conflict and reach that are very much in line with some of the ideas put forward above. Israel, racked by the first identifiable failure of her forces to achieve their objective, nevertheless has a maritime arm that makes sense in her special situation. Many other countries not examined in any detail above — Argentina, Chile, Greece, Indonesia, Italy, Nigeria, Pakistan, Peru, Turkey — have some of the characteristics of medium power at sea, used for national purposes, and follow to greater or lesser degree some of the principles suggested.

Only in the northern tier of medium powers, on both sides of the Iron Curtain, is another approach apparent: the contribution of maritime forces to an alliance. The dependence of the Eastern European countries on Soviet naval power is so obvious that it is seldom remarked; even the Polish navy has minimal reach and can sustain independently only the lowest level of conflict. But The Netherlands, Germany, Denmark, Norway and Canada all specialise and to a large extent subordinate their national force requirements to alliance needs. For these states, limits and risk at sea are conditioned, if not governed, by the net assessments of the alliance.

This leaves Britain, with perhaps a more complex web of history and existing maritime heritage than any nation on earth, a bewildering succession of strategic ideas over the past three decades, a political system that allows quite sharp shifts of policy, and a diminishing but still large economic stake at sea. Probably because they are so close to the writer's experience, the tensions, the limits and the risk-assessments in the British planning process seem to have been quite unique in their complexity and, probably, their lack of ultimate rationality.

The central tension has been between reliance, on the one hand, on independent state power, and on the other on collective security. By simple extension this moves into autonomous strategies and force structures on the one hand and contributory forces on the other. Like a tug-of-war that goes on for ever, this tension has no absolute resolution; however contributory they may be the forces will have some autonomy, and however autonomous they are they will be useful in some circumstances as a contribution. But where the tell-tale coloured ribbon on the tug-of-war stands at any particular moment may, in the event, be critical.

The unsurprising conclusion reached by this study is that Britain has gone too far, and was in danger before 1982 of going a great deal too far, in the direction of a contributory policy, especially at sea. The factors that led to this have been addressed by other writers and require no further analysis here; it is simply worth saying that in the writer's view Britain is too populous, rich, maritime and, quite simply, important to adopt a 'strategy' of reliance on collective security and contributory forces. She ought to maintain significant autonomy, enough to operate the necessary chemistry of power, as in fact she showed herself prepared to do at some cost and great risk in 1982. The oddities of British pragmatism, the inconsistency between declared policy and actual practice, were that year exposed in a way that would have been hilarious if anyone had been unworried enough to laugh.

To the challenge the maritime, amphibious and shore-based air forces rose magnificently and it is right to pay tribute to the people who carried the business — nationally trained, led and motivated. But it is also fair to think for a moment of the rearguard action that had been carried out since 1966 or thereabouts by the service staffs, and some dedicated civilians, in the Ministry of Defence. Though they seldom articulated it, and indeed it would have been impolitic to do so, they fought hard to maintain the maximum autonomy in terms of level of conflict and reach. In so doing they brought into being a force of nuclear-powered fleet submarines; kept the best seagoing logistic organisation possessed by a medium power, efficient world-wide operational communications, high-grade anti-submarine assets, air defence that gave an opponent formidable problems, ships and troops capable of amphibious assault; and, in a brilliant counter-attack, reprovided fixed-wing aircraft organic to the fleet for attack and defence. But the rearguard action was becoming perilous; ship-based airborne early warning had not been, could not on a NATO basis be, justified; amphibious capabilities and too many frigates were due to go.

Even though the Falklands proved that the service planners, for all their overemphasis on quality, had got it largely right and the politicians and pundits disastrously wrong, the tensions in British policy remain and the tug-of-war has by no means shifted to the side of autonomy. Partly this is due to vested interests in the services and outside, partly to the now-powerful NATO establishment, partly to moments of inertia in the processes of Whitehall and partly to the voices that ask where the next Falklands is to be. (These last asked a similar question after Kuwait, the Indonesian confrontation, the Beira patrol, the Cod disputes and Belize.

So far their failure rate has been 100 per cent.)

Such an excursion into British matters must be excused, coming from this source as it does. It is time this study returned to the general topic by way of conclusion.

It has not attempted to provide a blueprint for medium-power maritime forces. Even strategic plans, and much more force structure and organisation, must spring from a nation's own character, interests and resources. What the study has done, it is hoped, is explain how a medium power may hope to maintain control over its destiny, and especially how the sea aspect of this control may be managed.

There are those who suggest that in maritime terms there will after the next decade or so be no medium powers as such. The superpowers, they say, will lord it in the oceans with weapon potential of great ferocity and precision, and all the other navies and maritime air forces will cower in the backyards of their exclusive economic zones. The writer does not share that view, any more than he shares the notion of multipolarity that was fashionable in the early 1970s. Superpower at sea will go on being a fact and will in absolute terms increase, but the mutual constraints on it will also increase and the pressure needed to pull its trigger will be correspondingly greater. However, the physical resources available to small and medium powers — in the form of weapon systems handy for the middle levels of conflict — will also increase in number and effectiveness, often at manageable cost. Thus the capacity of and need for medium powers to take independent action in support of their interests at sea will not significantly diminish, any more than will their need to exert a catalytic effect on an ally in emergencies that they can no longer handle themselves.

The tools of the trade, both conceptual and material, are readily available. The resources are often less certain, and it is only by the judicious use of the tools and a proper assessment of limits and risk that the medium power can hope to attain a realistic maritime strategy within its means. But if it follows that course, thinking the matter through with the minimum of assumptions, it has a chance of maintaining maritime policies and forces that will, in support of its national interests and in a wide range of circumstances, be decisive.

APPENDIX

Notes on the Sea Dependence Tables 3.2 and 3.3

Maritime Factors

Seagoing Trade is the first and most obvious maritime factor to be compared with both population and GDP. The *United Nations Bulletin of Statistics* regularly publishes figures for cargoes loaded and unloaded, in thousands of tonnes; the latest year for which figures were available, at the time the research was done, was 1978. The figures were adjusted to base-dates for each country, summed and applied directly to both GDP and population, giving the peculiar expressions:

$$\frac{\text{Thousand tonnes}}{\text{Milliard dollars GDP}} \quad \text{and} \quad \frac{\text{Thousand tonnes}}{\text{Millions of people}}$$

Each number so produced is an indicator of maritime dependence; the higher the number, within its family, the greater the dependence. It would probably have been preferable to use the value, rather than the tonnage, of goods loaded and unloaded; but these figures were not published at that time. In any event there is nothing unusual in the direct comparison of diverse parameters to produce indices for a particular purpose; it is frequently done in analytical and technical work.

The method lacks refinement, though, for several reasons. First, it takes no account of cabotage. The raw data do include a cabotage column but at this stage no adjustment has been made. Second, no assessment can be reached of a country's dependence on trade going through an entrepôt; for example, West Germany is dependent to an undetermined extent on traffic going through Rotterdam. Finally, the figures for entrepôt trade themselves may give a somewhat distorted view of dependence in those countries where it is on a large scale; this applies to the Netherlands and Belgium (as well as Hong Kong and Singapore, which were treated in the raw data but are not included in the tables as they are not medium powers).

Fish Catches are factors that are relatively easy to analyse. They are listed in United Nations statistical documents. Again, the base year of 1978 was the latest available; the source was the *FAO Year Book of Fishing Statistics*, 1979. The indices in this case are produced by

$$\frac{\text{Thousand tonnes catch}}{\text{Milliard dollars GDP}} \quad \text{and} \quad \frac{\text{Thousand tonnes catch}}{\text{Millions of people}}$$

These indices are, of course, quite crude as indicators of food-dependence. A full analysis would have to take account of the use to which the catches are put, whether for export, animal-feed processing or domestic human consumption.

The Size of the Merchant Marine, for those states that have significant shipping industries, is another parameter — derived in this case from the *Fairplay Shipping Yearbook* — that can be compared with GDP and population in a similar manner. A merchant marine of less than a million tonnes is taken as negligible. Again, the indices produced could be further broken down to establish specific sorts of dependence. However, as in all the other categories so far mentioned, the cruder figures are probably the more robust; infinite refinement may produce infinite irrelevance.

Ship Building and Repairing may only marginally be a factor in maritime dependence, since offshore procurement is now a very common practice even in the most seafaring of nations; the arguments for national autonomy in ship construction are much less strong than they were. Yet it is a fact that most nations with a maritime outlook do have such industries, and the indices have therefore been computed to add to the evidence.

The Offshore Zone. All the factors above are fairly well documented and generally have a data base which, even if not of the best order of accuracy, is subject to central scrutiny by impartial organisations and therefore has a good deal of consistency. More difficult for several reasons are the offshore estates of nations: their continental shelves and fishing zones.

First, it is clearly desirable to indicate not only the current production of such areas but their potential. However, states can be quite secretive even about current figures; they will certainly not wish to publish potential resources unless it is in their interests.

Moreover, in many cases the potential is simply not known; for example, knowledge that the North Sea oil (as distinct from gas) province existed dated from the mid-1960s at earliest, and this was in a highly-developed country whose need for indigenous fuel resources was evident.

Second, in the case of living resources the data for separate states' fishing zones are often not available, and certainly not on a common data base. The *FAO Yearbook*, the only comprehensive document, divides the world into 20 or so areas and details the catches from each; but an area may take in the offshore waters of a dozen or more countries as well as the high seas to seaward of them.

In consequence, the indices for dependence on offshore zones are much less reliable than those so far mentioned. None the less an attempt has been made to generate them.

Offshore oil production as tabulated in *Offshore Magazine* (20 June 1981) has been compared with GDP and population in the same way as the earlier parameters. A statement is also made on the percentage of each state's total production that is attributable to offshore operations. These assessments give an indication of the vulnerability of each nation's economy to offshore oil. This has been combined with an assessment of fish production from the offshore zone, including some assessment of its potential. The offshore dependence index is governed by all the foregoing factors.

Presentation of the Data

The *Which?* type presentation was chosen to give immediacy to the findings, which a simple matrix of numbers would not. The number of stars allotted was based on a logarithmic scale. When all states including the smallest were considered, the one-stars tended to be the most numerous; but medium powers, which are the only ones considered for the tables in this book, gravitate naturally towards the higher ratings.

BIBLIOGRAPHY

Ambrose, E. *Rise to Globalism: American Foreign Policy Since 1938*, 3rd revised edn (Penguin Books, London, 1983)

Barnett, A. D. *Uncertain Passage* (Brookings, Washington, 1974)

Barnett, C. *The Collapse of British Power* (Methuen, London, 1972)

Barston, R. P. and Birnie, P. (eds), *The Maritime Dimension* (George Allen and Unwin, London, 1980)

Bereiweriso, L. O. F. 'New Maritime Policy and its Effect on Nigeria', *Seaways*, March 1985, pp. 12–13

Bhargava, G. S. *India's Security in the 1980s* (International Institute for Strategic Studies, London, Adelphi Paper No. 125, 1976)

Boczek, B. A. *Flags of Convenience* (Harvard University Press, Harvard, 1962), p. 94

Bolt, C. *A History of the USA* (Macmillan, London, 1974)

Bonsignore, E. 'The *Madina*-Class Frigates', *Military Technology*, No. 1/85, p. 30

Booth, K. *Navies and Foreign Policy* (Croom Helm, London, 1977)

Bouchard, Lt. J. and Hess, Lt. D. J. 'The Japanese Navy and Sea-Lanes Defense', US Naval Institute, *Proceedings*, March 1984, pp. 90–7

Bowett, D. W. *Self-Defence in International Law* (Manchester University Press, Manchester, 1958)

Brionowski, A. (ed.), *Understanding ASEAN* (Macmillan, London, 1982)

British Atlantic Committee, *Diminishing the Nuclear Threat* (London, 1984)

British Maritime League, *Report* of Conference, 21 June 1984

Brownlie, I. *International Law and the Use of Force by States* (Oxford University Press, Oxford, 1963)

Buchan, A. *Change Without War* (Chatto and Windus, London, 1974)

Buzan, B. *A Sea of Troubles? Sources of Dispute in the New Ocean Régime* (International Institute for Strategic Studies, Adelphi Paper No. 143, 1978)

Cable, J. *Gunboat Diplomacy*, 2nd edn (Macmillan, London, 1981)

——— *Britain's Naval Future* (Naval Institute Press, Annapolis, 1983)

——— 'Surprise and the Single Scenario', RUSI, *Journal*, March 1983, p. 38

——— 'Interdependence — a Drug of Addiction?', *International Affairs*, Summer 1983, pp. 365–79

Cahn, A. H., Kruzel, J. J., Dawkins, P. M. and Huntziger, J. *Controlling Future Arms Trade* (McGraw Hill, New York, 1980)

Chapman, J. W. M., Drifte, R. and Gow, I. T. M. *Japan's Quest for Comprehensive Security* (Frances Pinter, London, 1983)

Chesworth, Air Vice Marshal G. 'Maritime Alliance: Practice and Future', *Maritime Strategy Seminar*, 15 October 1981, *Report* (Navy International, Nautical Institute, RUSI, 1982), pp. 26–30

Chichester, M. and Wilkinson, J. *The Uncertain Ally: British Defence Policy 1960–1990* (Gower, Aldershot, 1982)

Clementson, Sqn Ldr J. 'No More Dominoes: ASEAN and Regional Security', RUSI, *Journal*, December 1984, p. 36

Cockcroft, A. N. 'Development of Routeing in Coastal Waters', *Journal of Navigation*, Vol. 38 (1985), p. 78

Colombos, C. J. *International Law of the Sea*, 6th edn (Longmans, London, 1967)

Cosby, I. P. S. G. 'Self-Defence as a Basis for Maritime Forces', unpublished paper presented at the Seminar on Medium Maritime Power, Gosport, July 1982

Coutau-Bégarie, H. *La Puissance Maritime Sovietique* (Economica, Paris, 1983)
Crane, J. *Submarine* (BBC, 1984)
Defence, Secretary of State for (UK), *Statement on the Defence Estimates 1966*, Cmnd. 2901 (HMSO, London)
——— *Statement on the Defence Estimates 1980*, Cmnd. 7826 (HMSO)
——— *Statement on the Defence Estimates 1981*, Cmnd. 8212 (HMSO)
——— *Statement on the Defence Estimates 1982*, Cmnd. 8529 (HMSO)
——— *Statement on the Defence Estimates 1983*, Cmnd. 8951 (HMSO)
——— *Statement on the Defence Estimates 1984*, Cmnd. 9227 (HMSO)
——— *The Future UK Strategic Deterrent Force* (DOGD 80/23)
——— *The Falklands Campaign: the Lessons*, Cmnd. 8758 (HMSO, 1982)
——— *Statement on the Defence Estimates 1985*, Cmnd. 9430 (HMSO)
Director of Public Relations (Navy), UK, Broadsheets 1983 and 1984 (HMSO, London)
Draper, G. I. A. D. 'The Legal Limitations upon the Employment of Weapons by the UN Force in the Congo', *International and Comparative Law Quarterly*, Vol. 12 (1963), p. 401
Edwards, Capt. B. E. D. 'High Noon in the Gulf', *Seaways*, November 1984, p. 3
Ethell, J. and Price, A. *Air War South Atlantic* (Sidgwick and Jackson, London, 1983)
Facer, R. *Weapons Procurement in Europe — Capabilities and Choices* (International Institute for Strategic Studies, Adelphi Paper No. 108, 1975)
Ferreira, D. P. C. *The Navy of Brazil: an Emerging Power at Sea* (National Defense University, Washington, 1983), p. 40
Friedman, N. *Submarine Design and Development* (Conway Maritime Press, London, 1983)
——— 'Real Time Ocean Surveillance', *Military Technology*, No. 9/84, pp. 76–81
Fujii, Y. 'Recent Trends in Traffic Accidents in Japanese Waters', *Journal of Navigation*, Vol. 35 (1982), p. 91.
Fujimaki, S. 'Japan in the Eastern Sea', paper given at the Ninth Greenwich Forum, September 1983
Gerencser, M. and Smetek, R. 'Artificial Intelligence on the Battlefield', *Military Technology*, No. 6/84, p. 86
'Gisborne', 'Naval Operations in the Malacca and Singapore Straits', *Naval Review*, July 1967, p. 45
Giles, D. 'Want of Frigates', *Naval Forces*, No. 2/1984, p. 58
Gorshkov, Admiral of the Fleet of the Soviet Union S.G. *The Sea Power of the State* (Pergamon Press, Oxford, 1978)
Grant, B. *The Security of South-East Asia* (International Institute for Strategic Studies, Adelphi Paper No. 142, 1978)
Handlin, O. *The History of the United States*, Vol. 2 (Holt, Rinehart & Winston, New York, 1967), p. 655
Henderson, Sir N. *The Birth of NATO* (Weidenfeld and Nicholson, London, 1983)
Hastings, M. and Jenkins, S. *The Battle for the Falklands* (Michael Joseph, London, 1983)
Hill, J. R. 'The Role of Navies', *Brassey's Annual 1970* (William Clowes, London, 1970)
——— 'Maritime Forces in Confrontation', *Brassey's Annual 1972* (William Clowes, London, 1972)
——— *The Rule of Law at Sea*, unpublished thesis, University of London (King's College), 1973
——— *The Royal Navy Today and Tomorrow* (Ian Allan, Shepperton, 1981)
——— *Anti-Submarine Warfare* (Ian Allan, Shepperton, 1984)
——— 'Maritime Forces for Medium Powers', *Naval Forces*, No. 2/1984, p. 29

——— *British Sea Power in the 1980s* (Ian Allan, Shepperton, 1985)
Hoffman, S. 'Security in an Age of Turbulence: Means of Response', *Third-World Conflict and International Security Part II* (International Institute for Strategic Strategic Studies, Adelphi Paper No. 167, 1980)
Hooton, T. 'Naval Mines', *Military Technology*, No. 9/84, pp. 27–33
Howard, M. *The Causes of Wars* (Temple Smith, London, 1983)
Jane's Fighting Ships, 1983–84 (Jane's, London, 1983)
Jane's All the World's Aircraft, 1984–85 (Jane's, London, 1984)
Jane's Weapon Systems, 1984–85 (Jane's, London, 1984)
Jennings, J. S. 'Problems Arising from North Sea Development', paper given at the Ninth Greenwich Forum, September 1983
Kahn, H. *On Escalation* (Praeger, New York, 1965)
Kapur, A. *The Indian Ocean: Regional and International Power Politics* (Praeger, New York, 1982)
Kapur, H. *The Awakening Giant* (Sijthoff and Noordhoff, Amsterdam, 1981)
Kelleher, C. M. *Western European Navies and the Future* (Royal Netherlands Naval College, Den Helder, 1980)
Kennedy, P. M. *The Rise and Fall of British Naval Mastery* (Allen Lane, London, 1976)
Kitson, F. *Low Intensity Operations: Subversion, Insurgency and Peacekeeping* (Faber and Faber, London, 1971)
Koburger, Capt. C. W. (USCGR) 'Swords and Surfboats: Cost Effective Maritime Law Enforcement', Nautical Institute Seminar, 10 November 1983, *Report*, p. 6
Kohli, Admiral S. N. *Sea Power and the Indian Ocean* (Tata-McGraw Hill, New York, 1978)
Labayle-Couhat, J. (ed.) *Combat Fleets of the World 1984/85* (Arms and Armour Press, London, 1984)
Lacoste, Vice Admiral P. *Stratégie Navale* (Nathan, Paris, 1981)
Larus, J. 'India: The Neglected Service Faces the Future', US Naval Institute, *Proceedings*, March 1981, p. 78
Laqueur, W. *The Road to War 1967* (Weidenfeld and Nicholson, London, 1968)
Leenhardt, Rear Admiral Y. 'The Role of the French Navy in the National External Action Policy', *NATO's 16 Nations*, April–May 1984, p. 40
Leggett, E. *The Corfu Incident* (Seeley Service, London, 1974), p. 24
Lellouche, P. (ed.) *La Sécurité de L'Europe dans les années 80* (Institut Français des Rélations Internationales, Paris, 1980)
Lider, J. *Military Thought of a Medium Power* (Institute of International Affairs, Stockholm, 1983)
Liska, G. *Alliances and the Third World* (Johns Hopkins University Press, Baltimore, 1967)
Luttwak, E. *The Political Uses of Sea Power* (Johns Hopkins University Press, Baltimore, 1974)
Macfarlane, N. *Intervention and Regional Security* (International Institute for Strategic Studies, Adelphi Paper No. 196, 1984)
Mahan, A. T. *The Influence of Sea Power upon History* (Little, Brown, Boston, 1890), p. 23
Mande, Brig. Y. A. 'India's Security Environment', USI *Journal* (New Delhi), October–December 1983, p. 307
March, E. J. *British Destroyers* (Seeley Service, London, 1966), pp. 267, 398, 467
Marder, A. J. *The Anatomy of British Sea Power* (Frank Cass, London, 1964), pp. 261, 277
Martin, L. W. *The Sea in Modern Strategy* (Chatto and Windus, London, 1967)
McDougal, M. S. and Burke, W. T. *The Public Order of the Oceans* (Yale University Press, New Haven, 1962)

McGeoch, Vice Admiral Sir I. 'National Security and Maritime Defence', *Oceanic Management: Conflicting Uses of the Celtic Sea and Other UK Waters* (Europa, London, 1977)
Menon, Capt. K. R. 'The Sea Denial Option for Smaller Navies', US Naval Institute, *Proceedings*, March 1983, pp. 119–22
Military Balance, The, 1983–84 and *1984–85* (International Institute for Strategic Studies, London)
Moineville, H. *Naval Warfare Today and Tomorrow* (Blackwell, Oxford, 1983)
Namboodiri, P. K. S., Anand, J. P. and Sreedhar, *Intervention in the Indian Ocean* (ABC Publishing House, Bombay, 1982)
Namier, L. B. *Diplomatic Prelude 1938–1939* (Macmillan, London, 1948)
Neutze, Cdr D. R. 'The Gulf of Sidra Incident: A Legal Perspective', US Naval Institute, *Proceedings*, January 1982, pp. 26–31
Nitze, P. *et al. Securing the Seas: The Soviet Naval Challenge and Western Alliance Options* (Westview Press, Boulder, 1979)
O'Connell, D. P. *The Influence of Law on Sea Power* (Manchester University Press, Manchester, 1975)
O'Neill, R. C. (ed.) *Insecurity! The Spread of Weapons in the Indian and Pacific Oceans* (Australian National University Press, Canberra, 1978)
——— (ed., with D. M. Horner) *Australian Defence Policy for the 1980s* (University of Queensland Press, Queensland, 1982)
Owen, H. (ed.) *The Next Phase in Foreign Policy* (Brookings, Washington, 1973)
Ranft, B. M. and Till, G. *The Sea in Soviet Strategy* (Macmillan, London, 1982)
Ranken, Cdr M. B. F. (ed.) *Greenwich Forum VI, World Shipping in the 1990s* (Westbury House, London, 1981)
Rosinski, H. *The Development of Naval Thought* (Naval War College Press, Newport, 1977)
Roskill, S. W. *The War at Sea* (HMSO, London, 1955–61)
——— *The Strategy of Sea Power* (Collins, London, 1962)
Safran, N. *Israel — The Embattled Ally* (Belknap Press, Harvard, 1978)
Scheina, R. L. 'The Malvinas Campaign', US Naval Institute, *Proceedings*, May 1983, p. 116
Seyersted, F. *United Nations Forces in the Law of Peace and War* (Sijthoff, Amsterdam, 1966)
Skolnick, Capt. A. 'Too Light on Lasers?', US Naval Institute, *Proceedings*, December 1984, p. 30
Smith, D. *The Defence of the Realm in the 1980s* (Croom Helm, London, 1980)
Sochaczewski, J. M. 'The Role of Communications in NATO', *Military Technology*, No. 6/84, pp. 150–6
Sokolsky, J. J. 'The US Navy and Nuclear ASW Weapons', US Naval Institute, *Proceedings*, December 1984, p. 153
Starkey, R. J., Jr 'The Renaissance in Submarine Communications', *Military Electronics*, April 1981, p. 44
Strategic Survey, 1982–83 and *1983–84* (International Institute for Strategic Studies, London)
Tange, Sir A. 'Australian Regional Defence Commitments', address at the *Seapower '81 Seminar* (Australian Naval Institute)
Taylor, T. *European Defence Co-Operation* (Chatham House Paper No. 24, 1984)
Teller, E. 'The Nature of Nuclear Warfare', *US Air Force Magazine*, January 1957
Till, G. *Maritime Strategy and the Nuclear Age*, 2nd edn (Macmillan, London, 1984)
——— (ed.) *The Future of British Sea Power* (Macmillan, London, 1984)
The Times Atlas of the Oceans (ed. A. D. Couper) (Times Books, London, 1983)

Todd, D. *The World Shipbuilding Industry* (Croom Helm, London, 1985)
Treves, T. 'The UNLOS Convention of 1982: Prospects for Europe', paper given at the Ninth Greenwich Forum, September 1983
Tsipis, K. *The Future of the Sea-Based Deterrent* (MIT Press, Cambridge, Mass., 1973)
Turner, Admiral S. 'Missions of the US Navy', *US Naval War College Review*, March 1974
Urick, R. J. *Sound Propagation in the Sea* (DARPA, Washington, 1979)
Veazey, Capt. S. E. 'New Shape in Ships', US Naval Institute, *Proceedings*, February 1985, p. 40
Veremis, T. *Greek Security: Issues and Politics* (International Institute for Strategic Studies, Adelphi Paper No. 179, 1982)
Wagner, Lt Cdr Cort D. 'Australia', US Naval Institute, *Proceedings*, March 1983, pp. 84–90
Waters, D. W. 'Seamen Scientists Historians and Strategy', Presidential Address to the British Society for the History of Science, 1978
Watt, D. C. 'How British Governments have Viewed the Sea', Closing address at the Ninth Greenwich Forum, September 1983
Wemyss, Rear Admiral M. La T. 'Submarine and Anti-Submarine Operations for the Uninitiated', RUSI *Journal*, September 1981, p. 26
Winton, J. *Convoy: The Defence of Sea Trade 1890–1990* (Michael Joseph, London, 1983)
Woodward, Rear Admiral Sir J. 'The Falklands Experience', RUSI *Journal*, March 1983, pp. 25–32
Yost, D. S. *France's Deterrent Posture and Security in Europe* (International Institute for Strategic Studies, Adelphi Paper Nos. 194 and 195, 1984–5)
Young, E. 'New Laws for Old Navies', *Survival*, November–December 1974, pp. 262–7

INDEX

Abadan crisis 120
Aboukir, HMS 163
access 30–2
accommodation for ships' companies 184
active and passive sonar 175
  see also sonar
Afghanistan 52, 205
afloat support 5, 226
aim:
  in higher level operations 132
  limitation 111
  of battle 142
  of conflict 85
  political or military 111, 132
air defence 171–4, 202
  big spender 189
  by fighters 172
  by ships 173
  seduction of missiles 174
  target indication 172
  warning 172
air traffic control 102
aircraft:
  airborne early warning (AEW) 5, 151, 172, 210, 226
  base requirements 166
  fixed-wing ship-based 5, 62, 159, 202, 226
  fixed-wing shore-based 58, 167, 168, 201, 203, 207, 209
  increment to surface forces 202
  landing facilities 166
  limited endurance 167
  limited roles in single type 167
  lofted sensors 166
  mobility 166
  operational command and control 214
  payload 164
  range 166
  rotary wing 168
    see also helicopters
  supply and reinforcement by 83, 120
  surveillance value 167
  table of characteristics 165
  vulnerability 167
  weapon carrying ability 166
aircraft carriers:
  big spenders 188
  UK policy 150
  US policy 163
airfields 62
Alford, Jonathan 6
alliances 66–73
  and port visits 98
  care of 109, 158
  communication problems 182
  formality of 70, 220
  price of 71, 198–9, 204, 206, 209
  support for 36, 147, 212
    see also NATO and individual countries
allies:
  ad hoc 73
  and reach 151, 154–5
  as providers of cover 129, 201, 211
  attitude to non-superpower disputes 71, 202
  in general war 146
  lack of interest in administrative threats 56, 198
  level of trust 72
  non-superpower 72
  point of intervention 224
  superpower 67, 70, 71, 142, 147, 155, 176, 212, 219
  UK conflict against 25
Amerigo Vespucci, Italian training ship 99
Amethyst, HMS 120
ammunition stocks 62, 90, 153, 159
Amoco Cadiz, tanker 107
amphibious forces 5, 82, 91, 204, 224
amphibious operations 61, 120, 139–40, 146, 150, 164
Angola 205
anti-ship operations 177–82
  guns 178
  means of attack 178
  mining 180–1
  missiles 179
  over-provision for 181
  ships good targets 177–8
  torpedoes 179

anti-submarine warfare (ASW) 84, 174–7
against nuclear-powered submarines 204
big spender 189
demands massive resources 177
five-phase process 175
requires variety of systems 175
sonar 174–5
weapons 176–7
Aqaba, Gulf of 141
ARAPAHO concept 184, 202
Archer, Dr Clive 6
Ardent, HMS 163
area of operations
higher level 134–7
low intensity 114–15
Argentina 15, 16, 31, 42, 43, 54, 60, 85, 92, 136, 149, 197, 225
armament industries 154, 210
Armilla patrol 115, 119, 139
Army, British 3
Ascension Island 59
ASEAN 27
ASROC 176
Atlantic, Battle of the 142, 145–6
Atlantic, Standing Naval Force 154
Atlantic, use of 147
Australia 15, 16, 27, 31, 42, 43, 54, 145, 153, 201, 210
ANZUS Treaty 69, 199, 220
strategy 24, 189, 224
Austria 15, 16
autonomy 26–7, 48, 146, 189, 218, 222, 225–6
AWACS 210
Awati, Vice Admiral M.P., IN 6

Bab-el-Mandeb 141, 142
Backfire bomber 172
Bahrain 33
Balance of Power 22
Bandar Abbas 121
Bandar Khomeini 57
Barents Sea 82
Barnett, Correlli 46, 222
Baruch, Bernard 80
bases 46, 59, 90, 152, 202
for allies 199, 221
pirate 125
battle 35, 142–3, 146
battle group 82, 146
battleships 89
Beagle Channel 54
Beira Patrol 111, 226
Belgium 15, 16, 42, 43, 154
Belize 112, 226
blockade 35, 57, 81
boarding 104, 117
bombardment 62, 140, 146
bombs 59, 89, 168, 177
Bonsignore, Ezio 185
Booth, Kenneth 6
bottom arrays 175
Brazil 6, 15, 16, 31, 42, 43, 44, 47, 145, 201
area of interest 149
armament industry 210
claim to patrimonial sea 55
defence budget 185
economic power 64
navy 69
nuclear policy 207
relationship with superpowers 53, 220
strategy 23–4, 197, 224
treaty structure 69
Britain *see* UK
British Pacific Fleet 145
Buchan, Alastair 27–8
budgets, defence 47, 185, 207, 209
bulk carriers 33
bullying, charges of 114, 117, 119
Buzan, Barry 56

Cable, Sir James 6, 59, 85, 152, 177
cabotage 32, 42
Cambridge seminar 5
Canada 12, 15, 16, 31, 42, 43, 55, 113, 222, 225
capitalist economies 8
Caribbean 4, 69
Caroline, the 113, 114
Castex, Admiral Raoul 34
catalysis 221, 223, 224
CENTO 71
Ceylon 33
Chad 22, 54, 205
channels of fire 173
Chapultepec, Act of 69
Chatfield, Admiral of the Fleet Lord 5
Chile 15, 16, 31, 42, 43, 54, 149, 225
China 15, 16, 62, 219
incursion into India 68
power status 18–19
Churchill, Sir Winston 80
Clausewitz, Carl von 85

coastal state:
  and disaster control 106
  constabulary function 99–107
  counter-piracy function 125
  interests in general 36
  interests in resources 33
  Law of the Sea Convention 37
coastguard 105, 106, 107, 200, 213
cod disputes 4, 84, 85, 112, 114, 118, 226
codes and cyphers 95
coercion 21, 51
Colomb, Captain Sir John 34
command, control and communications 59, 81, 86, 91, 102, 106, 108, 143, 181–2, 214–15, 220
command of the sea 35
Compton-Hall, Cdr Richard 161
concepts, use of 79
conflict 9
  analysis 1971–9 71
Conqueror, HMS 183
conquest 9
constabulary function 34, 88, 99–107, 124, 200, 209
container ships 33, 158
continental margin 37, 38
continental shelf 11
contribution to alliance 3, 4, 145, 226
convoy 82, 175, 203
  ONS 5 142
Corbett, Sir Julian 34, 142
core force 24
Corfu Channel incident 45
Cosby, Ivan 6
costs 185–9, 201
counter-intelligence 95
Couper, Professor Alastair 40, 158
Coutau-Bégarie, Hervé 6
cover 129, 201
Crotale 173
Cuba 43, 140
Custance, Admiral Sir Reginald 34
customs 33, 55, 103

data acquisition:
  above water 172, 178
  and handling 182
  requirement in low intensity operations 118
  underwater 174
de Gaulle, General Charles 8, 22, 223
de Tocqueville, Alexis 17
deception 139
decoys 173
deep sea-bed regime 39
defects, operational 153
demonstration of resolve 115, 119–20
demonstration of right 37, 115–18
Denmark 15, 16, 42, 43, 94, 154, 225
dependence, to be avoided 212, 222
detente 66
detention 58, 105–6
deterrence 3, 22, 35, 61, 70, 79–81, 84, 88, 91, 92, 108, 145, 218
  see also nuclear strategic deterrence
Diego Garcia 68
diplomacy:
  and coercion 51
  and offshore resources 34
  and supranational organisations 218
  and trade 158
  as substitute for military power 65, 197
  French 22
  naval 96–9
disaster control 106–7
discrimination against foreign shipping 32, 102
Djibouti 96, 216
dog, shaggy, as low intensity asset 118
Dominica 96
Dreadnought, HMS 209
Duval, Admiral Marcel 6

Eagle, HMS 161
Eberle, Admiral Sir James 6
Eccles, Admiral, USN 81
economic power 8, 12, 30, 197
  and risk 45
  and seabased resources 33
  as element of threat 52
  in French strategy 22
economic zone *see* exclusive economic zone
Ecuador 55
educational base 8
effectiveness 89–92, 164
Egypt 15, 16, 17, 31, 42, 43, 116–17
Eilat, Israeli destroyer 128, 179
electronic countermeasures 159, 173
electronic intercept 172
Empire Roach, MV 117

endurance of maritime units 118
enlightenment, as national objective 13
entrepôt trade 42
environment, marine 37, 94, 104
escalation
  risk of 114–15, 118, 129, 198, 224
  theory 86
Ethiopia 205
European Economic Community 18, 54, 105
evacuation of nationals 121
exclusion zone 84, 135–6, 141
exclusive economic zone 11, 37, 58, 100, 104, 125, 149, 155
exercises 97, 153, 215
  with allies 109, 221
Exocet 179
expatriates 121
exploitation of resources 33, 47, 55, 82, 103
exponential, the ruthless 186–7
exports by sea 31
extended vital interests 12–14, 20, 21, 53, 56, 61, 67, 149
external trade, dependence on 7

Falkland Islands 54, 60–1, 92
Falklands Campaign 13, 82, 135, 137, 142, 151, 163, 174, 184, 185
Farragut, Admiral 179
fast attack craft 59, 161, 184
Fife, HMS 96
financial institutions, influence 8
Finland 15, 16, 42, 43
fire-and-forget weapons 90
Fisher, Admiral 'Jacky' 200, 209
fisheries 34, 37, 41, 55, 56, 82, 100, 213
  disputes 116
  distant-water 151
  regulation 102–3, 105
flags of convenience 31, 32, 42
foreign policy 9
Fox, Ambassador 113
France 5, 6, 15, 16, 31, 42, 43, 44, 53, 54, 62, 96
  Algerian emergency 122
  and ESRO 189
  and Indian Ocean 59
  and Israel 70
  and NATO 22, 67, 220, 222
  armament industry 210
  blue water reach 154
  defence budget 185
  economic power 64
  frigates for Saudi Arabia 184
  nuclear policy 80, 108, 145, 223
  nuclear testing zones 13, 120
  overseas deployments 97
  Spiny Lobster War 151
  strategy 22, 197, 224
  surveillance 94
  value to alliance 199
freedom of navigation and overflight 37
freight rates 31
French foreign service 8
frontiers 10, 19
fuel 161, 162, 164

Gabon 44
gas, undersea extraction 34
Gaullism 53, 222–3
General Belgrano, ARA 84, 135, 180, 183
general war 87, 145–8, 178, 206
Germany, Federal Republic 15, 16, 31, 42, 43, 44, 219
  defence budget 185
  economic power 64
  regional navy 154, 199, 225
Ghazi, PS 177
Gibraltar 59, 116, 120
Goa 205
Goalkeeper 173
good order at sea 99–107, 200
Gorshkov, Admiral of the Fleet of the Soviet Union 97, 139
Greece 15, 16, 42, 43, 154, 205, 225
  reaction to Cyprus incursion 92, 95
Greenland-Iceland-UK gap 175
Grenada 205
Grotius, Hugo 36
Gueritz, Rear Admiral Edward 6
guerre de course 35
Gulf of Oman patrol *see* Armilla patrol
Gulf, the 52, 54
Gulf States 27
Gulf War 54, 57, 83, 115, 136, 141, 211
gun 59, 62, 173, 178, 181

Hancock, USS 141
harassment 56
Harpoon 179
Harrier aircraft 167, 188

Hart, Liddell 85
hegemony 12, 23
helicopters 159, 160, 175
  see also aircraft, rotary wing
higher level operations 87, 132–44
  aim 132–3
  amphibious landing 139
  and aircraft 167
  and ASW 176
  and submarines 171
  and surface ships 164
  and torpedoes 180
  area 135–7
  battle 142–3
  bombardment 140
  command and control 215
  difference from low intensity operations 132
  passage, denial of 140–1
  passage, opposed 137–9
  scope 133–4
  sea areas, denial of 141–2
  sea use and sea denial 137
  transition to 164
hijacking 58, 126
Hoffman, Stanley 71
home base 87, 149
Hong Kong 80, 123, 202
Hormuz, Strait of 57, 119
hostile act, difficulty of perceiving 128
hostile intent, even greater difficulty 128
hovercraft 188
Howard, Professor Michael 35

Iceland 33, 44, 56, 59, 84, 111, 154
Ikara 176
illegal immigration 104, 123–4
in-flight refuelling 59, 168
in-port inspection 104
India 6, 15, 16, 27, 31, 42, 43, 44, 71, 83, 149, 153, 210, 219
  agreement with Soviet Union 68, 220
  Indo-Pakistan War 1971 119, 132–3, 137, 141
  nuclear policy 88, 207
  reach 198
  relationship with superpowers 53
  strategy 22–3, 197, 224
Indian Ocean 27, 59, 97, 198
Indonesia 13, 15, 16, 27, 54, 60, 62, 85, 95, 123, 225
information handling 101, 106, 182
initial casualty concept 128
initiative:
  as element of rules of engagement 127, 134
  need for medium power to keep 21, 221
innocent passage 37, 45, 55
inspection 103
instructions to sea users 102, 117
insurance, marine 57
intellectual power 8, 12, 34, 51
intelligence 92–6, 101, 122
interdependence 11
internal tensions 9
internal waters 11, 104
International Court of Justice 40, 45
international law 36–40, 54, 56, 61
International Maritime Organisation (IMO) 104
international organisations for dispute settlement 72
International Sea-Bed Authority (ISBA) 39
invasion 10, 61
Iran 15, 16, 27, 31, 42, 43, 211
Iran-Iraq War *see* Gulf War
Ireland, Republic of 122
Irish Republican Army (IRA) 122
irredentism 10
island-grabbing 60, 205
Israel 8, 15, 16, 20, 26, 31, 42, 43, 62, 135
  defence budget 185
  navy 132
  neighbour problem 54
  nuclear policy 207
  strategy 24–5, 197, 211, 225
  tripartite guarantee 70
  see also Yom Kippur War
Italy 15, 16, 31, 42, 43, 64, 154, 225

Japan 6, 15, 16, 31, 42, 43, 189
  armament industry 210
  economic power 8, 18, 64, 65
  fisheries 34
  Maritime Safety Agency 107
  military power 17
  reach 198
  strategy 23, 197, 224
  treaty with USA 23, 68, 220
  victory at Tsushima 89
Jones, Nicely-Nicely 5
jurisdiction:

and self-defence 113
at sea 36, 99
map 38
relation to state security 122

Kahn, Herman 85, 86
Kapur, Ashok 22, 27
Keflavik 85
Kelleher, Professor Catherine 149, 154
Kellogg-Briand Pact 39
Kennedy, Paul 46
keywords 25
Kharg Island 57, 149
Kimm, Captain Peter 6
Kinley, Geoffrey 6
Kissinger, Henry 25
Kitson, Sir Frank 111
Korean airliner shoot-down 117
Korean War 137, 141
Kuwait 43, 120, 226

La Réunion 216
land warfare 86
landing craft 160
lasers 162, 203
Lasswell, Harold 13, 61
law at sea 36–40
municipal law 99–100
Law of the Sea Convention 1982:
incomplete accession to 39, 65
length 39
provisions 37–9
leadership 91
Lebanon 62, 70, 211
levels of conflict 85–7
and reach 151–2
as basis for planning 197
levels of operation *see* levels of conflict
Liardet, Captain Guy 6
Liberator VLR aircraft 174
Liberia 43
Libya 56
lifesaving 106
limited conflict 84, 86
limits 223–4
declaration 115, 134
of low intensity operations 111–15
Liska, George 27
logistic organisation:
and effectiveness 91
and reach 152, 206
disjunctions in NATO 221
for surface ships 162
UK 226
see also afloat support
low intensity operations 87, 111–31, 200
aim 111–12
amphibious 120–1
area 114–15
command and control 130, 215
counter-piracy 124–6
counter-terrorist 122–3
cover 129
demonstration of resolve 119–20
demonstration of right 115–17
evacuation of nationals 121
force characteristics required 122, 123, 130
frequency 136
illegal immigration 123–4
offshore installation protection 126–7
rules of engagement 127–9
scope 112–14
suitability of surface ships 164
summary 129–30
weapon options 118
Lusitania, SS 134
Luxembourg 19

McConnell, James 6
Macfarlane, Neil 205
McGeoch, Vice Admiral Sir Ian 6
Madina class 184
Mahan, Alfred T. 30, 34, 37, 79
maintenance 90, 184
Malacca Strait 55, 123
Malafon 176
Malaysia 13, 54, 62, 85, 123
manganese nodules 34
maritime power:
and vulnerability 44
comparison 42–3
components 30–6
evidence of 218
influenced by law 36
mobility 89
material efficiency 89–90
materiel:
air defence 171–4
aircraft 164–8
and interests 157–8
anti-ship 177–81
anti-submarine 174–7
command, control and

communications 181–2
costs 185–9
platforms 157, 158–71
platforms and systems 183
submarines 168–71
surface ships 158–64
Mayotte 216
media 60
medium powers:
alliance requirements 66–73, 219–20
and air defence 174
and ASW 176, 204
and big spenders 188–9
and bombardment 140
and cover 129
and cream-puff systems 187
and general war 145, 206
and gold-plated systems 188, 206
and good order 101–5
and levels of conflict 85–7, 197–8
and low intensity operations 121, 200
and materiel 157
and nuclear-powered submarines 208
and nuclear warfare 147, 206, 223
and rules of engagement 128–9
and sea control 82
and sea denial 83–5
characteristics 5, 20–2, 26, 218
choices remain open 221
counter-terrorist operations 127
dilemmas 64, 219
force requirements 200–9, 225
maritime policy co-ordination 212–13
medium maritime powers 46–8
national needs 200
planning problems 195
relationship with superpowers 53
salvage laws 107
strategic basis 21, 26, 158
surface ship dilemma 164
merchant marine 31–2, 41, 44, 46, 55, 206, 213
technical developments 158
Mexico 15, 16, 31, 42, 43, 123
military power 9, 12
at sea 34–6
expense 64
numerical comparisons 16–17
risks and penalties 45
mine countermeasures 180–1
mining 57, 59, 180–1, 201
Ministry of Defence UK 3, 5, 226
missiles:
air defence 173, 183
and ARAPAHO concept 184
anti-ship 58, 84, 172, 179, 203
anti-shore 62
anti-submarine 176
as targets 171–3
ballistic 171, 173
first use 134
Moineville, Hubert 85, 161, 183, 195
mukhti bahini 123
multipolar world 23, 27
Muscat 119

Nailor, Professor Peter 6
narcotics smuggling 104
Nasser, Gamal Abdel 88
nation-building 10
nation-states:
characteristics 7, 15
independence 11–12
maritime tasks 200
power 8–9
primacy 218
vital interests 9–14
vulnerabilities 9–14
national control 21
NATO:
and Gibraltar 59
and UK defence policy 3, 25
area 67
exercises 109
force goals 4
France leaves military structure 22, 220
levels of operation 86
maritime forces 4, 146
role in Norway 150
staff and command structure 67, 220, 221
Standing Naval Force Atlantic 199
transatlantic reinforcement 175
treaty 4, 67
US nuclear commitment 223
value of UK's position 199
Naval Review, the 5
naval staff 3, 4, 5
necessity, as principle of self-defence 113
negative security assurances 70
neighbours 53–4

Nelson, HMS 179
Netherlands 15, 16, 26, 31, 42, 43, 59, 154, 211, 219
neutrals 57, 137, 139
New Hebrides 4, 120
New Jersey, USS 140
New Zealand 13, 15, 16, 17, 31, 42, 43, 69
Nigeria 15, 16, 31, 42, 43, 58, 132
Nimitz, USS 56
Nimrod 167
Nixon doctrine 68
non-alignment 22, 219
normal conditions (cf. peace) 87, 88–110
  constabulary duties 99–107
  counter-intelligence 95–6
  disaster control 106–7
  effectiveness 89–92
  intelligence gathering 92–3
  material efficiency 89–90
  organisation 91
  port visits 97–9
  presence 96–9
  readiness 88–9
  strategic deterrent patrols 107–8
  surveillance 93–5
  threat 52
  training 90–1
  value of surface ships 164
Northern Ireland 4, 10, 122
Norway 15, 16, 19, 26, 31, 42, 43, 45, 154
Norwegian Sea 82
nuclear bombardment 62, 80
nuclear power 169
nuclear strategic deterrence 107–9, 207, 223
nuclear warfare 206
nuclear weapons 36, 108
  big spenders 188
  effect on strategy 80
  first use 134
  French programme 22
  general war 145
  industrial back-up 108
  Israel 25
  use at sea 146

O'Connell, Daniel 127, 128
O'Neill, Robert 199
Officer of the Guard 118
offshore installations 37, 58, 103
  protection 126, 201
oil:
  offshore well 44, 58
  spills 107
  undersea extraction 34
Oman 4, 52, 211
Onishi, Dr Seiichiro 6
operational intelligence 92
optimising of forces 208
organisation:
  and deployment 212–16
  as element of effectiveness 91–2
Organisation of American States 69, 72
Owen, Dr David 119

passage:
  of shipping 137–9
  of warships 56, 100
  rights of 37, 45, 116
Pakistan 15, 16, 71, 83, 225
Palestine 123–4
Paracel Islands 60, 136, 137, 139
patrimonial sea 55
Pax Britannica 46
peace *see* normal conditions
peaceful co-existence 72
Peloponnesian wars 82, 204
Pepys, Samuel 143
performance, relation to cost 187
Peru 33, 55, 225
Philippine Sea, Battle of 183
phosphorites 34
pilot 103
piracy 57–8, 124–6
planning 89, 195–212
  alliance and its price 198–9
  and risk 205–6, 223
  constabulary 200–1
  cyclic process 195, 196
  deficiencies and options 210–12
  for higher level operations 202–3
  for short war 147
  force requirements 200–9, 223
  level of conflict 197, 223
  optimising maritime forces 208–9
  organisation and deployment 212–16
  reach 197, 223
platforms and systems 183–5
Poland 220, 225
political direction 91, 146, 214
political independence 10–12, 19, 20, 53
pollution 37, 100, 104

port state jurisdiction 104
ports 42, 62, 103, 158
  entry regulations 55
  visits by naval forces 97–9, 151
Portugal 154, 185
potato, as constabulary weapon 106
power:
  and vulnerability 44–6
  as national objective 13, 61
  balance of 22
  definition 7
  economic 8
  elements 7–9, 218
  intellectual 8
  maritime 30–50
  means of 21
  military 9, 88
  responsiveness 64
presence 96–9, 151
procurement 90, 209–12
propaganda 51
proportionality:
  and submarine warfare 171
  as principle of self-defence 113
protection of shipping 138
public image 119, 127, 140, 161
Punch 98

Qaboos, Sultan 52

radar 159, 162, 172, 178
Ranft, Professor Bryan 6
range 168
reconnaissance 59
rectitude, as national objective 13, 61
Red Crusader case 105
replenishment at sea 162
requisition of merchant ships 31
research and development 210–11
resource enjoyment 11, 33, 39
  constabulary function 99–107
resources, human and industrial 209
respect, as national objective 13, 61
rights of user 10
Rio Treaty 69
risk 45, 85, 138, 152, 204, 223–4
Rodzhestvensky, Admiral 89
roll-on/roll-off 33
Rosinski, Herbert 30
Roskill, Stephen 83
Royal Air Force 3, 107
Royal Marines 150
Royal Naval College 5
Royal Navy 4, 46, 61, 71, 107, 208
rules of engagement:
  and submarines 171
  basis in law 40
  in amphibious operations 139
  in battle 142
  in higher level operations 133, 134
  in low intensity operations 127–9, 215
Ruiz, Captain 6

sabotage 58, 126
salvage 107
San Luis, ARA 180, 201
sand and gravel 34
Sandys, Duncan 80
sanitised areas 138
Saudi Arabia 43, 184–5, 211
scenarios 80, 149, 152, 197, 221, 222, 224
scope of operations 112–14, 133–4
sea:
  as 'great common' 30
  size 81
  surface, as basis for sea use 83
sea-bed:
  exploitation 34
  jurisdiction 37
sea blindness 47
Sea Cat 183
sea control 81–2, 84
Sea Dart 173
sea denial 83–5, 122, 137, 140–2, 146, 150, 171, 202, 224
sea dependence 40–4, 47, 228–30
sea-skimming missiles 179
Sea Sparrow 173
sea use 30, 47, 82–3, 101, 122, 137, 150, 202, 224
sea users 36
  need for information 101
  rights under international law 37
search and rescue 106
Seaways 65
Sea Wolf 173
Selden, John 36
self-defence:
  and low-intensity operations 111
  anticipatory 114, 128
  as justification for war 40, 60
  basis of Japanese strategy 23
  in Falklands campaign 135–6
  includes defence of ships under flag 118

principles 113
self-determination 61
seminars on medium maritime power 6
sensors 171–82
air-defence 171–4
anti-ship 177–82
anti-submarine 174–7
training on 91
Sevaistre, Rear Admiral Olivier 6
Sharpe, Captain Richard 6
Sheffield, HMS 128, 184
shipbuilding 33, 41, 210, 213
ships' lives 5
Sidra, Gulf of 56, 128
Singapore 43, 58
skill, as national objective 13
Slessor, Marshal of the RAF Sir John 80
small powers 19–20, 195, 201
Small Water Plane Area Twin Hull (SWATH) ship 188
solidarity, as national objective 13, 61
sonar 159, 161, 162, 174–5
sonobuoys 175, 176
South Africa 15, 16, 31, 42, 43
South America 54, 69, 109
South Atlantic 4, 59, 69
see also Falklands campaign
Soviet Union 15, 16, 31, 42, 43, 47, 62
and Afghanistan 52
and India 23
as main threat to UK 3
frontier regime 100
invasion of Czechoslovakia 12
lead times 209
military doctrine 79
military power 17, 18
navy 66, 67, 97, 160, 206
Spetsnaz forces 62
strategic rocket forces 178
treaty with USA on prevention of incidents at sea 107
space 93, 163, 177, 189
Spain 15, 16, 31, 42, 43, 59, 85, 94, 116, 154
Spanish Civil War 124
speed 124
Spiny Lobster War 24, 151
Spratly Islands 60, 136, 137, 139
statistical data 7, 15–16, 42–3, 228–30
status quo 112
stocks 90
straits 37, 45, 81
strap-on systems 157, 185
strategic deterrent patrols 107–9
strategy:
effect of preoccupation with threat 51
medium power 21
must serve national interest 216, 218
preservation of vital interest 14, 158
relation to power 7
relation to size and shape studies 200
starting point 196–7
surprise 163, 178
see also individual countries
submarines:
and higher level operations 133, 134
ballistic missile 63, 108, 147, 207
coastal 201
data gathering 170–1
design factors 169
difficulty of communication 170, 182
effect of nuclear power 169
endurance 170
higher level operations 171
indiscriminate weaponry 171
powerful anti-surface asset 203
striking power 170
submerged passage 39
superpower forces 176
supply by 83
tactical operation 174
subversion 51
Suez 88, 137, 139
superior fleet 117
superpowers 17–19, 52, 53, 58, 66–70, 79, 177, 198
see also allies, threats
surface warships 59, 159–64
ability to carry multiple systems 160
characteristics table 160
degraded by sea conditions 161
design factors 159
in force requirements 200
in low intensity operations 164
not optimum sensor platforms 162
optimising for correct level 208

payload 159, 160
public impact 161
suitability for port visits 99
sustainability 161
visibility 162–3
vulnerability 84, 163
Surinam 59
surveillance 93–5
counter-terrorist 122
incidents 94
sustainability 152–4, 160, 184
Sweden 15, 16, 31, 42, 43, 154
Switzerland 15, 16, 30
Syria 70

tactics, effect of preoccupation with threat 51
Tanganyika 120
technology:
and resource exploitation 34
developments in shipping 158
effect on law 36
effect on weapons and platforms 183
in communications 182
territorial integrity 10–11, 19, 20, 53, 82, 200, 207
territorial sea 11, 37, 58
terrorists 62, 121, 122–3
Thatcher, Mrs Margaret 124
Third World 18
threat 51–66
administrative 55–6, 63
at sea 55–63
bombardment 62
mine 181
missile 138
non-superpower 53–5, 59, 63, 198
of force 9, 12
pattern of 71
strategic before technological 197
subsurface 138
superpower 53, 58–9, 63, 177, 198
terrorist 62
Till, Dr Geoffrey 6, 81
Timor 60, 136, 137
Tiran, Strait of 116–17
Tlatelolco, Treaty of 220
Torgo, Admiral 89
Tomahawk 179
torpedoes 59, 89, 171, 176, 177, 179, 183, 210
Total Exclusion Zone *see* exclusion zone
towed arrays 162, 175, 176, 203
trade:
and access 30–2, 150
as cause of dispute 39
as parameter of sea dependence 41
does not protect itself 64–5
missions 33
protection 35, 81, 137, 204
surface 83
traffic separation schemes 100, 104
training 90–1, 108, 153, 215
Tropic of Cancer 67
tropicalisation 153
Tsushima, Battle of 89
Tunb Islands 60
Turkey 15, 16, 94, 154, 225
descent on Cyprus 92, 95, 132, 137
Turner, Admiral Stansfield, USN 81
Tuvalu 19

Ultra Large Crude Carriers (ULCC) 158
uniqueness:
of medium powers 20
of nations 5, 7
UNITAS exercises 109
United Kingdom 15, 16, 31, 42, 43, 45, 62
aim in Falklands Campaign 132
alternative strategy for 5
amphibious operations 120
and NATO 67, 222
and 6 per cent multiplier 186
as medium power 6
blue water reach 154
command and control 92
confrontation with Indonesia 13, 123, 226
continental shelf legislation 100
defence policy 25
historic reach and scope 219
intelligence on Argentina 95
interests 4
maritime assets 226
maritime policy 225
merchant marine 31, 55
NATO requirements 204, 222, 225
navy *see* Royal Navy
nuclear policy 109, 145
overseas deployments 97
research and development 211
SAS/SBS 62
strategic assumptions 197
strategy post-1968 3, 225–6

strategy pre-1968 3
surveillance 94
tripartite guarantee to Israel 70
value to NATO 199
United Nations 19, 30, 66, 68
Charter 10, 12, 13, 39, 113, 114, 138
forces 59, 117
General Assembly 12, 60
Law of the Sea Conference 37, 65
Security Council 62
UNCTAD liner code 32, 55
United States 15, 16, 20, 31, 42, 43, 62
and Australia 24
and Brazil 23–4, 69
and India 23, 68
and Israel 24–5, 70
and Japan 23, 68
and UN Law of the Sea Conference 39
Central American policy 52
Indian Ocean deployment 119
military power 17
Marine Corps 204
Navy 4, 66, 146, 147
Sixth Fleet 70
sponsorship of Iran 211
Treaty with Soviet Union on Prevention of Incidents at Sea 127

Vattel 33
Venezuela 15, 16, 31, 42, 43
very short take-off and landing (VSTOL) aircraft 202
vessel traffic services 200–1
Vienticinco de Mayo, ARA 135, 166
Vietnam 113, 136, 137, 140, 141
Vietnamese boat people 124
vital interests 9–14, 20, 21, 48, 66, 93, 158, 218, 223
vulnerability:
and power 44–6
and protection by military force 35
in ship procurement 33
merchant marine 32
of medium powers 53, 64
of small powers 19

war:
as current phenomenon 9
justification in self-defence 39
Warsaw Pact 109, 146, 220
water conditions, effect on sonar 162, 169
wealth, as national objective 13
created by merchant marine 31
created by trade 30
weapons:
expenditure 138
options 118
practices 116
relation to rules of engagement 134
use of 117
see also bombs, guns, missiles, torpedoes
Webster, US Secretary of State 113
well-being, as national objective 13
Wellington, Duke of 91

Yom Kippur War 132, 133, 135, 141, 174
Young, Elizabeth 6

zero-sum games 44
Zionism 24
zones of peace 219

For Product Safety Concerns and Information please contact our EU
representative GPSR@taylorandfrancis.com
Taylor & Francis Verlag GmbH, Kaufingerstraße 24, 80331 München, Germany

www.ingramcontent.com/pod-product-compliance
Ingram Content Group UK Ltd.
Pitfield, Milton Keynes, MK11 3LW, UK
UKHW020157260926
475702UK00047B/502
* 9 7 8 0 3 6 7 7 1 2 1 9 8 *